MANAGING CHILDREN'S SERVICES IN LIBRARIES

MANAGING CHILDREN'S SERVICES IN LIBRARIES

Fourth Edition

Adele M. Fasick and Leslie Edmonds Holt

LIBRARIES UNLIMITED

AN IMPRINT OF ABC-CLIO, LLC
Santa Barbara, California • Denver, Colorado • Oxford, England

Library of Congress Cataloging-in-Publication Data

Fasick, Adele M.
    [Managing children's services in the public library]
    Managing children's services in libraries / Adele M. Fasick and Leslie Edmonds Holt. — 4th ed.
        p. cm.
    Includes bibliographical references and index.
    Previous ed.: 2008.
    ISBN 978-1-61069-100-0 (acid-free paper) — ISBN 978-1-61069-373-8 (eBook)
    1. Children's libraries—United States—Administration.   2. Public libraries—United States—Administration.   I. Holt, Leslie Edmonds.   II. Title.
    Z718.2.U6F37 2012
    025.1'97625—dc23   2012032470

ISBN: 978-1-61069-100-0
EISBN: 978-1-61069-373-8

17   16   15   14   13   1   2   3   4   5

This book is also available on the World Wide Web as an eBook.
Visit www.abc-clio.com for details.

Libraries Unlimited
An Imprint of ABC-CLIO, LLC

ABC-CLIO, LLC
130 Cremona Drive, P.O. Box 1911
Santa Barbara, California 93116-1911

This book is printed on acid-free paper ∞
Manufactured in the United States of America

Contents

List of Figures   xiii

Section I: The Library in Its Community: Challenges and Changes   **1**

Chapter 1: Why Do We Need Libraries for Children?   **3**

Purposes of Children's Libraries   3

Changing Priorities   4

Types of Children's Libraries   6
   Public Libraries   6
   School Libraries   6
   Special Libraries   7

Planning Services for All Children   7
   Preschool Children   8
   School-Age Children   9
   Transitional Users   9
   Adults   10
   Differences Unrelated to Age   11

Types of Services   12
   Building Collections   13
   Making the Collection Accessible   13
   Delivering Information Services   14
   Providing Educational and Recreational Programs   14
   Outreach   14

Marketing Services   15
Evaluation and Accountability   15

Looking Forward   16

Chapter 2: Getting to Know Today's Children   **19**

Demographic Changes   19

Changing Educational Trends   20
Homeschooling   20
Online Schools and Classes   20
High Stakes Testing   21
e-textbooks   21

Changing Uses of Media and Technology   22

Changes in Reading Formats   23
Schools   23
Public Libraries   24

Changes in Information Seeking   24
Digital Resources   24
Group Searching   25

Changes in Employment Outlook   25

Section II: Planning Services: Challenges and Changes   **29**

Chapter 3: Strategic Planning   **31**

Mission Statements for Strategic Planning   31
Public Library Mission Statements   31
School Library Mission Statements   32
Children's Libraries in Other Settings   33

Moving from Mission to Departmental Goals   33
Environmental Scan   34
Strategy Formulation through Objectives   35
Hallmarks of Useful Objectives, Activity Statements, and Indicators   36
Collaborative Planning   37
Working with Objectives   38
Visualizing the Strategic Planning Process   39

Chapter 4: Evaluation   **41**

Evaluating Achievement   41

Outcome Evaluation   41
Knowing Where You Stand—Routine Collection of Data about Services   42
Evaluating Specific Programs or Activities   44

Statistical Evaluation 45

Qualitative Evaluation 45

Using the Results of Evaluation 45

Causes of Failure to Meet Objectives 46

Reporting Evaluation Results 47

What Is an Annual Report? 47

Who Prepares the Annual Report and When? 48

Preparing the Annual Report 49

Audiences for Annual Report 49

Theme of the Report 49

Telling the Story with Graphics 50

Pictures 50

Use Several Different Channels 51

Chapter 5: Budgeting and Fundraising **53**

Preparing the Budget 54

Staff Time 58

Adding New Programs and Services 58

Managing the Budget 59

Accountability 59

Fundraising 60

Friends/Parent Support 61

Foundations 62

Corporate Support 63

Grant Support 64

Locating Grant Opportunities 64

Chapter 6: Facilities and Space Planning **69**

Maintaining Library Space 69

Day-to-Day Issues 70

Looking Good 70

Adult Friendly 71

Changing Spaces 71

Planning Interiors 72

Housing the Collection 74

Furnishings 74

Infrastructure 75

Planning for Technology 75

Other Considerations 75

New Libraries   76
    Evaluating Space   77

Section III: Developing and Managing Collections:
    Challenges and Changes   **79**

Chapter 7: Collection Development in a Multimedia World   **81**

Changing Nature of Library Collections   81
    Selection of Print Materials   84
    Selection of Digital Materials   84

Sharing Resources   86

Weeding the Collection   86

Selection Policies   88

Keeping Up with Changing Needs   89

Chapter 8: Acquisition, Automated Systems, and Access   **93**

Materials Acquisition   94

Automated Systems   96
    Cataloging and Classification   96
    Changes in Automated Systems   99

Circulation   100

Access   100

Shelving Materials   101
    Marketing the Collection   102
    Promoting Electronic Media   103

Chapter 9: Intellectual Freedom and Privacy   **105**

Issues in Intellectual Freedom   105

Specific Issues with Digital Resources   108

Basic Steps for Preserving Intellectual Freedom
    in Youth Services   110
    Step One: Know the Documents Supported by the American
        Library Association   110
    Step Two: Have a Selection Policy in Place   114
    Step Three: Be Prepared to Deal with Challenges   114

Children's Right to Privacy in Public and School Libraries   116

Basic Steps for Preserving the Privacy of Library Users   117
    Step One: Develop a Privacy Policy   117
    Step Two: Review Your Privacy Practices   118

Step Three: Protecting Children from Social Media Misuse   118

Talking Points for Explaining Library Policy   120

Section IV: Managing Services: Challenges and Changes   121

Chapter 10: Programs and Services for Children   123

Reading Enhancement Programs   123
Steps in Planning a Storytime   124
Making Preschool Programs Available to Offsite Children   125
Reading Development Programs for School-Age Children   126

Helping Children Find Information   126
Information Services in Libraries   127
Alternative Delivery Programs   128
Homework Help   129

Enrichment Programs for Children   129

Programs to Increase Library Visibility   130
Preparing for an Event   131
Attracting a Large Audience   131
Planning an Author Visit   132
Other Programs to Increase Library Visibility   133

Chapter 11: Outreach and Cooperative Programs   135

School and Public Library Cooperation   135
Resource Sharing   137
Communication   137
School Programs and Services   139
Sharing Space   141

Working with Child-Serving Agencies   142

Public Library Outreach   143
Outreach to Daycare   144

Chapter 12: Marketing and Maintaining a Public Profile   147

Branding   148

Developing a Marketing Plan   149

Public Relations   150
Quality Library Services   151
Meeting the Public   152
Handouts: Flyers, Posters, Bookmarks, and Brochures   153
Electronic Media Promotion Services   153
News Releases   155

Public Service Announcements	156
Media Interviews	156
Paid Advertising	158
Evaluating Marketing and Public Relations	159

Section V: Creating a Productive Work Environment: Challenges and Changes — **161**

Chapter 13: Recruiting and Retaining Staff and Volunteers — **163**

Staffing Plan	163
Process of Hiring	165
Interviewing	166
Orientation of New Staff	168
Staff Retention	169
Ongoing Staff Training	169
Rewarding Staff Achievement	171
Handling Potential Conflict Situations	172
Conflict about Work Habits	172
Dealing with Grievances	173
Performance Appraisal	175
Using Volunteers	176

Chapter 14: Leadership and Staff Communications — **181**

Working with Other Departments	181
Creating an Effective Departmental Team	184
Balancing Communication Channels	185
Face-to-Face Communication	185
Telephone Calls	185
Texting	186
Electronic Mail	186
Put It in Print	187
Occasions for Sending Memos	187
Letters	188
Reaching the Entire Department	189
Sharing Ideas with Other Youth Librarians	190
Networking within a System or Region	190
Broadening Your Network	191
Choosing a Professional Association	192
Attending Conferences	193

Section VI: Looking toward the Future: Challenge and Change   **197**

Chapter 15: Changing Media—Changing Services   **199**

    Transliteracy   199

      Merging Media Platforms   200

      Encouraging Interactivity in the Library   200

      Inclusive Services for All Media for All Patrons   201

    Changing World of Publishing   201

    Acquiring and Providing Digital Materials   202

    Maintaining an Atmosphere that Welcomes Change   203

      Encourage New Ideas and Suggestions   204

      Allow Experimentation   204

      Allow Criticism of Imposed Change   205

      Don't Stop Talking   205

    References and Additional Resources   207

    Index   215

List of Figures

Figure 1.1 How Library Intersects with Children and Media   5

Figure 3.1 Steps in Strategic Planning   32

Figure 3.2 Planning Flow from Goals to Activities   39

Figure 4.1 Planning Evaluation of Programs   44

Figure 4.2 Information Collected for Reports   48

Figure 5.1 Steps in Preparing a Budget   55

Figure 5.2 Sample Public Library Budget   56

Figure 5.3 Sample School Library Budget   57

Figure 7.1 20th-Century Children's Library Collection   82

Figure 7.2 21st-Century Children's Library Collection   82

Figure 7.3 Materials for Different Age Groups   83

Figure 8.1 Cataloging Specification Decisions   98

Figure 9.1 Ideas and Media Aimed at Children   106

Figure 9.2 Library Bill of Rights   110

Figure 9.3 Free Access to Libraries for Minors   111

Figure 9.4 Access to Resources and Services in the School Library
Media Program   113

Figure 9.5 Sample Request for Reconsideration of Library
Resources   115

Figure 10.1 Types of Library Services for Children   124

Figure 13.1 Sample Job Description   164

Figure 13.2 Elements of Educational Presentation   171

Figure 14.1 Basic Communication Links in Public Library   182

Figure 14.2 Basic Communication Links in School Library   183

Section I

The Library in Its Community: Challenges and Changes

Children's librarians today see dramatic changes in the communities they serve: the nature of education and learning, the print and digital media they collect, and the lives of the children who use their libraries. Section I looks at the background of children's libraries, their relevance to the community, and the children they serve.

CHALLENGES

- Children's reading habits are changing year by year as ebooks displace print books in book sales and at home and school.
- Families are becoming more stressed as more single parents raise children on their own, more children live in poverty, and more children live in homes where English is not commonly used.
- Communities are changing as immigration patterns and changing birthrates change demographic profiles.
- Spending on public institutions is decreasing, and libraries and schools often have to seek funding from private individuals and corporations.
- Children's use of media is changing their interests and patterns of reading and learning.

CHANGES

In Section I we describe changes that are affecting communities and the children who live in them and use school and public libraries. We suggest ways in which librarians can adjust to ongoing community change by diversifying collections and services, remaining aware of new social and demographic patterns, and integrating children's media skills and interests into plans for library collections and services. Reading these chapters will introduce you to strategies for making your library a vital part of your community.

1

Why Do We Need Libraries for Children?

Why do communities spend money on libraries for children? At a time when traditional government services and expenditures are being questioned, why should libraries be supported? In several states school libraries are being closed, and public libraries are having their hours cut back. Suggestions have been made that with so much information and recreational materials online, children don't need libraries anymore. How can librarians explain to the public that their services are as important as ever? How did libraries for children become an important part of our society, and how long will they remain important?

PURPOSES OF CHILDREN'S LIBRARIES

Among the reasons for the success of children's libraries was the importance of reading skills necessary for workers in factories and offices. Children moving from farming communities to cities needed greater reading skills than their parents as America moved from a rural to an urban economy, and immigrant children needed to learn to read and write in English. Libraries introduced both of these groups to books and built reading skills. As children had access to more books and reading materials through library use, they read more, enjoyed it more, and learned more. Public libraries and some school libraries used storytimes and other book-based programs to build pre-reading skills of preschool and kindergarten children. Schools taught basic reading skills in the classroom, but libraries offered resources for the practice in reading needed to develop fluency.

Library services are offered to individuals, so the reading done in a library can match the specific interests and talents of users. Young people need stimulation, structure, and reading practice, and those could be found in library collections and services. The library has always been all about learning that focuses on the individual child's interests and abilities.

By the middle of the 20th century, children's libraries were the great success story of the library community. They received overwhelming support from parents and teachers and were often seen as the most important reason for taxpayers to support public libraries and school districts to provide library service.

Gradually as the 20th century moved on, libraries became more than just a resource making books available to all children. After World War II, more audiovisual materials were produced for children, and libraries collected many of them. Stories and music for children were provided on vinyl records and later cassettes, CDs, and DVDs. The growth of the internet late in the century led to an important revolution in services. At first it was just the catalog that went online, but as the years passed, informative and entertaining websites for children were developed, music became a product to be downloaded to MP3 players, and videos proliferated. At first children's librarians reacted by setting up computer labs or clusters where children could use software or do word processing. Soon the computers were integrated into the library itself, and as laptops, smartphones, and tablets became gateways to the online world, digital and print materials mingled in the same environment.

important

Even though children and their media have changed, some things remain constant. The children coming into our libraries vary greatly in age and background. They come from many different ethnic and social groups. Often they have learned to speak many different languages. No matter how different the children and how changed the media they prefer, libraries still have a mandate to provide collections and services for all.

The library as a public institution offers well-defined services for all children. All children need to find these things when they use a library, no matter what kind of family they come from:

- Access to recreational formats, especially books, which may not be available elsewhere
- Access to information and knowledge at a level they can understand
- Tools to help them hone their skills and manipulate the information they are learning
- Trained personnel to help them find information and materials relevant to them
- Security in a safe environment
- Opportunities to interact with other children and develop social skills

CHANGING PRIORITIES

A century ago children's libraries were important because they made a scarce resource—books—available to all children in a community. They provided entertainment and information in formats that were difficult to find outside of schools, and even schools had a very limited supply of books. Now in the early years of the 21st century, both entertainment and information resources are available to children not only in school but in virtually all homes. Access to television is almost universal for American children, and access to computers and the internet is fast approaching universality.

Not only do kids have many forms of media available, they tend to use it for many hours during the day. According to a recent study

Each day, school-age children pack almost eight hours of media exposure into 5 and a half hours of time. By using more than one medium at a time, also known as media multitasking, children can up their media consumption and squeeze more technology into their few non-school hours (Rideout, 2010).

Libraries are no longer the sole source of stories, music, news, or information, but this does not mean they are obsolete. Information overload can be as difficult to handle as information scarcity, and children growing up in the midst of a glut of media often find it difficult to understand and to process the facts they find. The role of libraries has changed from being one of the few suppliers of print information and recreation to being one of the few institutions that can organize a never-ending stream of information media and help children make sense of it. Librarians are no longer gatekeepers with a defined collection of materials, but rather Sherpas guiding children through the tangles of digital offerings both inside and outside of the library building. Their roles have evolved but have not lost their value to the community.

so true!

Libraries operate at the intersection of children and media. To do that successfully, librarians need to be comfortable with many kinds of media. Information is becoming increasingly agnostic—not limited to any one platform, but capable of being read, viewed, and understood in several different formats. Some individuals prefer one format to another, but many of today's young people move happily from one to another. The public expects libraries to provide a wide range of services and materials, although not every library will offer every possible variation.

Figure 1.1
How Library Intersects with Children and Media

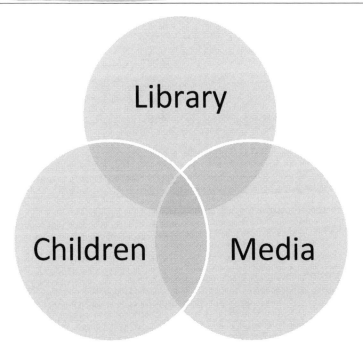

TYPES OF CHILDREN'S LIBRARIES

Children's libraries got their start when public libraries started collecting materials for children, although at first they usually defined children as those ages 12 and older. Gradually the age restrictions on children who used the library were dropped; collections expanded to include picture books, and parents were invited to start borrowing materials even for children too young to read. Now public librarians define their patron group as all the children in a community from ages 0 to 12 or 14. School and special libraries for children have more specific audiences.

Generally they are the most inclusive type of library, setting fewer limitations on clientele than school or special libraries. Although children's libraries are similar in their goals and services, there are differences in their functions and goals.

Public Libraries

Mission. The mission of most public libraries is to serve all of the children in a community, including various ethnic groups; those with special needs; temporary residents, such as migratory workers; and those who are being homeschooled.

Services. Public libraries collect a wide range of materials, both print and non-print, for all age groups, designed to meet the needs of special groups within the community. They also offer reference services and programs designed to encourage reading and other educational activities. These include storytimes for young children, reading groups, summer reading programs, and sometimes clubs.

Staffing. Professionally trained library staff are generally in charge of public libraries. They do the administrative work and perform many of the services provided. Library assistants, clerks, shelvers or pages, maintenance staff, and volunteers provide auxiliary services to keep the libraries functioning. An elected or appointed library board is the governing body under the direction of the city or county government. State and provincial libraries often set standards for the local library.

Funding. Public libraries are tax-funded institutions. Local taxes are generally their major support, supplemented by state and federal monies. They may also receive money from donations, grants, bequests, and endowments.

School Libraries

Mission. The goal of school libraries is to provide access to high-quality resources in a variety of formats that support curricular and instructional goals and respond to diverse student needs and interests and to ensure that students and teachers have equitable access to the library and its resources, including current technology. School libraries often include professional collections for teachers and sometimes resources for parents. They do not generally provide materials or services for preschool children or for those attending other educational institutions.

Services. School libraries collect materials for students and teachers to support the school curriculum. Recreational materials, especially those that encourage reading, are also frequently collected. In addition, the libraries serve students by providing reference services and library instruction. The staff works with teachers to suggest and provide materials to support class projects and interests. They may also hold storytimes for primary grade children and book clubs for readers.

Staffing. School libraries in most states and provinces are staffed by librarians who are certified teachers as well as certified school librarians. The staff may also include library assistants, clerks, and parent or student volunteers.

Funding. Funding for school libraries comes from local and state tax funds supplemented by grants and sometimes federal funds. Gifts and donations in kind are provided from parents and community groups. Because school libraries are an integral part of the school system, their funding depends on the general education budget of the community and the state. Recently many municipalities and states have been reducing their funding for school libraries, sometimes reducing hours of opening, sometimes requiring school librarians to serve several schools in a district, and sometimes transferring school librarians back into the classroom and allowing the libraries to be staffed by a clerk or volunteer parents.

Special Libraries

Mission. The mission of special children's libraries is determined by the mission of the parent organization. Museums, hospitals, churches, and community groups are types of organizations that may provide libraries for children. Their goal is to further the aims of the institution by providing materials and services for children who participate in the organization. These goals determine the types of materials provided: museums collect in the field of the museum whether science or art; church libraries support religious classes by offering supplementary materials; hospitals offer background on medical conditions and often recreational materials; and community groups may build collections that give background about sports, hobbies, or specific ethnic groups depending on the nature of the institution.

Services. The services provided by special libraries vary widely. In addition to a collection, these libraries often provide reference services, occasionally reading groups or storytimes, or classes related to the mandate of the organization.

Staffing. Some large institutions employ a professional librarian; many others rely on volunteers. Retired librarians and library school students are frequently volunteers in special libraries. The public library may offer some help to special libraries in the community.

Funding. Special libraries receive funding from the budget of the institution they serve. Large, well-funded institutions often provide generously for materials and services; many other special libraries struggle along with donated books and volunteer services.

PLANNING SERVICES FOR ALL CHILDREN

If the goal is to reach kids, it must be their needs and perspectives that shape what we do. That perspective will be varied, and varied approaches must be used to reach kids how, where and when they are receptive (Sullivan, 2010, p. 78).

As media converges and books, the internet, DVDs, and social networks offer much of the same content in varied formats, librarians are shifting the focus of their service from offering collections of materials to being access points for many forms of entertainment and information. In the children's department or at school, a child who borrows the latest Newbery Medal winner may follow up by posting a comment on the library blog, preparing a video book review to post on YouTube, or perhaps enter the library's Facebook site to discuss the book with friends.

Some typical library users:

- A Head Start student comes with her grandmother to a library story program. The booklist of stories will be available online for her parents to view and talk about with the child at home.
- A 12-year-old uses a home computer to check resources in the school library's homework help center. Unable to locate the information she wants about wildlife sanctuaries in South India, she has an online chat with the librarian, who helps her find a map and pictures.
- Three fourth-grade boys come to the library to participate in a gaming meet. The librarian arranges a schedule for them and others as they arrive. After playing, the boys add an entry to the library blog commenting on the games and suggesting others the library might purchase.
- A small group of fifth-graders in a local school exchange email with the public librarian to arrange a library visit. They are searching for books and pictures about the history of textile mills in their community.
- Two Chinese-speaking preteen newcomers to the community come into the library to find dual-language books for themselves and a video with Chinese captions for their grandmother.

One important difference among the children served by a library is their age. In planning services, librarians must be sure they meet the needs of each age group, from toddlers to young teens. Both materials provided and interactions with them vary by age. Most libraries break their child users into groups.

Preschool Children

Preschool children may be infants brought to the children's department by parents or caregivers. Some libraries provide playpens where these babies can be left for a short time. Books of nursery games and rhymes for reading to babies as well as CDs and simple DVDs serve these youngest clients. Some libraries offer brief storyhours for babes in arms.

When children reach the toddler stage (when they begin to walk), the range of materials and services increases greatly. Toddlers require special materials— sturdy boardbooks, music CDs, and appropriate DVDs as well as toys. If programs are offered for the underthrees, provision must be made for a high ratio of adults to children. Often parents are required to attend and participate with their child. The difficulty of controlling the activities of toddlers means that direct supervision of each child must be available at all times.

By the time children reach the age of three or so, their needs and behavior are quite different from those of the toddlers. Children of this age can handle standard picture books, and a wide range of materials should be available to meet their varied and growing interests. In many libraries, some computers are designated for use by preschoolers and their caregivers. Three- and four-year-old children do not require as much adult supervision as toddlers, but they still can't be left alone. Programs for them can be held in larger groups and require less personnel time. Because preschoolers are interested in learning about almost everything, they are an appreciative audience for library programs. Many of the programs and services provided by traditional children's departments or schools with an early education program are aimed at preschool children's language growth and development of pre-reading skills. In designing facilities for children's departments and school libraries, furniture suitable in size and design for preschoolers is important. Provision of a program room separate from the main library spaces is often useful.

School-Age Children

Some school-age children (kindergarten to fifth or sixth grade) have a school library available as well as the public library. And school-age children spend five to eight hours a day in class, so programming and special services aimed at this group are often more limited than those for preschool children. Many librarians provide special programs and reading clubs for school-age children after class and during the summer months.

In most communities there is heavy use of the public library by schoolchildren both for recreational and school-related materials. School libraries first meet the students' academic needs, but often have recreational activities as well. A large proportion of the materials in an average children's department are suitable for school-age children. Most of the reference service provided in the department will be for this age group, so the reference collection is usually slanted toward their needs. Because schoolchildren come to the public library in the late afternoon, evenings, weekends, and holiday periods, they tend to make heavy demand during these times. Crowded conditions often occur when schoolchildren congregate in the library during school breaks. Many public libraries provide collections and programs to help children with their homework and actively work with local schools to coordinate library activities for students.

School-age children begin to develop interests and preferences for what to read and learn about. Reading skill is more varied as is the ability to do computer research, so even within this age group there are wide variations of needs and interests. School librarians have the advantage of access to school performance records and grade-level expectations to help them tailor services for individual students. Children's librarians need to develop surveys of informal ways to tell what children need and want.

Transitional Users

Most children's departments are planned to serve children under the age of 12 or 13. Many children move quickly and happily into the adult department, but others find it difficult to make the adjustment. Children often need help to navigate the larger adult collection and may need the more personal help offered by staff in the children's room. Children whose reading skills are limited or whose native language is not English are more likely than others to have difficulty in making this transition. Parents also may expect older children to watch younger siblings, and that keeps them in the children's department.

Children's departments in libraries without specialized young adult staff have a responsibility to provide bridging materials and services to help transitional users become independent users of adult services. A selection of teenage books, magazines, and other media are often necessary in a children's department.

School librarians need to help prepare students for reading at the next level as well. This means having collections in elementary school for gifted readers and providing information literacy instruction so that elementary students will be comfortable in the middle school library. Middle and high school libraries need to have adult material that is age appropriate for gifted students and easier materials for students who are not reading or learning at their grade level.

Adults

Although adults are not the primary target audience for services offered by the school library or in the children's department, many services are designed for adults. Adult users of a children's department or school library might include:

- Parents choosing books for children
- Homeschooling parents looking for materials and services
- Teachers in both public and non-public schools
- Daycare and youth workers in the community
- Students of children's literature
- Family literacy or English as a second language programs

The needs of adults are often different from those of the children. Literature students may ask for historical children's books that would not be kept in most children's collections; youth workers may want materials aimed very specifically at their programs; and parents sometimes request the inclusion or exclusion of materials expressing particular points of view. All of these requests must be considered and addressed.

Many libraries offer family programs or school open houses and encourage parents and children to use the school library or children's department together. Some libraries require children to be accompanied by parents or an adult when in the children's department. Parents and caregivers may expect the school or children's librarian to provide parent-centered reference and parenting materials. For example, in Suffolk County, New York, the public library manages the Community Resources Database, which contains information on health and social service agencies that help parents and children; see https://211longisland .communityos.org/cms/ (accessed Aug. 29, 2012). Use of the children's department by adults may necessitate the provision of adult-sized furniture or study carrels, and sometimes affects the overall noise and activity level considered acceptable. Some libraries provide rocking chairs or other comfortable furniture to encourage adults to read to children. Occasionally adults in the children's department may pose a threat to children, and some librarians prefer to limit use of the children's area to adults accompanying children or those who are students or teachers using children's materials. → Scary ⏜

Differences Unrelated to Age

Besides age differences, there are other factors that affect the way children use libraries and their need for services. Each school or community has a different mix of elements that may affect library services, and an effective librarian considers them in planning.

Ethnic Diversity

Children whose home language is not English may want materials and programming in other languages. Selecting, acquiring, and cataloging foreign-language materials for children can be difficult and time consuming. If the school or community includes several groups speaking different languages, the librarian may need to ask neighborhood groups for help in locating appropriate materials. Providing services such as storyhours for different language groups is an even more complex task and, unless library staff members have the necessary language skills, requires use of outside personnel.

Many communities and schools serve African Americans, Asian Americans, or other racial minorities. These librarians will want to include materials by and about these minority cultures. The library may provide special cultural programs aimed at these groups; often this is done in cooperation with community groups.

→ I didn't know this. cool.

For example, many school and public libraries celebrate Dia de los Ninos/Dia de los Libros (Children's Day/Book Day) which is April 30. Founded in 1996 and supported by several divisions of the American Library Association, Dia provides a way of honoring children and books. Its goal is to link children of all cultures to bilingual or multilingual books and engage parents, teachers, and librarians in cultural learning through books (Naidoo, 2011, p. 201).

Not all materials for non-English speakers will be in their home language. Librarians may collect materials that reflect the background and heritage of the various groups. Folktales and legends from particular cultures are important to increase children's sense of their heritage. Storyhours featuring English translations of stories from a particular cultural group may be a regular part of the program.

Homeschooled Children

Many librarians work with parent groups to provide programming and materials designed for families whose children are being homeschooled. Most communities have homeschooling parent groups who will work with the library in planning these. In some states, school librarians are required to lend materials to homeschooling families and provide students with computers and information literacy instruction.

Homeschooled children benefit from individualized instruction but may lack access to resources and support systems for augmenting their learning. Homework help programs can offer an excellent resource for these students (Intner, 2011, p. 150). Some libraries have a collection of textbooks that also expand learning resources for homeschooled students, or librarians identify online courses and educational resources that these students can use at home or in the library.

Special Needs

Children with physical or mental differences have special needs that the library can serve. The needs of children with disabilities affect collection development, the layout of the library, and programming. These children must be considered when designing the overall program of a school library or children's department. The federal Americans with Disabilities Act (ADA) directs public institutions to provide facilities and services to children with a variety of disabilities. State and local governments often have specific regulations about how to design space, and local advocacy groups often can provide guidelines for providing services.

School librarians should work with special education teachers to be sure that the school library is included in the special education student's individual learning plan. The school librarian should follow all school regulations when developing services that provide the least restricted environment for mentally, physically, and behaviorally different students. Librarians in the public library are not regulated so specifically, but they, too, should be as inclusive as possible.

Unattended Children

Library services should be provided not only to children who come to the public library for a specific purpose, but also to those who habitually spend after-school hours there. These children, sometimes referred to as latchkey children or self-care children, are not primarily interested in the library's collection but in having something satisfying to do. The number of these children will vary from one community to another, but their needs should be considered in setting library policy. School libraries should have clear rules about when students can come to the library unaccompanied by a teacher and what supervision needs to be provided for the school library to be open before and after school.

Other groups that may require particular services are transient children, those whose parents are migratory workers or who are on temporary assignments or contract work; children of the homeless living in shelters or elsewhere; and hospitalized and institutionalized children. The specific groups will vary from one school or community to another, but librarians should assess the needs of all groups in the community when planning a program of services.

TYPES OF SERVICES

Libraries offer a basic menu of services for children or students, although the details and method of delivery varies from one community or school to another.

While each type of service is distinct, they operate together to create the whole program of services to children.

Building Collections

Providing a collection of materials is a basic task of any library, although not all the materials may be in the library's physical site. A school or children's department collection includes fiction and nonfiction books; magazines; nonprint materials such as ebooks, DVDs, and CDs; and offsite electronic resources through databases, websites, and appropriate social network resources.

Books are still the backbone of most children's collections (for now) and are divided into categories of some or all of the following:

- Boardbooks
- Picture books
- Books for beginning readers
- Chapter books
- Graphic novels
- Nonfiction and reference books
- Foreign-language books
- Historical children's books
- Parenting and teacher books for adults
- Textbooks, workbooks, and other learning materials

The development of information technology has expanded the definition of a collection. A school library or children's department will typically try to combine the provision of onsite materials with that of access to offsite information. Collection development includes selecting databases, choosing link sites for the department's webpage, and deciding on the purchase or licensing of other electronic media.

Managing the children's collection involves setting priorities, selecting and purchasing materials based on library policies, and weeding worn or outdated materials. It also requires making the collection accessible.

Making the Collection Accessible

A collection of materials is of little value unless users can find items they want. The services for making resources accessible include cataloging and classification of materials, reference services to help individuals or groups find specific information for school or personal needs, and readers' advisory services to help individuals or groups find materials for recreation or education. Signage and recommended lists of materials also help make library materials easier to find.

Online catalogs provide information about where and in what format materials are housed and make it possible to access or borrow materials from other libraries. Another access point is the library's webpage, from which children can search the catalog and the library's databases as well as recommended webpages. Web access should be high speed, and both schools and public libraries need to make electronic resources available to homes, recreational centers, and other locations where children gather.

Delivering Information Services

Answering children's questions is a basic part of a librarian's work. Questions include requests for specific books or other materials as well as for homework help or other information. These are the services that bring children and collections together, and they may include

- Recommending books or other materials
- Answering reference questions in the library or through telephones, email, online chats, texting, or cell phones
- Teaching children how to use the catalog, databases, and internet searching
- Helping parents, teachers, and caregivers to find materials for children

School and children's librarians need to listen carefully to library users, develop good interview skills, and be available to answer questions in a thoughtful, unhurried way. The range of questions is wide, and with children it is important not only to give an accurate answer, but one the child can understand and use.

Providing Educational and Recreational Programs

The familiar storyhours for toddlers, preschoolers, and older children are designed to develop literacy and encourage reading. Game days, summer reading clubs, art and craft programs, author visits, and the like are designed to give children cultural and recreational experiences that might not otherwise be available to them.

Some programs sponsored by libraries are not directly linked to educational goals. These might include craft programs, dancing, filmmaking, gaming groups, and language classes. Often these programs use outside personnel as leaders, but the planning, registration, and publicity may be handled by the library. These programs can draw new users to the library and give the librarian an opportunity to tell children about all the school or public library does. It is also good practice to have programs that are fun to help children and families have a positive view of the library.

Outreach

Some children's departments offer programs and services outside the library building. Most school librarians offer programs in the classroom as well as the library and interact with teachers by attending staff meetings. Many children's librarians visit daycares and schools, but librarians also serve boys and girls clubs, camps, recreation centers, or other places that children gather. Outreach can include materials for circulation or programs. Some libraries participate in community fairs or school reading events; others host programs on public television.

The library may establish partnerships with organizations or agencies that serve children and families. Partnership activities may include joint training of staff such as public librarians attending curriculum training at the school district or school librarians attending a presentation by a children's author at the public library. School and public librarians can also share homework alerts from teachers, or other regular communications. Partners can be health related with the partnership providing health information to families or library materials for hospital patients. Many local museums, schools, and libraries share exhibits and activities for children.

Marketing Services

Unless people know what the library has to offer, they will not take advantage of the collections and services. Parents of young children are eager to find resources for them, but many do not think of using the library. "Libraries are a beloved tradition in America, commanding respect, pride, and even a willingness to support the occasional bond issue. Yet, for an institution that has been around this long, the library has simply faded into the background for many in the general public" (Sass, 2002, pp. 37–38). School libraries are often seen as an extra because parents and taxpayers do not know what services they provide. Librarians must work hard to ensure that their community is aware of all the materials and services the library offers.

Examples of library marketing:

- Drafting media releases to announce programs
- Providing a new book column in local newspapers, including foreign-language papers
- Taping public service announcements for radio and television
- Developing an attractive children's department website
- Posting videos of library events on YouTube and other outlets
- Producing an e-newsletter or a children's department blog

Specific methods will vary according to the community and will change with evolving technology, but the principle of informing people about library services is a constant. Public and school libraries are service organizations, and the community should be informed about their collections and services.

Evaluation and Accountability

An additional responsibility of school and children's librarians is to evaluate the success or impact of the services offered. Most librarians who serve children work for agencies that use tax funds, but even in private schools or libraries there is increased interest in accountability. This includes both how funds are allocated and spent and what benefits are gained by offering library services for children. So evaluation has become part of the job for school and children's librarians. Evaluation may include:

- How many children or students attend a program or use a service
- Circulation and online "hit" statistics

- Improved grade or academic performance linked to library use
- Positive attitude toward reading, improved reading scores
- Awards or commendations of library staff
- Positive comments from library users

Many of the factors that librarians use to plan services and activities such as "identifying the users, figuring out what users need, determining how to meet the users' needs are the same factors that inform the evaluation process" (Intner, 2011, p. 159). Whether librarians use surveys and focus groups, self-evaluation, or head counts, the purpose of evaluation is twofold. First, evaluation assures users and the public that the library benefits actual children in purposeful and important ways. Second, evaluation helps staff to improve and change services based on facts about what works for users and what doesn't.

Being a school or children's librarian requires understanding that services and programs need to be varied both because children vary from age to age, from school to school, and from community to community. And communities and schools change over time, so library services and programs need to change from year to year. School and public libraries are not one thing, but many services and programs that are needed and used by children and families. The challenge for school and children's librarians is to choose, design, and coordinate the best possible programs to serve children in their school or community. The reward is that the work is not boring, varies from day to day, and, if done right, helps all sorts of children be successful students and happy people.

LOOKING FORWARD

Twenty-first-century libraries are part of a revolution in communication and education, and nowhere is this more evident than in children's services. Children's libraries today are heirs to a long tradition of public services to children, but they cannot rest on their laurels. As the world changes, libraries must change, too, if they hope to continue their central position in communities. Collections, services, and planning will be fluid and ever-changing as librarians meet the challenges of a changing society.

IF YOU WANT TO KNOW MORE ...

Bertot, John Carlo, Paul T. Jaeger, and Charles R. McClure, eds. 2011. *Public Libraries and the Internet*. Santa Barbara, CA: Libraries Unlimited.

Cerny, Rosanne, Penny Markey, and Amanda Williams. 2006. "Knowledge of Client Group." In *Outstanding Library Service to Children: Putting the Core Competencies to Work*. Chicago: American Library Association.

Diamant-Cohan, Betsy. 2010. *Children's Services: Partnerships for Success*. Chicago: American Library Association.

Feinberg, Sandra, Barbara Jordan, Kathleen Deerr, Marcellina Byrne, and Lisa Kropp. 2007. *The Family-Centered Library Handbook*. New York: Neal-Schuman.

Intner, Carol. 2011. *Homework Help from the Library: In Person and Online*. Chicago: American Library Association.

Naidoo, Jamie Campbell, ed. 2011. *Celebrating Cuentos: Promoting Latino Children's Literature and Literacy in Classrooms and Libraries.* Santa Barbara, CA: Libraries Unlimited.

Rideout, V., U. G. Foehr, and D. Roberts. 2010. *Generation M2: Media in the Lives of 8- to 18-Year-Olds.* Menlo Park, CA: Henry J. Kaiser Family Foundation. Available at http://www.kff.org/entmedia/upload/8010.pdf (accessed Aug. 29, 2012).

Sass, Rivkah K. 2002. "Marketing the Worth of Your Library." *Library Journal* 127 (11): 37–38.

Sullivan, Michael. 2010. *Serving Boys through Reader's Advisory.* Chicago: American Library Association.

Walter, Virginia. 2010. *Twenty-First Century Kids, Twenty-First Century Librarians.* Chicago: American Library Association.

2

Getting to Know Today's Children

The United States Census of 2010 revealed that children growing up today have changed in significant ways from those of the 20th century. Although the basic structures of children's lives are similar to those of their parents, differences in the demographic, economic, and education patterns of the country have affected many of them. Librarians in both school and public libraries need to understand how some of these social factors affect the children they serve.

DEMOGRAPHIC CHANGES

Children growing up in 21st-century America face a number of challenges. The unsettled world situation, declining economic security, and drastic shifts in employment opportunities have caused many families to be less able to ensure a good future for their children. Children have declined as a percentage of the overall population, while the over-65 age group has increased. During the 1960s, when children were 36 percent of the population, education was at the center of social concern. Schools and libraries benefitted from the interest of communities in doing their best for youngsters. In 2009, children made up only 24.9 percent of the population, and much of society's interest was focused on the health and welfare needs of older adults. At the same time the absolute number of children has grown, and their educational and welfare needs are greater than ever.

SOME BASIC FACTS ABOUT AMERICAN CHILDREN

- 1 person in 4 is less than 18 years of age (lowest percentage of children ever)
- 1 child in 5 lives in poverty (among African Americans it is 1 child in 3)
- 1 child in 3 lives in a single-parent family (among African Americans it is 2 children in 3)
- Almost 1 child in 3 lives in a home where no one has full-time, year-round employment
- 2 babies in 5 are born to teenage mothers
- 1 teen in 20 is neither in school nor a high school graduate (Data Center, 2012)

Although communities vary widely in their composition, almost all of them have been affected by the overall trends in American society. High unemployment has meant more children live in economically insecure families even in prosperous suburbs. Communities across the country are more diverse than ever before, and almost all school districts and libraries serve some children whose families speak a language other than English at home. Single-parent families, families with same-sex parents, and families headed by grandparents are present in most communities and give a picture of family life not always represented in children's books. The American population is also shifting geographically. In the 2010 census, population grew in the West and South far faster than it did in the Midwest or Northeast. Some of this change is due to immigration from other countries, but most of it is the result of movement from one state to another.

CHANGING EDUCATIONAL TRENDS

Homeschooling

Among the changes that have taken place in American schools over the past ten years has been the increasing number of children who are homeschooled. Approximately one and a half million children were homeschooled in 2007, the last year for which the United States Department of Education has figures. That number is almost 3 percent (2.9%) of all school-age children, up from less than 2 percent (1.7%) in 1999. The biggest reason for homeschooling children is to provide a religious and moral education; other reasons include dissatisfaction with local schools, fear of bullying or violence in schools, distance from available schools, or children with special needs.

Children who are being homeschooled often do not have access to a school library, so many of them depend on public library services to supplement the curriculum they are following. Some public libraries provide meeting rooms for homeschooling parents to get together and provide lessons or discuss issues. Online resources for homeschooling parents and children are also much in demand.

Online Schools and Classes

Online courses are being used by both homeschooled and in-school children. According to a 2007 report from the North American Council for Online Learning, this practice

at the k-12 level has grown so much in recent years that the main issue in most states is no longer whether or not online learning is occurring, but rather how it is being implemented. As of September 2007, 42 states have significant supplemental online learning programs (in which students enrolled in physical schools take one or two courses online), or significant full-time programs (in which students take most or all of their courses online) or both. Only eight states do not have either of these options, and several of these states have begun planning for online learning development. In addition to the spread of online learning programs to most states across the country, the majority of existing online programs show considerable growth in the number of students they are serving. (North American Council, 2007, p. 7)

[handwritten margin note:] Why is that the last year of data?

The National Center for Education Statistics reported that in 2009–2010, 55 percent of public school districts reported having students enrolled in distance education courses. Among those districts, 96 percent reported having students enrolled in distance education courses at the high school level, 19 percent at the middle or junior high school level, 6 percent at the elementary school level, and 4 percent in combined or ungraded schools (National Center, 2011, p. 14).

High Stakes Testing → FUCK THIS BULLSHIT!

The climate of education in the United States has been altered by the passage of the No Child Left Behind legislation in 2002. That bill required states to test children in public schools and to reorganize schools in which children's scores did not improve over the years. There has been a great deal of discussion and arguments about the bill because of its emphasis on testing as a means of evaluating both teachers and schools. Arne Duncan, secretary of education in the Obama administration, has described some of the perceived weaknesses:

The act's emphasis on test scores as the primary measure of school performance has narrowed the curriculum, and the one-size-fits-all accountability system has mislabeled schools as failures even if their students are demonstrating real academic growth. The law is overly prescriptive and doesn't allow districts to create improvement plans based on their unique needs. It also has not supported states as they create teacher evaluation systems that use multiple measures to identify highly effective teachers and support the instructional improvement of all teachers (Duncan, 2012).

In the short term, the impact of the mandatory tests has been to cause schools to focus more narrowly on curricular needs. In some school districts this has led to less use of recreational reading materials in libraries. Some parents, too, have demanded materials that are clearly related to educational goals rather than to the enjoyment of reading. Kindergarten curricula guides have shifted to more direct preparation for reading and learning. In many districts, the kindergarten classes of today look more like the first grade classes of ten or fifteen years ago than traditional kindergartens. Many librarians and specialists in early education believe it is important to let parents know that purely recreational reading has an important place in the lives of young children.

This is sad and frustrating

In the upper grades the emphasis on testing has led to diminishment of education in arts and music. In some schools librarians may be required to cut back on collection in areas outside of the curriculum. Some parents rely on public libraries to provide materials to supplement children's education in these areas. Many libraries are providing more programming for children to make up for the changes in school curriculum.

e-textbooks

Although K–12 schools have been slower to adopt e-textbooks than colleges and universities, they are starting to move in this direction. In 2011, McGraw-Hill, one of the largest educational publishers, released its first entirely e-textbook curriculum. In the past most publishers have provided e-textbooks at this level primarily as supplements to print textbooks. In early 2012, Apple released a free program to enable teachers and authors to prepare textbooks for use on iPads. This trend is too new to assess how it will affect libraries, but it seems likely that it will influence both the collections and services they provide. Some students and teachers may request more print resources to back up e-textbooks, while others may prefer a greater variety of ebooks. Because many schools do not have the resources to provide ebook readers to all students for the e-textbooks, many have instituted a Bring Your Own Device (BYOD) policy. Librarians in some school districts may take on the job of providing reading devices for use in classrooms. Public libraries may be expected to make more reading devices available for lending to patrons.

CHANGING USES OF MEDIA AND TECHNOLOGY

As many commentators have noticed, today's children live in a media-rich world. A Kaiser Foundation study of the media use of young people from 8 to 18 years of age released in 2010 reported that the amount of time spent consuming media grew from 6 hours and 21 minutes to 7 hours and 38 minutes during the past 5 years. Because many young people use more than one type of media at the same time, they "pack a total of 10 hours and 45 minutes worth of media content into those daily 7 ½ hours" (Rideout, Foehr, and Roberts, 2010, p. 2).

Even among children 8 and under, a substantial proportion spend several hours each day watching, or at least being exposed to media. According to a study published in 2011, "Children age 8 and under spend an average of about three hours (3:14) a day with media, including screen media, reading, and music. Most of that time is spent with screen media: an average of 2:16 a day. Music and reading occupy an average of about a half-hour a day each" (Rideout, 2011, p. 17). Some of this exposure comes because television is always present in many homes no matter what other activities are being carried on. "More than a third (39%) of children 8 and under live in homes where the television is left on all (10%) or most (29%) of the time, whether or not anyone is watching it" (Rideout, 2011, p. 19).

Although television occupies more time in children's lives than any other media, computer use is also a major factor. The studies referred to above report that 72 percent of children below the age of 8 have a computer in their home. Almost half of the 2- to 4-year-olds have used a computer, and 9 out of 10 in the 5 to 8 age group have tried one. The average age for starting to use a computer is three and a half years.

Mobile media is also used by a growing number of young children. Among the 5- to 8-year-old group, approximately half have used a cell phone or other mobile device to play games, watch a video, or use apps (Rideout, 2011, p. 21). The digital divide shows up sharply in the use of mobile devices, with higher-income families having far more access to them than those in lower income groups. According to a 2011 report: "More than a third (38%) of lower-income parents don't have any idea what an 'app' is, compared to just 3% of higher-income parents. And just 14% of lower-income parents have ever downloaded any apps for their children to use, compared to 47% among the higher-income families" (Rideout, 2011, p. 21). Many lower-income families are unfamiliar with the nature of apps for mobile devices, while more than half of higher-income parents have downloaded apps for their children.

During the last ten years or so, the nature of the digital divide has changed. Computers are now widely available in homes, schools, and libraries, giving most children some access to online materials. High-speed internet access, however, varies considerably with income and with geographic region, making easy use of many computer-based materials difficult for some groups of children. Similarly, television is almost universally available to children, but cable access and the many channels it provides is much more limited. Digital recording devices are also more often available in upper-income homes, so many families cannot time shift educational programs or record them for re-watching.

Another change in technology use that has started to affect classrooms and libraries is the growth of communication through Skype. This free program offers free telephone calls between people in different parts of the country or of the world. Calls are sent over the internet rather than through conventional telephone lines and thus escape phone company charges. Many immigrant communities have found Skype an important tool to enable individuals to maintain contact with family and friends overseas.

Many children's librarians use Skype calls as a means of bringing children's authors into the library without having to pay the costs of travel or accommodation. Many authors have prepared presentations that include pictures, readings, and conversation with individual students. Of course this is not the only way Skype can be used in libraries and schools. Students can speak with groups of children overseas, exchanging details about their localities and learning about other places. Experts in various fields of study can talk to classes or groups. This use of communication is almost certain to grow as people discover new ways of utilizing the tool.

CHANGES IN READING FORMATS

The distinction between reading and using media has become blurred as more and more content is being produced that blends text with video or audio files. No matter whether these materials are used on a computer screen or, increasingly, on a mobile device such as an iPad, Kindle, or other tablet, they require some equipment. As we have seen from the figures above, this equipment is unevenly provided to children. How are we to meet these needs?

Schools

Many schools are moving toward having digital materials available to children in classrooms and school libraries, but the expense of maintaining equipment is difficult for most districts. Even when computers are donated to schools, they are often not maintained effectively and become outdated and unusable after several years. Parents groups sometimes give money, equipment, and volunteer time to help schools maintain their programs, but this is not a practical solution for the average school district. A major shift to digital rather than print sources for textbooks and curricular reading is not likely to happen until the economy improves, but over the long term digital formats will almost surely become more common.

Some school districts have implemented a program to encourage students to bring their own devices, such as iPads, to school, while the district provides them for students whose families cannot buy them. This solution seems unlikely to be satisfactory in the long term because it calls attention to economic inequalities between students.

Public Libraries

Digital materials are available in most public libraries. Children's departments, however, have not adopted these materials as quickly, although many now supply ebooks for borrowing. Many middle grade novels are being published as both ebooks and print versions. More picture books are being produced as apps, and children are reading them on tablet devices. Because of the disparity in home access to digital reading devices, families in upper-income communities are likely to be more interested in having the public library provide digital books and apps for children than those in lower-income areas. Decisions made by the school districts about using digital reading materials in classrooms are also likely to influence the demand in public libraries.

The availability of ebook readers in American homes has grown sharply during the past few years. A January 2012 Pew Research Center study (Rainie, 2012) reported that the ownership of digital readers nearly doubled over the 2011 holiday season. Nearly one in five adults now owns either a dedicated ebook reader or a tablet computer. As might be expected, ownership is higher among younger, college-educated, affluent people than among those in other demographic groups. Owning a digital reading device has not yet become a majority pattern, but considering that tablet computers were only introduced in 2010, the growth is impressive and suggests that within a few years most people will own one. Librarians will have to plan on satisfying patrons who do much of their reading in this format.

CHANGES IN INFORMATION SEEKING

Digital Resources

Reference services to children and teens have been changing dramatically ever since the introduction of online information sources. Although some schools and libraries have been slow to adapt to these changes, the transformation from print to digital is now almost complete. In a study at the University of Maryland, researchers found that almost all of the children they studied (ages 7 to 11) were familiar with the Google search engine and used it to find information (Druin, 2009). Most teachers and librarians are also aware that Google is the first place most children look when trying to get information for homework assignments or personal information. Many adults who work with children have also found, as these researchers did, that children's searching methods are often flawed. Frequently children do not find the information most useful to them or they spend far too much time searching before locating what they need.

Librarians in school and public libraries have devised ingenious plans for teaching children how to use library resources in searching for information, but many have not acknowledged that much of the information they are searching

agree.

for is not to be found in the physical library collection. Children need instruction in searching for information online and finding what they need both in the library and from their classroom, home, or other location where they might have online access. During the coming decade, as more and more young people have access to mobile technology, they will carry their information sources around with them on smartphones or whatever technology replaces those. The librarians' task will be to teach young people how to search effectively on a variety of platforms.

Search engines are not the only source of information for young people. Online video collections (for example, YouTube) are also an important source of information. In response to the educational use of their videos, YouTube in 2011 announced it would host an education channel to group together videos with a limited selection of videos for educational use.

The growth of social media sites has made accessible another source of information popular with young people. Sharing information with friends, asking questions about homework, recommending books and other media—all of these are frequently done on social media pages. For some information this is an effective search strategy. The librarians' task will be to show the strengths and weaknesses of relying on social media for information.

Group Searching

Another trend in information seeking is collaboration. Schools are beginning to emphasize collaboration in learning, and this leads naturally to working with others in search for information. The reason for the increasing emphasis being placed on collaboration is the changing workplace. Many projects in business, science, technology, and the arts are group projects in which problems are defined, solutions sought, and products developed by groups rather than by individuals working alone.

When teachers encourage students to work together in collaborative study, they often arrange desks in clusters to facilitate the use of shared tools. Librarians, too, will be expected to make arrangements for children to work together at a computer and to share the use of print and visual sources. This trend in education is already affecting the way librarians arrange their furniture and their resources.

CHANGES IN EMPLOYMENT OUTLOOK

The younger children among library patrons and school students are probably unaware that their career paths are a source of worry to parents and teachers. The 21st century has seen a changing job picture in North America and many other countries.

- The growth of technology has meant that fewer unskilled workers are required in factories and in agriculture as automation takes over many routine tasks.
- Both manufacturing and markets are now global, so tasks that once had to be performed locally can now be handled by facilities in different geographic areas in different parts of the world.

- Companies, both large and small, must constantly reinvent themselves to meet changing market needs; otherwise, even long-established businesses may disappear, disrupting employment opportunities in their communities.
- Jobs in service industries are predicted to grow over the next ten years. About a quarter of all new jobs are likely to be in the health services and assistance field.
- The fastest growing job sectors during the 2010–2020 decade are likely to be in the health care and social assistance sectors, while manufacturing jobs are likely to decline. Jobs requiring a master's degree will grow the fastest, while those needing only high school graduation are expected to be slowest (U.S. Bureau of Labor Statistics, 2010). This trend has already started and is likely to accelerate.

Most of the children attending our schools and using libraries today can expect to hold several jobs over their working life. The era of lifetime employment in one company appears to have ended for almost everyone who is not planning a career in a family business. Not only will employees have to get used to different employers and changes in working conditions, they are likely to find sharp differences in their working condition even in the same job. Changes in technology and in patron expectations will mean that employees will have to be able to adapt quickly and learn new skills. The skill set any student has at graduation time will need to be upgraded constantly over the years. Adaptability to new situations is a habit children should develop during their school years.

Another increasing trend in employment is the growth of collaborative working. Many modern workplaces are designed to group workers together in large open spaces rather than isolating each person in a small office or cubicle. One reason for this is to encourage collaboration and facilitate open discussions between individuals that may lead to problem solution and innovation. Collaboration between individuals and groups has led to much of the growth in technology and science. Today's schoolchildren will be well-served if they learn to work collaboratively on projects during their education. Traditional education methods that stress competition between individual students are less common in schools today than they were in earlier times.

Predictions about how employment trends should affect K–12 education vary, but many people agree that Science, Technology, Engineering, and Math, the so-called STEM subjects, should be encouraged. Job growth in these areas has outpaced that in the traditional humanities subjects of literature and the arts. Although almost no one would suggest that children concentrate entirely on STEM subjects, many educators believe they should be emphasized in schools. Library collections and services in these areas can certainly be strengthened by taking advantage of the many STEM resources being made available in print and online. The well-known preference of many children for nonfiction materials rather than stories has sometimes been lost in a drive to encourage reading with little emphasis on the content being read. Reading is important as the basis for education, but when basic skills have been mastered, encouraging a reading habit is likely to depend on the provision of stimulating content in areas of interest.

Today's children face a challenging world full of opportunities and difficulties. Preparing them to live in this world is the task of youth librarians, whether in school or public libraries.

IF YOU WANT TO KNOW MORE ...

Cooper, Linda Z. 2002. "A Case Study of Information-Seeking Behavior in 7-Year-Old Children in a Semistructured Situation." *ASIS* 53 (11): 904–922.

Cooper, Linda Z. 2005. "Developmentally Appropriate Digital Environments for Young Children." *Library Trends* 54 (2): 286–302.

Data Center 2012 from Kids Count. http://datacenter.kidscount.org (accessed Aug. 29, 2012).

Dresang, Eliza. 2005. "The Information-Seeking Behavior of Youth in the Digital Environment." *Library Trends* 54 (2): 178–196.

Druin, Allison, Elizabeth Foss, Hilary Hutchinson, Evan Golub, and Leshell Hatley. 2010. *Children's Roles Using Keyword Search Interfaces at Home.* Mountain View, CA: Google Inc.

Druin, Allison, Elizabeth Foss, Hilary Hutchinson, Evan Golub, Leshell Hatley, Mona Leigh Guha, and Jerry Fails. 2009. "How Children Search the Internet with Keyword Interfaces." Proceedings of Interaction Design and Children (IDC 2009), Cuomo, Italy, 89–96.

Duncan, Arne. 2012. "After 10 Years, It's Time for a New NCLB." *Washington Post*, January 8. Available at http://www.ed.gov/blog/2012/01/after-10-years-it%E2%80%99s-time-for-a-new-nclb/ (accessed Aug. 29, 2012).

Gutnick, Aviva Lucas, Michael Robb, Lori Takeuchi, and Jennifer Kotler. 2010. *Always Connected: The New Digital Media Habits of Young Children.* New York: The Joan Ganz Cooney Center at Sesame Workshop.

Hanson, Cody W. 2011. "Issues for Information Access on the Mobile Web." In *Library Technology Reports.* Chicago: American Library Association.

National Center for Education Statistics. 2011. "Distance Education," NCED 2012-008, p. 14 (http://nces.ed.gov/pubsearch/pubsinfo.asp?pubid=2012008; accessed Jan. 14, 2012).

North American Council for Online Education. 2007. http://www.inacol.org/research/docs/KeepingPace07-color.pdf (accessed Aug. 29, 2012).

Rainie, Lee. 2012. *Tablet and E-book Reader Ownership Nearly Double over the Holiday Gift-Giving Period.* Washington, D.C.: Pew Internet Project. Available at http://pewinternet.org/Reports/2012/E-readers-and-tablets.aspx (accessed Aug. 29, 2012).

Rideout, Victoria. 2011. *Zero to Eight: Children's Media Use in America. Common Sense Media.* Available at http://www.commonsensemedia.org/sites/default/files/research/zero toeightfinal2011.pdf (accessed Aug. 29, 2012).

Rideout, Victoria, Ulla G. Foehr, and Donald F. Roberts. 2010. *Generation M(2): Media in the Lives of 8- to 18-Year-Olds.* Menlo Park, CA: Henry J. Kaiser Family Foundation Study. Available at http://www.kff.org/entmedia/upload/8010.pdf (accessed Sept. 5, 2012).

U.S. Bureau of Labor Statistics. *Occupational Outlook Handbook, 2010–11 Edition.* Available at http://www.bls.gov/oco/oco2003.htm (accessed Aug. 29, 2012).

Weber, Sandra, and Shanly Dixon. 2007. *Growing Up Online: Young People and Digital Technologies.* New York: Palgrave Macmillan.

Section II

Planning Services: Challenges and Changes

> Organizing is what you do before you do something, so that when you do it, it is not all mixed up.
>
> —A. A. Milne

Schools and libraries set goals, decide on how to evaluate progress toward these goals, and create budgets that prioritize planned activities. School and children's librarians also need to plan for changes to the space, whether it is a new computer table or a whole new library space.

CHALLENGES

- A strategic plan is difficult to create in the midst of constant change in library practice, technology, and family life.
- Children's librarians need to improve evaluation techniques to meet the growing demand for accountability in their delivery of identifiable benefits to the children who use the library.
- Children's librarians must offer consistent programs and services even though funding is not assured year to year.
- Libraries need to reorganize space and upgrade electrical and communication systems to accommodate e-materials.

CHANGES

Chapters in this section describe planning, evaluation, and budgeting techniques essential for successful management of resources as well as maximizing service in the school or public library. We have added information on space and facilities planning as it is an important component in serving children, teachers, and parents effectively.

3

Strategic Planning

Strategic planning is the process by which staff in a library, or any organization, decides where to spend its money and resources and what will be done or accomplished during a specific time period. It should be presented in a document that enables administrators and the public to know why the library deserves support for its activities and what benefits the community can expect from them.

MISSION STATEMENTS FOR STRATEGIC PLANNING

Strategic planning for library departments starts with reading and understanding the library's mission statement.

Public Library Mission Statements

Mission statements are broad general statements about the overall purpose and aims of a library. Some mission statements are very succinct, such as the one from the New York Public Library:

The mission of The New York Public Library is to inspire lifelong learning, advance knowledge, and strengthen our communities. (http://www.nypl.org/help/about-nypl/mission; accessed Sept. 5, 2012)

The Seattle Public Library states its mission this way:

The Seattle Public Library brings people, information and ideas together to enrich lives and build community. (http://www.spl.org/about-the-library/mission-statement; accessed Sept 5, 2012)

Figure 3.1
Steps in Strategic Planning

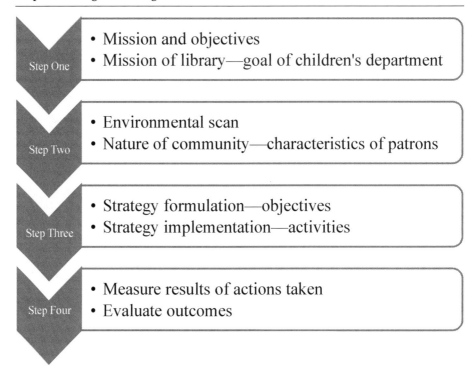

Step One
• Mission and objectives
• Mission of library—goal of children's department

Step Two
• Environmental scan
• Nature of community—characteristics of patrons

Step Three
• Strategy formulation—objectives
• Strategy implementation—activities

Step Four
• Measure results of actions taken
• Evaluate outcomes

The goals of a library and of a department grow out of the library's mission statement. A mission statement sets forth in general terms the purpose of the institution. Examining the mission statement of your library and developing departmental goals that can be clearly related to it helps ensure that the department is on the right track. Having a defined set of goals and objectives demonstrates to administrators and to the public that a department has a clear view of what it is trying to do for its patrons and for the community at large. A children's department goal of serving every child in the community by "promoting easy access to a vast array of ideas and information" grows naturally out of the mission statement of the Seattle Library.

School Library Mission Statements

School libraries also have mission statements. Here is an example from Eldorado Intermediate School in Chestnut Ridge, New York:

The mission of the Eldorado Library Media program is to ensure that students, staff and community have access to and possess the knowledge and skills to effectively use information in both print and digital formats. In doing so, the library media program supports and fosters lifelong learning. (http://www.eram.k12.ny.us/education/components/scrapbook/default

.php?sectiondetailid=41830&PHPSESSID=aee042f01b80b57b0f5b47961b48e8c4; accessed Aug. 25, 2012)

Children's Libraries in Other Settings

Not all children's libraries fit into the traditional administrative structures of public libraries or schools. Hospitals and museums may also house children's libraries dedicated to the needs of patrons of the parent institution. Usually the institution has a mission statement that can be a guide for the specific goals of the children's library. The Brooklyn Children's Museum, for example, has a mission statement that easily fits into the activities of children's library services:

The mission of Brooklyn Children's Museum is to actively engage children in educational and entertaining experiences through innovation and excellence in exhibitions, programs, and use of its collection. The Museum encourages children to develop an understanding of and respect for themselves, others and the world around them by exploring cultures, the arts, science, and the environment. (http://www.brooklynkids.org/index.php/aboutus/whoweare; accessed Aug. 27, 2012)

MOVING FROM MISSION TO DEPARTMENTAL GOALS

Many institutions have mission statements that are quite general and therefore can be interpreted in different ways. Nonetheless, it is the statement that justifies expenditures on children's services and serves as the basic support for a librarian's program of services. It is usually wise to incorporate reference to the mission statement in departmental goal setting. A good mission statement is a source of guidance and inspiration; it defines the unique contribution of your library (or the children's department) and should be easy to say, read, and remember (Wallace, 2004, p. 16). Some children's departments create a departmental mission based on the mission of the larger library to use as a guide in planning, budgeting, and fundraising; others simply refer to the institution's mission statement as the basis for planning.

Goals that grow out of mission statements:

Mission Statement—We strive to inform, enrich, and empower every person in our community.
Department Goal—Create services that reach every child in the community.

                              * * * *

Mission Statement—To guarantee that students and staff have access to and are effective users of ideas and information.
Departmental Goal—Develop an effective information literacy program for students in each grade.

In the examples above, the departmental goals show a strong link to the stated mission of the library. In writing or talking about the department's goals, library staff should emphasize the way in which the goals carry out the library's mission. This is the foundation a department head can use to defend specific programs developed under the goals. To some extent it protects the library's activities from defunding by making clear how each activity plays an important role in carrying out the library's overall mission.

The process of establishing, attaining, and evaluating goals is a continuous one; each goal must be examined periodically to see whether it is still appropriate. Goals grow out of the mandate of the library, and in many libraries they are intended to remain unchanged for three to five years. Objectives and activities undertaken to achieve the goals usually are reviewed and if necessary changed on a yearly basis.

Specific activities and programs are chosen to achieve the objectives of a department's goals. They should grow naturally from the goals of an organization and should relate to specific library goals. It should be possible for library staff and the public to see how the activities work to carry out the stated library goals. Here are some examples of these relationships:

Goal—Create services that reach every child in the community
Activities—

1. Provide storyhour programs for daycare centers throughout the community
2. Establish a weekly Spanish-language storyhour at the library
3. Offer email and chat session reference service for children who cannot get to the library
4. Develop rotating collections of books and other materials for teachers in charter schools and for groups of homeschooling parents

Each of these activities clearly relates to the goal of the department, which grows directly out of the library's mission.

Environmental Scan

Gathering Information. "Environmental scan" is a rather elaborate name for looking around the community, collecting information, and talking to people who are the intended audience for an activity. To investigate how the department should go about providing storyhours for daycare centers, for example, library staff would begin by finding out how many daycare centers there are in the community and where they are located. Many lists of accredited daycare centers may be kept by the local government, or an internet search will give information about most of them.

Having identified the daycare centers you want to serve, your next task is to find out whether they are interested in the service. Information about the programs that would be available can be posted on the library website and centers invited to apply. To reach most of the centers, it will be necessary to contact them directly. Telephone calls usually work best because mail and email requests rarely receive replies. Telephone calls are time-consuming, so the library may use volunteers to make the preliminary calls. If possible, a telephone call could be followed by a personal visit to the daycare center, or a daycare representative may visit the library. Face-to-face interaction will give the library staff a good idea of what kind of programs a center might want and information about the attitudes and goals of the center.

Getting Feedback. It is important to get feedback from the potential audience for a program, but there is some danger in simply asking what services individuals or groups would like. To avoid raising unrealistic hopes, the library might provide a list of possible services, such as weekly or monthly storyhours, rotating collections of books, or occasional programs. The library staff must make clear that this phase of questioning is only to establish which services would be appreciated, because the library will not be able to provide every service requested.

To encourage ongoing exchange of ideas and feedback on programs, a librarian could establish a daycare page on its website or social media site, or initiate email communication with providers. Evaluation sheets distributed at programs elicit some responses, but typically very few adults take the time to fill them out, and telephone calls to evaluate programs should be discouraged because they are extremely time consuming. Both daycare providers and children's librarians are busy people who will appreciate simple and efficient communication methods.

Collecting Statistics. Another strand of environmental scanning to support the decision to provide storyhours for daycare centers is to document the need by collecting statistics. The department should have available the demographic information about how many preschool children live in the community and what proportion of them are in daycare centers or other group care facilities. In some communities most preschool children of working parents are cared for by members of the extended family; in others the majority of families choose to have one adult stay at home with the children or to have a nanny. In these communities, encouraging individual visits to the library may be a higher priority than establishing services for group facilities. Another important factor is to find out whether other organizations or community groups are providing the same type of service, although very few other groups offer storyhours or early literacy programs similar to library programs.

Strategy Formulation through Objectives

Objectives are statements that focus work on some specific aspect of a goal. Each goal could have several appropriate objectives that suggest activities the librarian might undertake. Objectives give specific, measurable, and time-oriented indications of how well a department is moving toward the attainment of goals by meeting the stated needs of those served or describing what benefits or outcomes library users will attain.

Objectives should have a time frame. They should indicate what you want to accomplish by a certain date so that you can check on how well you are doing. For example, an objective might be "Reference service through chat sessions will be available at least three hours daily by the end of 2015." Sometimes objectives are broken down into stages: "Class visits will be set up for at least 50 percent of elementary schools by the end of the 2014 school year and 80 percent by the end of the 2015 school year." Most departmental objectives are designed for periods of from one to three years. Very few challenging objectives can be met in less than one year, and very few plans can be made for more than three years. Short-term objectives for specific programs or projects are often useful supplements to the overall departmental objectives.

Activities describe or list specific actions the children's department will take to achieve the objectives. The activities should relate directly to the objective and be as specific as possible. Rather than "improve the collection" or "offer programs," activity statements might say "purchase 20 percent more Chinese-language books this year" or "arrange 10 class visits to local elementary schools."

Indicators are statements that describe how achievement will be measured. It is the specificity of objectives and the fact that they are measurable that make them useful. Goals can be nonspecific, because they only point the direction in which the library is moving. Many goals will never be completely achieved. Objectives and activity statements, on the other hand, spell out what the department intends to do and how staff members expect to do it; indicators define how they will know whether or not they have achieved their aims. At the end of the time period it is easy to see whether or not the objectives have been met.

Hallmarks of Useful Objectives, Activity Statements, and Indicators

An objective should describe an intended outcome for the user rather than a procedure done by library staff. Activity statements specify what the department is doing (the input); objectives specify why it is being done—what the impact to the user or community will be. The emphasis should be on the value given to the patron rather than on the action taken by the library. An objective of "Have the reference desk staffed by a librarian on school days" is not as useful as "Provide correct and complete answers to children's reference questions during after-school hours." An activity might be "hire one more professional children's librarian to provide reference service during after school hours." The indicator might state "children's reference questions will be answered correctly and completely at least 80 percent of the time." The first example states what you are going to do but does not necessarily indicate an outcome. Having someone on the reference desk reading library journals and glaring at every kid who comes near might reach the first objective but would not improve your reference service. When writing objectives you should be sure the intended outcome is obvious to other people and not just to you and that the standard of success stated in the indicator is realistically possible to obtain and is a true measure of the objective.

A children's department plan includes three things:

- what is to be accomplished (Objective)
- what specific activities will be done to accomplish the objective (Activity Statement)
- how success will be measured (Indicator)

Collaborative Planning

After the environmental scan has collected relevant facts and documented the need for services, the library staff will set up objectives and decide on the specific activities to offer. Enthusiastic staff members can often think of dozens of programs and activities that would be fun to plan, but trying to do too much at once can lead to failure and discouragement. It's important for the staff to set realistic objectives for the department and plan activities that relate directly to meeting the department's objectives.

Budget constraints may limit the scope of activities that can be offered, but sometimes additional money can be found for well-designed and valuable programs. Often a new program starts with a small pilot project. Storyhours could be offered, for example, to three daycare facilities to test how much time and money would be necessary to expand the service. The expenses involved in sending personnel out to daycare centers would include the cost of losing that person's in-library work time, transportation costs, and probably the purchase of additional books to be lent to the daycare staff for follow-up reading to children. If these costs are high, the librarian may apply for a grant to cover them, but should also attempt to find some way of continuing funding for successful programs after the grant runs out.

To devise realistic objectives, encourage input from all levels of staff in the department. The first step is to call a staff meeting to discuss the project. The department head reminds the staff of the departmental goals and talks about the reasons for setting objectives. Every staff member is encouraged to suggest areas where objectives would be useful and what the objectives might be. It is also a good idea to seek input from library users or interested community groups (teachers, scout leaders, preschool caregivers, etc.) through surveys on the library website or focus groups or less formally through conversation with children and adults. General comments and ideas can be invited on the library website or blog. Asking users about their needs and priorities can help focus objectives on the real needs of the community served. The next step is the formation of a committee to prepare written objectives. If the staff is small, the entire group may work on the document, or the department head may draw up a draft for discussion. Once the department has agreed on objectives the department head should get approval from library administration and share the children's department's objectives with other library departments to insure cooperation and coordination with other library staff.

Objectives should be clear, specific, and realistic. While some librarians feel that there are aspects of service that cannot be quantified, objectives should, at the least, indicate how those things that are not quantifiable are to be judged: the enthusiasm at storyhours, greater response from teachers, and so forth. Objectives should be attainable but challenging. They must strike a balance between an overambitious "consult with all teachers about their assignments" and statements that require no change of service—"answer reference questions." The purpose of setting objectives is to move you toward meeting goals. There is no point in setting them unless some value is achieved by attaining them.

Staff members who will be responsible for meeting the objectives need to accept them as reasonable. If staff members believe objectives are plans sent down by administrators who do not understand the day-to-day operations of the department, they may not implement them eagerly. For this reason, even though an individual or a small committee may be responsible for drafting objectives, they should be discussed and revised by all members of the department, both professional and nonprofessional.

If staff members have not worked with formalized objectives before, they may see them as a threat. To avoid this, the department head may encourage the staff to set limited and easily met objectives the first time around. If the employees see that objectives can benefit them by providing a means of documenting their achievements, they may be ready to set more challenging objectives on the next round.

First-time users of objectives may go to the other extreme and set unrealistically ambitious objectives. One way to avoid this is to measure on a short term, usually monthly, basis how well the objectives are being met. If objectives are too ambitious, it will become apparent in a month or two. The objectives can then be modified to be more reasonable in time for the formal assessment at the end of the year.

Working with Objectives

Objectives can enhance the effectiveness of a department only if the staff remains aware of them. Some departments use visual reminders, such as notices on the staff bulletin board, to remind people about departmental activities that meet objectives. These can take various forms:

> We plan to order ten graphic novels this month. How many have you reviewed so far?
> We agreed that each staff member would post one blog entry each month. Have you done yours?

As with all notices on bulletin boards or used as email taglines, these must be changed frequently or people will cease to notice them, much less read them. It helps, too, if bright colors and entertaining graphics are used to draw attention to the message. Brief reminders can also be used as taglines on staff email or crawl lines on a staff section of a website. This technique should not be overdone or the messages will become an intrusion and annoyance.

At staff meetings and more informally in conversations, department heads can mention objectives. This should never be done in a threatening way, but as a good-natured reminder of the department's objectives. Monthly reports should include progress made toward meeting objectives.

Although objectives are formal statements designed to be formally evaluated, there must be some flexibility in their use. Occasionally an unexpected disaster such as a fire will cancel out all of the previously planned objectives. Even lesser events such as a succession of staff illnesses or resignations, changes in the library administration, or community problems caused by a plant closure or agricultural crisis may require modification of a department's objectives.

When it becomes clear that some objectives are going to be unreachable, a staff meeting and discussion can lead to modifications to make the objective realistic. Naturally, these changes should not occur every year or the setting of objectives becomes meaningless. Like all management tools, however, objectives must be modifiable in light of actual events.

The department head should assess objectives on an ongoing basis throughout the year. If it is clear that objectives are not being met, it is better to make adjustments early rather than announce at the end of the year that there has been a disastrous failure. Oftentimes objectives need to be modified; at other times, it may be best to forget about a particular objective and to work on the underlying problems that the failure to meet it may reveal. If objectives are being met, it is useful to let the staff know how well they are doing. Blogs, wikis, websites, and staff meetings can be used to announce successes in meeting objectives on a monthly or quarterly basis.

Visualizing the Strategic Planning Process

The work plan of a children's library is determined by the mission of its parent institution whether a public library, a school, or another entity. The logical flow of departmental goals from that mission should be clear to all. It can be visualized this way:

Figure 3.2
Planning Flow from Goals to Activities

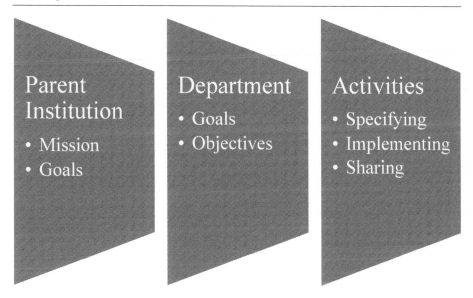

Although the specific process of setting goals and objectives may vary in degree of formality and the number of people involved, some basic principles should be maintained:

- Collect information about the environment
- Invite input from the community
- Set objectives as a collegial process
- Plan specific activities to fulfill the established objectives
- Leader acts as a coach to encourage staff to meet objectives

IF YOU WANT TO KNOW MORE . . .

All About Strategic Planning, Free Management Library. Available at http://management help.org/plan_dec/str_plan/str_plan.htm (accessed Aug. 30, 2012).

Brophy, Peter and Kate Coulling. 1996. *Quality Management for Information and Library Managers*. Brookfield, VT: Aslib Gower.

Crittendon, Robert. 2002. *The New Manager's Starter Kit; Essential Tools for Doing the Job Right*. New York: American Management Association (see especially chapter two).

Fincke, Mary Beth, Mary Frances Zilonis, and Carolyn Markuson. 2002. *Strategic Planning for School Library Media Centers*. Lanham, MD: Scarecrow Press.

Matthews, Joseph R. 2005. *Strategic Planning and Management for Library Managers*. Westport, CT: Libraries Unlimited.

Staerkel, Kathleen, Mary Fellows, and Sue McCleaf Nespeca, eds. 1995. *Youth Services Librarians as Managers: A How-to Guide from Budgeting to Personnel*. Chicago: American Library Association.

Wallace, Linda K. 2004. *Libraries, Mission & Marketing: Writing Mission Statements That Work*. Chicago: American Library Association.

4

Evaluation

One of the great mistakes is to judge policies and programs by their intentions rather than their results.

—Milton Friedman

EVALUATING ACHIEVEMENT

Once a department has formalized its goals and objectives, it is tempting to sit back and consider the job done, but this is a mistake. Your task is only half done until you know that the goals set and the services based on them are actually benefiting the people you serve. We can look at a busy library with its satisfied patrons and think we have achieved our goals. Unfortunately, appearances don't always tell us the complete truth. Just because more easy readers are being acquired doesn't mean that the audience for these books is satisfied. Summer reading programs reach many enthusiastic children, but have we reached the ones who need the library most? We need to judge programs on facts, not on impressions. In these times of budget constraints for libraries and schools, it is especially important to demonstrate that resources are being used effectively and offering solid value to the community.

OUTCOME EVALUATION

While attendance at programs or use of the library's collection is a strong statement of support for the library's function, it does not tell the specific impact that library activities have on users or the community. So in addition to gathering data on how much the library is used, information on how using the library has helped people should also be collected.

Outcome measures provide a systematic way to find out whether services are meeting or exceeding the objectives set for them:

- what works best for the people who use your services
- how to change programs and services as your community changes
- how to best use the resources you have and get the resources you need to provide library service to children

In addition to increasing the knowledge of youth services staff, outcome evaluation (OE) provides the following:

- OE helps staff "work smart" by providing a system to measure success and specific information to use to adapt or change programs and services.
- OE strengthens library planning and budget allocation.
- OE allows library staff to understand and describe the impact of its program and services on its users.
- OE enables communication among youth services staff and between library departments, including administration.
- OE enhances communication with the community, donors, and program partners.
- OE provides accountability for public agencies, including libraries.
- OE is required by the federal government and will be increasingly required by agencies using state and local funds.
- OE may be required by private donors as well (Dresang, Gross, and Holt, 2006).

Techniques used to measure impact include systematic observation, interviews, surveys, or focus groups with specific user groups. While these techniques may be new to some librarians, other service agencies including the United Way, the Girl Scouts, and many community health organizations are using these techniques and might provide training locally for library staff new to using them. Some outcome evaluation need not be complicated. Evaluating a single activity or a time-limited set of activities such as series of storytimes can be done simply. The measurements are straightforward and the collection of data fairly simple. Observing how many children attend a program, how many participate in program activities such as singing along with the group, and whether the number of children actively participating increases as the programs continue gives useful results. Noting which individual stories or songs increase children's participation rates gives results that can be used to improve future programs. Systematic observation of program participants and recording the data can help librarians plan new programs. Asking children what they learned or enjoyed during a program can give good information about how a particular program helped (or did not help) meet a particular objective. Evaluating more complex programs or areas of service may take a longer time and include the collection of more data, but the essential point of view is the same: to put the user at the center of the evaluation and measure the effects of the programs on patrons. Outcome evaluation is enhanced when the library staff is drawing on a systematic knowledge of what the library is doing and how services are being used.

Knowing Where You Stand—Routine Collection of Data about Services

Any department manager should know the current status of services and activities provided. Some statistics are routinely collected by most libraries, and the children's librarian should keep track of changes in these measurements. A guide to ways of measuring services is the American Library Association's *Output Measures for Public Library Service to Children: A Manual of Standardized Procedures* (Walter, 1992). Although these measures are twenty years old, many of them are still important in children's departments. The measures included in this guide can be supplemented by measurements of electronic services, resulting in a list similar to the following:

- Collection measurements: books circulated; books and other materials used in-house; ebooks circulated; trends in types of materials used and in format of materials
- Programming measures: attendance; number of views of video; number of questions and comments both online and in person
- Reference services: number of questions asked in-house; number of email questions; chat, text messages
- Google analytics: number of hits on websites; number of page views; unique number of viewers; time spent on pages
- Community relations: contacts with schools or daycare centers; number of cosponsored programs
- Reading groups sponsored and number of individuals participating in them

These measures are usually collected routinely and are useful for a variety of purposes and provide many clues for possible changes in the library:

1. Circulation figures, recording the number of people attending programs, and contacts with other agencies are easy ways to keep track of what is being done. These figures give indications about the types of materials and programs popular in the community and the agencies interested in working with the library.
2. Periodic recording of reference questions for limited time periods is useful as a way to find out why patrons are using the library. Many libraries collect statistics about reference questions, including those asked in person, online, and by telephone, for a two-week period each spring and fall. The figures are analyzed by categorizing them as directional, short answer, or in-depth queries. If the majority of questions asked by patrons in the library are simple queries about the location of the photocopy machine or the periodical collection, it suggests that additional signage is necessary. If large numbers of questions on the same topic are asked by many patrons, the librarians may decide to develop pathfinders or resource lists on these subjects.
3. Google analytics or another online record source provides automatic counts of visits to the department's homepage and blog or wiki, the number of unique viewers, and the time spent on various pages. Visits to the department's Facebook page can be collected and reported to the page administrator weekly. These visits indicate the level of interest in topics covered or programs announced on Facebook.
4. School libraries collect many of these same statistics modified by school practice. Circulation figures are important, as well as the number and types of reference questions. Discussion of these statistics with teachers often helps them to assess how well students understand class assignments.

Formal assessment of how well objectives are being met is usually done on a yearly basis, although the time frame for the objective may be longer than that. Annual assessments are useful to ensure that the department does not get too far off track in meeting its planned goals. The annual evaluation is usually a formal report made available to all staff members so they can see how well the department is doing and pinpoint areas that need improvement. Most yearly assessments become part of the library's annual report that is given to the library or school board, the state library agency, and the public.

Evaluating Specific Programs or Activities

This knowledge of what the department is doing overall serves as the background for evaluating specific programs. The process is shown in figure 4.1.

The first section of this chart is determined while the programs objectives are being devised. Library staff should be clear about the outcomes desired. They should also agree on the measurements needed to determine whether the outcomes are reached. These could be set up as follows:

- Objective: to increase use of the library by the Filipino American community
- Activity: hold eight dual-language English/Tagalog storytime programs during the summer
- Desired Outcome: participation by at least 15 children in each of the storytime programs

Some evaluation measurements stated in the indicator or activity statements are obvious: in this example, the number of programs and attendance at each are the important factors; for collection development, the number of books purchased in a particular area can be counted; for staff development, the

Figure 4.1
Planning Evaluation of Programs

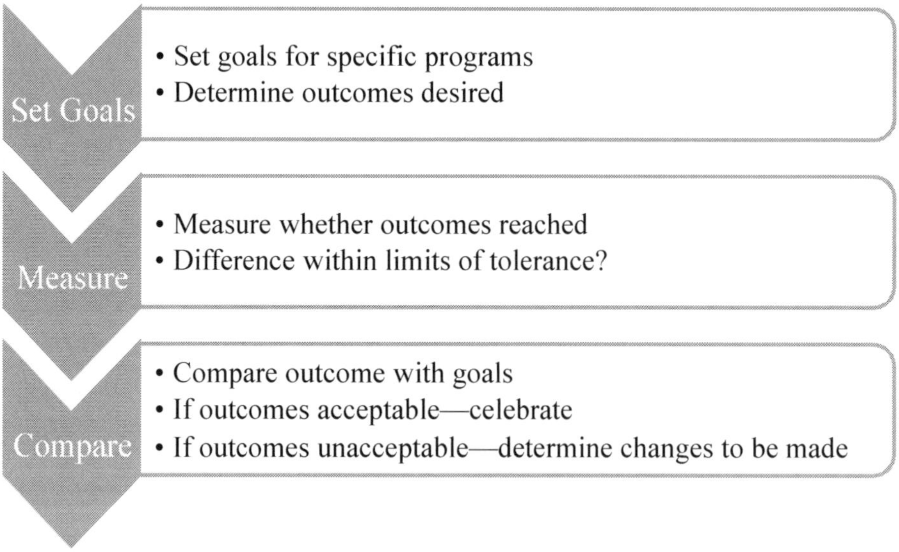

Set Goals
- Set goals for specific programs
- Determine outcomes desired

Measure
- Measure whether outcomes reached
- Difference within limits of tolerance?

Compare
- Compare outcome with goals
- If outcomes acceptable—celebrate
- If outcomes unacceptable—determine changes to be made

courses or workshops attended are obvious measures. Other types of objectives such as those concerned with the number of reference questions successfully answered or the amount of reading guidance given may require sampling and counting techniques. When deciding on evaluation measures, keep in mind the principle that because outcomes should reflect changes for library users rather than the library itself, it is important to gather information from users and sometimes nonusers. This is often done by using surveys, interviews, or focus groups to get input directly from adults and children who are served by the department.

Statistical Evaluation

Using some or all of these measures can help the librarian decide whether objectives are being met. The decision as to which measures to use in evaluation is made at the time the objectives are set. In the example of the dual-language storytimes, the number of programs, the number of attendees, and the circulation of materials in the hour after each event would be recorded, providing a statistical basis for evaluation. To judge whether the department has had a positive impact on library users requires additional information.

Qualitative Evaluation

A wide-reaching underlying objective, such as increasing the use of the library by the Filipino American community, calls for data collection over a longer period of time. This level of outcome evaluation might be handled through a survey or focus group for parents or caregivers of children who attend the programs. Do the parents feel more comfortable in the library? Do they read to their children at home more often than they used to? Have any of the parents or children participated in other library activities such as summer reading programs, or do they intend to do so? This level of evaluation requires more time and effort than a simple collection of data, but it gives more information about the impact of library services on the lives of patrons.

USING THE RESULTS OF EVALUATION

Whatever method is used to evaluate how well a department is meeting its objectives, it is important to remember that the method should be decided upon when the objectives are first set. If this is not done, the department staff may find themselves unable to decide whether or not their objectives are met.

When objectives are successfully met, staff members can congratulate themselves on a job well done and are frequently eager to move on to setting new objectives for another year. Successful results should be reported to the staff, the public, and the authorities responsible for the library. Various reporting strategies will be discussed later in this chapter.

The failure to meet objectives is much more difficult to deal with. If a department has set itself the objective of contacting 50 percent of the teachers in their jurisdiction, but manages to reach only 25 percent, the staff may feel demoralized and discouraged. The task of the department head in this situation is to help the staff analyze the reason for failure and move toward either reaching the objective or setting one that is more realistic.

It is important that no one member of the staff be made to feel responsible for failure to meet a departmental objective. If there is a problem with one member of the department, that should be discussed privately with the individual. Setting and attaining of department objectives are group processes. After the measurements have been taken to see whether or to what extent objectives are met, a staff meeting should be called. The degree to which each objective is met will be announced and the reasons for success or failure discussed.

Causes of Failure to Meet Objectives

Some of the causes of failure in certain situations are:

- Objectives are unrealistic when compared with the practice of most public libraries. An example would be to attempt to reach an objective of having 90 percent of the children in a community borrow at least one book.
- Objectives are unrealistic in terms of the personnel available: for example, to have at least ten class visits per week in a library with only two staff members.
- Conditions have changed, making the objective unreachable: for example, the assistant librarian has left and not been replaced, so the head of the children's department has been carrying out two library jobs for six months.
- Budget has not been sufficient to meet the objective: for example, an attempt to buy 500 Chinese-language books has revealed that these books are more expensive than had been expected, so only 400 books were actually bought.
- Personnel have not been able to manage change: for example, an attempt to train a staff member to sign storyhours for hearing-impaired children has failed because the staff member was unable to become proficient enough in signing within the time allocated.
- Occasionally the measurement chosen may not reflect the change resulting from the innovation. For example, the library began purchasing graphic novels for middle grade readers and decided to measure their impact by the increase in circulation. Circulation figures did not rise dramatically, but librarians have noticed that many children are coming to the library after school and reading the graphic novels in the library. The measurement chosen for evaluation did not match the actual impact of the action.

Frequently the cause of the failure to meet an objective gives a clear indication of the steps that need to be taken to ensure success next time. Occasionally the department head may feel that failure is due to the inadequacy or lack of interest of a particular staff member. In that case, the staff evaluation interview ought to focus on the objective involved. Setting and measuring objectives can, in fact, become a useful staff evaluation tool.

The most important point to remember in dealing with the failure to meet objectives is to focus on the reason for the failure and find a way to succeed. Failure should not lead to discouragement but to a renewed commitment to setting better objectives that can and will be met by the department.

In addition to evaluating success, evaluation often provides unanticipated results and information that can help the department become more effective.

A department may find new groups of people that could be served: for example, working with daycare centers may enable librarians to learn more about daycare workers who are interested in adult programs or reading groups at the library. Problems or issues for users may be identified: for example, many parents may find the sign-up system for library programs confusing or may need information in a language other than English. The information collected to evaluate success or failure to meet objectives plus other information gathered in the evaluation can be used as the basis for setting the next round of objectives.

REPORTING EVALUATION RESULTS

Discovering that the children's department has succeeded in achieving the goals set for itself is very satisfying and should be reported widely. Even if the department hasn't accomplished as much as hoped, it is important to document what has happened. Most library systems and municipalities have requirements for annual reports. If projects are funded by grant money, individual reports are usually required for the granting agency. The library, state agency, school district, or library board may also require monthly or quarterly reports. The discussion below talks mainly about annual reports, but the same concepts guide the development of reports given at other intervals. In addition to these required reports, it is generally good practice to keep the local community informed on an ongoing basis about what is happening at the library.

What Is an Annual Report?

Annual reports can take many different forms. The formal printed reports of earlier years have given way to shorter, more colorful formats with many pictures, available both online and in print versions. Many librarians make their reports available as PDF files on their websites so that patrons can easily download them for reading. The Chicago Public Library, for example, offers a lively report featuring pictures of patrons and staff and stories of how individuals respond to library services as well as tables of statistics (http://www.chipublib .org/dir_documents/ar_2009.pdf , accessed Aug. 29, 2012).

A smaller public library, the Mead Public Library, prepares a similar, if somewhat shorter, annual report for the public (http://www.meadpubliclibrary.org/ sites/default/files/10_annual_rpt_public_.pdf , accessed Aug. 29, 2012). Notice how both of these reports draw the viewer into the report with the emphasis not so much on the library and on what it is doing, but rather on the patrons and how they are benefiting from the library activities. They attract audiences because they follow these general principles for reports designed for the general public:

1. Report accomplishments NOT activities
2. Let users tell the story
3. Use pictures of library users, as they are more important than those of library staff
4. Create graphics for statistics—numbers of users, circulation, reference questions answered. Lists of numbers are boring or incomprehensible to many people.
5. Use pictures of celebrity visitors when available

Who Prepares the Annual Report and When?

Some directors give the responsibility for preparing the annual report to a specific individual or group such as the public relations department. Other directors expect each department to prepare a section of the report. No matter what the system used in your library, it is wise for the children's department to have as much input as they can in shaping the report. Even people in other departments of the library are not as aware as the department personnel about what has been going on. Although writing a report takes time, it is a task well worth doing. Your public will be glad to know what the department has been doing, so the annual report is an important part of marketing library services.

When do you start preparing an annual report? A good answer to this would be, the first day you arrive in the department. Collecting data and recording activities should be an ongoing process rather than an annual task. Some of the information that should be routinely collected is shown in figure 4.2.

Figure 4.2
Information Collected for Reports

Event	Information Collected	Additional Items
New Services	Description of change, especially innovations in tech or social media Expected impact	Pictures if possible Interviews with patrons
Programs Offered	Date Attendance Presenter Subject Evaluation	Pictures Publicity pieces News reports of event
Collection Added	Number of volumes or items Description of new type of collection	Perhaps picture of children using new materials
Staff Added	Brief biographical information Role in department	Picture Brief interview if available
Staff Leaving	Brief biographical information Appreciation of services	Picture
Renovations	Description of changes Impact on services Report of opening celebration	Before and after pictures Interviews with patrons
Gifts and Donations	Description of gifts Purpose or expected outcome	Pictures of donors Press coverage

Not all of this information will be used in the annual report, but it should be available so that the most important can be chosen not only for the annual report but for future media interviews or news releases.

Another useful source of information recording is for each staff member to keep a work journal. As described in an ALSC blog post, the work journal covers many activities:

A work journal is basically a "to-do" list with all the items crossed off (you know how awesome—and rare—that is). It is an account of your accomplishments, successes, failures, projects, programs, committee work, training sessions and anything else that you can think of. This valuable document will help you when it is time for your annual performance review, when you need to write a bio (and can't think of one interesting thing you've done, much less two) or when you apply for a new job. (Acerro, 2011)

These informal work notes will be very helpful in recording and publicizing the evaluations of departmental work as well as serving as a personal record for the individual.

PREPARING THE ANNUAL REPORT

Many states, provinces, and other jurisdictions have legal requirements about the format and contents of annual reports filed by libraries. These requirements must be observed, but often they are minimum standards and additional information can be included. Styles may vary depending on the abilities of staff and the tools they can use. Reports may follow any of these forms:

- A list of goals and outcomes and how they were met
- Brief, general statistical and factual material
- Statistical tables plus anecdotal reports of special events and services
- Statistics presented graphically with the addition of illustrations and text
- Brief online reports with links to more detailed statistical and factual information

Audiences for Annual Report

The library board, school board, or other governing body requires a full report with all the data available, but this is not the only audience for a library report. Library patrons and others in the community should have access to the information both in print format and online, and it is also important to release a report for community newspapers and other media. The same basic information with different formatting can serve each of these groups. They should all be kept in mind when the report is prepared.

Theme of the Report

Your report should be more than just a collection of facts and figures. You should analyze the material that has been collected and organize your facts so the reader understands the message. Some themes that might give a picture of the department's activities throughout the year might include the following:

- "Despite cuts in funding we have been able to increase our after school programs."
- "Exciting new collections of digital materials have strengthened our traditional services."
- "Extraordinary weather conditions damaged our library, but we have overcome obstacles and continue giving services to the community."

Knowing the goals and theme of the year will help you to arrange the material collected and to shape the report to include the major achievements and highlights of the year as well as changes such as new staff members and new programs or collections. You may also want to include goals for the following year. The amount of information given about each of these will vary depending on the audience for each version of the report.

TELLING THE STORY WITH GRAPHICS

Solid blocks of print and tables of statistics do not attract most readers, and many annual reports remain unread unless they are presented in a lively format. Every library now has the tools to turn their information into attractive charts and graphs. It is easy to experiment with different formats of graphs and charts to show the information you want to include. Minor differences in format can make a real difference in how easily people can understand the data you present. Ask for others' opinions so that you find the format that appeals to most people, especially those who are not as familiar with the library as the staff is. As many staff members as possible should have the chance to give suggestions about format. Young pages and clerks are often especially helpful in giving ideas for making the report readable for nonlibrarians. Look at journal articles and reports from other libraries both in print and online to get ideas about how to use graphics.

Another way to present figures painlessly is to turn them into averages and paint a picture of a typical user: for example, in West Alligator Springs, the average child with a library card

- visits the library 27 times a year
- uses the library databases 11 times a year
- reads 8 books during the summer reading program
- borrows 46 books a year

This kind of profile brings library statistics to life. It can be used to paint a picture of library users and staff or present other information.

Pictures

Most people, when confronted with a report whether online or in print, look at the pictures first and then turn to the text, so the pictures chosen for your reports are very important. Although shelves of attractive books have some appeal, there is nothing like a human face to attract the viewer. Whenever possible your pictures should feature library users. Pictures of events at the library, especially highly visual ones such as puppet shows or storytelling, attract many readers. It is also important to highlight some of the newer materials and services your library offers, because even today many people do not know about them. Instead of using just the familiar pictures of preschoolers poring over picture books, try to get one of a cluster of middle grade youngsters at a computer or reading graphic novels. Be sure to plan ahead and get permission from parents for using photos of their children in a report. If a program is covered in the press, the library can ask permission to reprint that photograph in both print and electronic versions of reports. Be sure to include a wide variety of children, boys and girls, different ages and ethnic groups, and children with disabilities.

Use Several Different Channels

The library's annual report will be made available through various formal channels as required in the jurisdiction, but your departmental report can also be disseminated in a variety of other ways including the following:

- Announce the release of the report on Facebook and Twitter and include a link to the report.
- Post the report on the library website with pictures on the front page and a link to the full report.
- Link a short video of highlights on the library website.
- Prepare bookmarks listing significant achievements and place them in books as they circulate.
- Make public service announcements (PSAs) for local radio and television stations.
- Send highlights from the annual report to electronic mailing lists.

The cycle of strategic planning, evaluation, and reporting is a continuous one. The annual report is a summary of the achievements of each year. Some years will be better than others, but each one should mark some successes and point the way toward future planning. It is a valuable tool for the library staff in deciding where they should put their efforts in coming years. The release of the annual report is also an occasion for calling attention to the library's services. It can be a marketing tool and serve as a basis for oral reports to parent groups and civic associations. With careful planning you can use your annual report not only to publicize your services, but also to improve them through increased community support.

IF YOU WANT TO KNOW MORE ...

Acerro, Heather. 2011. "Keeping a Work Journal." ALSC Blog, May 6. http://www.alsc .ala.org/blog/?p=2353 (accessed Aug. 29, 2012).

Basic Guide to Outcomes-Based Evaluation. Available at http://managementhelp.org/ evaluatn/outcomes.htm (accessed Aug. 29, 2012).

Dresang, Eliza T., Melissa Gross, and Leslie Edmonds Holt. 2006. *Dynamic Youth Services through Outcome-Based Evaluation.* Chicago: American Library Association.

Rubin, Rhea Joyce. 2006. *Demonstrating Results: Using Outcome Measurement in Your Library*. Chicago: American Library Association.

"'Things Are Changing Fast' SLJ's 2011 Technology Survey." 2011. *School Library Journal*, May, 28–33 (excellent examples of graphics).

Walter, Virginia. 1992. *Output Measures for Public Library Service to Children: A Manual of Standardized Procedures*. Chicago: American Library Association.

5

Budgeting and Fundraising

Can anybody remember when the times were not hard and
money not scarce?

—RALPH WALDO EMERSON

Managing the children's department or school library's money is an important
task. If budgets, accounting for the money as it is spent, and fundraising are done
well, children's librarians will get the most out of the resources available. Sloppy
handling of money or inattention to budgets or an unwillingness to fundraise will
ultimately shortchange the children and families served, because fewer books
will be bought and fewer programs and services will be supported. The other
issue is that it is just as important—and required—that those handling public
money or contributed money are accountable for how these funds are used.

In most libraries the board (public library or school) has the ultimate responsibility of accepting a balanced annual budget and approving expenditures
against the budget during the year. In the United States, public libraries and
schools get the majority of their funds from local property tax directly or as a
part of city or county government. Private schools get most of their funds from
tuition and endowments. Libraries and schools also may get funds from the
state or provincial libraries, fees, grants, and donations. Most libraries have an
annual audit of expenditures at the end of the year. This audit might be internal
or provided by an outside firm and usually involves checking that the library
has paid its bills, spent money as the board had planned, and used acceptable
accounting practices.

While the board is ultimately responsible for the budget, the library director or school superintendent and administrative staff prepare the budget, manage funds during the year, and organize and carry out fundraising activities.
The timetable for budget preparation, who participates in creating the budget,

and how funds are designated varies from library to library and from school to school, but at some point the manager of the children's department or the school librarian will be asked to submit a request for funds for the department. In some libraries, children's services are represented by the head of the public services department, which includes both adult and youth services. In other libraries, the branch heads take part in the budget-planning process, and they make decisions about the budget for children's services within their branches. Often the district head of libraries or the head of support services creates a budget to fund each school library in a district.

Constructing a budget requires time and effort, but, if carefully prepared, a budget is an important means of organizing library services. As organizational instruments, budgets help librarians determine priorities and achieve goals and objectives. A department's budget indicates the resources that will be needed to meet the library's goals and objectives. No matter how ambitious the proposed objectives are, they will become realities only if they are funded.

Libraries generally have two major types of budgets: the operating budget and the capital budget. Capital budgets deal with one-time expenditures, such as building a new library or making major renovations, upgrading computers, or a new phone/telecommunications system. A manager at the departmental or building level deals most often with operating budgets—the allocation of funds for the ongoing activities of the department or school library, though most managers can ask for furniture and equipment that are infrequent costs as part of the annual budget request.

PREPARING THE BUDGET

Because the budget is such an important document, the individuals involved in its preparation have the power to make influential decisions. Each library or school has its own way of constructing a budget. The children's or school librarian should understand who is involved and what is required to get financial support of library service to children. At the very least, anything connected with preparing budget reports or requests should be top priority for the department head or school librarian.

Budgetary changes should be realistic increments of the current budget. The department head must support each suggestion or request by carefully documenting the need for the increase. If the library system is operating under a flat budget, this will mean cutting back on some programs when new ones are added. If there are losses of revenue, departments may need to set priorities and reduce the budget systematically.

A budget grows out of the department's strategic planning; meeting the department's goals and objectives justifies budget requests. A manager should be able to defend budget requests on the basis of meeting the objectives set and approved by the administration. This holds true regardless of what budgeting system the library uses.

Budgets can be prepared in various formats. Many states and provinces mandate which budget format libraries must use. In other jurisdictions, the local municipality or school district selects the budget format to be used by all departments, including the library. For use within the library, however, budgets

Figure 5.1
Steps in Preparing a Budget

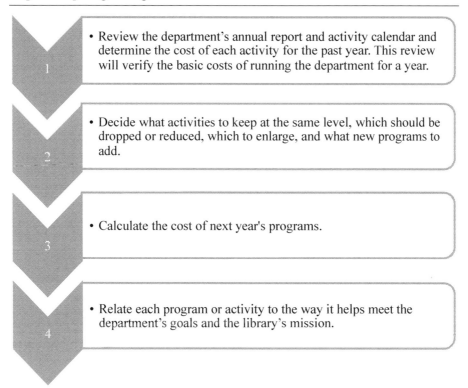

1 • Review the department's annual report and activity calendar and determine the cost of each activity for the past year. This review will verify the basic costs of running the department for a year.

2 • Decide what activities to keep at the same level, which should be dropped or reduced, which to enlarge, and what new programs to add.

3 • Calculate the cost of next year's programs.

4 • Relate each program or activity to the way it helps meet the department's goals and the library's mission.

may be reformatted, and more detailed breakdowns may be added to enable administrators to track trends and changes.

The line-item budget is the most traditional and commonly used type of budget. Most people are familiar with line-item budgets because they are often used for personal budgets. A line-item budget can be prepared based on the past year's budget by keeping the categories and calculating the cost for changes in spending in each budget year. In a line-item budget, amounts are listed for each item of expense (see figures 5.2 and 5.3).

These dollar amounts should be clearly related to programs or services but are based on the expenditures of previous years or on information about what other libraries spend. This type of budget makes it easy to see how the money is spent, whether the budget has been met, or whether spending is over or under the projected figures. A line-item budget also makes it easy to project how much funding is needed for the coming year, based on inflation. Also, it is as easy to cut a line-item budget as it is to add to it.

As well as completing the line items in the budget, the children's department head should provide a budget justification that explains both the details of how the budget with be subdivided and how the budget will meet the department's goals. Librarians can include what outcomes are expected. For example, the book budget might be divided into fiction and nonfiction and further divided

Figure 5.2
Sample Public Library Budget

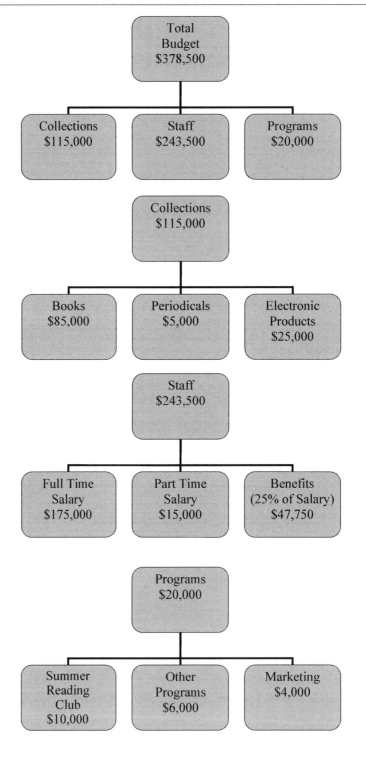

Figure 5.3
Sample School Library Budget

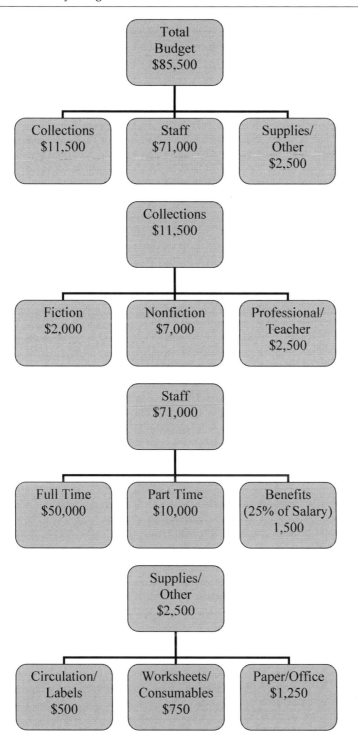

by picture books, readers, chapter books, and YA novels. Each category would have a dollar amount assigned.

An example of a budget narrative might be

The children's department (or school library) will add approximately 575 new books to the collection this year. These will replace and update old books and add the best of newly published items. Because the curriculum has changed in the schools, new science and nature books will be purchased for young readers, to meet the anticipated demand for this type of book. The outcome for children using the library will be they will find a better selection of books that will attract them to reading and meet their school home-work needs.

The actual format of the budget and the budget justification will be set by the library administrators and board. Following this format will make managing the budget easier. It usually helps to be able to estimate actual costs of items to be purchased, so decisions about how many programs will be provided, which performers or supplies will be used, and how many staff will be working in the department need to be made before the budget is finalized. It is also important to meet budget submission guidelines and to allow enough time to submit a reasonable and well-researched budget request.

Staff Time

In addition to determining program costs it is important to determine how much staff time will be needed to carry out the proposed budget. It is not real-istic, for example, to increase the collection development budget by 25 percent and not use more staff time to select and process the added materials. First, determine how much of each person's time is spent on each task. Staff can keep track of their activities for four or five days, over a two- or three-week period. After the personnel's time on particular tasks is determined, the cost in dollars of each aspect of service can be easily calculated. The department head can then create a program sheet listing each program and its objectives, the personnel requirements, and other costs. For example, if half of a librarian's time is spent on service to groups or teaching classes, the cost of providing that individual's share of this service amounts to half of his or her annual salary. Add up the por-tions of other people's time spent on this service to find the total personnel cost. How staff spends their time should support the goals of the department. If staff spend 90 percent of their time with fifth and sixth graders but a priority for the library is to improve early reading for kindergarteners, there is a disconnect. Goals need to be changed or staff reassigned to work with younger children.

Adding New Programs and Services

Once it has been decided that the new program will meet the needs of the community and fall within the department's objectives, the department head must prepare a specific description of the program and a budget request. The department head must determine how much professional, clerical, page, or vol-unteer time will be involved and estimate the amount of collection materials and supplies that will be needed. Time requirements for resources outside of the department, such as the library's technology support or publicity departments, should also be included.

While it may be difficult to determine in advance exactly how much time each task will take, a fairly accurate estimate can be based on the time involved in completing similar tasks for current programs. Because time estimates are usually low, about 10 percent should be added to the first figures suggested. After estimating the costs of personnel and materials, the total cost can be estimated. If the program is large and will require a major time commitment, it may be necessary to indicate what other program or service will be cut back.

In calculating the costs of a new program, service, or collection be sure to include the cost of its evaluation. The evaluation will indicate whether the new program meets its objectives. Although the evaluation will require time—and therefore money—it is an important part of overall planning.

MANAGING THE BUDGET

Specific planning for the upcoming budget year usually begins five or six months before the end of the current fiscal year, but in reality budget planning continues throughout the year. A library manager should always know where the department stands in terms of the current budget year. The library's accounting software can give an ongoing record of what has been spent and what remains. The department head or school librarian should take time to master the details of the budget reports and see how closely spending matches the projections in each category. While overspending is the major threat to budgets, underspending in any category is also an indication that something is wrong. This may mean the projected figures were not accurate, the need for the money was exaggerated, or the program is not being properly implemented. Also, librarians should be aware that if items are not received and paid for by the end of the budget year when the books are closed and audited, the cost will be charged in the next budget year. School and children's librarians should work closely with the district or library fiscal officer to avoid mistakes (Woolls, 2008, p. 149).

With a little effort, a manager can use a simple spreadsheet program on the department computer to keep track of the budget. Although it takes a few hours of work to become familiar with these programs, once the process is mastered, it will cut down on both time and effort in following budgets.

Accountability

Someone in the children's department or school library needs to track book and materials orders to understand how many of the books ordered actually are received. It may be that as many as 25 percent of materials ordered do not arrive at the library. Materials go out of print or are unavailable for purchase. It is important the library only pay for materials that arrive and that the children's librarian orders enough books to avoid underspending the collection budget. Likewise, the department needs a way to track all nonbook orders to both keep track of spending against the budget and avoid paying for items that were not delivered.

The children's librarian needs to learn and follow the library's procedures for paying performers, consultants, or other outside workers. If the library requires contracts, make sure these are in place before the work is done and follow procedures for paying non-staff workers in a timely fashion. If you hire a puppeteer, for example, before the event sign a contract stating, or get in writing, the specifics: how long the performance will be; if the library needs to have a sound system; or if there will be any other costs associated with the performance. Then follow through to make sure the puppeteer gets paid promptly or arrange to have the payment check to hand the performer at the end of the program.

Understand the rules for handling cash and *follow them to the letter*. Often the children's department or school library will be responsible for fines, lost materials payments, and other charges. Some libraries charge for computer time, printing, or use of copy machines, or may sell computer thumb drives, pencils, and other small items. Have clear rules about who will collect the money from coin-operated machines, what accounting needs to be done of that money, and where the cash is to be securely stored. Most libraries have a petty cash fund for staff to use to purchase small items from the store. This might include food for parties, craft supplies, stamps, or other items. Some libraries or school districts expect staff to purchase these items on their own and be reimbursed. Make sure to understand the rules and what receipts are required to assure that cash expenditures are carefully accounted for.

Good management of expenditures throughout the year is a requirement for all school and children's librarians. This assures that resources are spent as they are supposed to be according to the budget, that the children's department is getting the most out of the funds given it, and that money is not lost by negligence or theft. Learning as much as possible about the budget process will help children's and school librarians get support for services the department offers.

FUNDRAISING

While the regular budget process supports some activities in the school library or children's department, it rarely supports everything the department could or should do. Children's departments and school libraries need to find other sources of income to offer the quality services the community deserves (and often demands). Libraries, like other public institutions, have recently become more dependent on outside funding. School libraries have a tradition of raising money within the school, and many school districts have foundations to raise private and corporate funds. Many communities have cut back library funding at the same time as demand for library services is increasing. "If libraries are to sustain current levels of excellence, and if they are to grow to meet the needs of a technologically sophisticated age, they will have to discover new networks of funding" (Steele and Elder, 2000, v).

Although the major burden of raising funds for the library rests with the chief executive officer, the school or library development officer, or the library/school foundation, each department has a role to play in fundraising activities. The services provided by the children's department or the school library are highly valued in most communities. This means that children's department projects should have a broad appeal for potential funders. Children's librarians owe it to their patrons to try to raise money that will enhance services. Fundraising initiatives can be focused on private individuals, government and philanthropic foundation grants, or corporate sponsors. Typical goals of fundraising:

- Providing ongoing annual support
- Funding capital expenditures (a new building or upgraded computer equipment)
- Initiating a specific departmental project

In large- and medium-sized libraries and school districts, fundraising is likely to be done in an organized way with annual giving campaigns, fundraising events, corporate giving activities, and several grant applications a year. In these libraries, the children's librarian may be asked to suggest projects that need funding, visit potential donors, and help write grants that support children's work. In smaller libraries or in individual schools, the librarian might work with the library director or building principal and the library board to approach the local chamber of commerce, business association, or parent group for funds to support a particular program or to apply for funds from the state library.

Many individuals, even those who frequently use the library, have never thought of giving money to a school or public library. They assume the funding provided by tax monies is adequate. One of the first steps for a librarian who wants to raise money from local benefactors is to identify potential library supporters and educate them about the needs of the library. Fundraising is a business, and there is a growing body of knowledge to help the new or occasional librarian fundraiser. Expert Ken Burnett suggests that fundraising is getting more competitive and more targeted, and donors are getting harder to find and retain. He suggests that staff who fundraise should do their homework and set aside regular time for "essential reading" of books, journals, and websites about fundraising to be more effective and up-to-date (Burnett 2006).

Friends/Parent Support

Many school and public libraries have a Friends of the Library or a parent library support group. These are nonprofit organizations formed to promote a better understanding of the library's facilities, needs, and services. Often the Friends group plans and sponsors events, such as book sales, art exhibits, or performances, for the benefit of the library. Some Friends groups operate a library café or a store offering writing supplies or used books to library patrons. The group may organize volunteers to read to children or to help with special events. They also encourage gifts, endowments, and other donations. Friends groups may also have a membership fee to support the operation of the Friends and to donate directly to the library.

Schools sometimes rely on fundraising to purchase materials or other basic items needed for the library. Using parent and student volunteers, they join other school programs such as sports, music, or art in holding events to raise funds. These activities include holding a book fair where a portion of the profits go to the library, running a school store, having a car wash, holding a bake sale, or doing the school's can recycling. Book fairs are typically run with the help of a book fair company. The company will send the school librarian cases of books, promotional materials, and directions. The books are sold to students, teachers, and parents, and the school library gets to keep part of the profits. It is always good to hold the sales when parents are likely to be in the building for teacher's conferences or student performances (Martin and Zannier, 2009, p. 46).

In a small district in Michigan the school libraries have a full menu of fundraising activities to support materials purchase. This includes:

- Book Fair with celebrity storytellers
- Operating a school store that sells school supplies
- Book donations and time (volunteer) donations
- Birthday Book Club where families or students donate a book to celebrate a birthday
- Bookstore partnership where library gets part of the profits of book sales at a local bookstore
- Donations or grants from community groups
- Donations from the PTA and individual parents

Librarian Colleen Driscoll's advice is that "obtaining what your library needs does not always have to be an overwhelming, time-consuming, impossible task. Many small, doable projects can get you what is needed. Know your needs, seek out help, see what your community has to offer, be creative, and just try it" (Smallwood, 2011, p. 219).

A friends or parent group should have a way to receive money, plan for the donation use, and report back to donors on how the donations have been used. Budgets should be audited, and the financial accounting is usually done as part of the library's or school's money management. While most contributions to the Friends are small, total contribution to the library can be financially substantial. Friends-sponsored book sales are often the major fundraising project for libraries.

Friends groups are generally run by a group of its members, but their work may be coordinated by library staff. The children's department manager or school librarian should have Friends' projects developed, so when asked for ideas, the children's department will be able to explain the importance of their projects and be successful in getting the group's support. If staff does not suggest projects, funding may never be available for children's activities, or the Friends group will fund projects that are not a priority for the department.

Foundations

Many schools and libraries also have a library foundation in addition to or instead of a Friends group. The foundation, which is registered as a 501(c)(3) nonprofit organization, is allowed to seek corporate and foundation grants and donations that the school or library as a government agency may not be eligible for. The purpose of the foundation is to raise money for the library, and it has its own board and sometimes its own staff. As with Friends groups, the school or children's librarian should be prepared to suggest projects to be funded and work with foundation staff to meet with potential donors and help write and manage grants that are awarded.

An example of how a foundation might benefit the children's department is found in Hennepin County, Minnesota.

The Hennepin County Library Foundation has raised four million dollars for the library in the past 20 years, and in 2007 the Library Foundation announced a campaign to support the Hennepin County Library. The press release states that "Youth Development and Cultural Literacy & Diversity are Top Priorities. . . . The Foundation's commitment to secure $225,000 through a combination of private donor gifts, corporate and foundation grants and sponsorships will support initiatives and programming above and beyond [youth] services and programs currently available at the Hennepin County Library suburban system of 26 libraries and two Readmobiles that serve preschoolers to older adults in the metro area" (Hennepin County Library).

Corporate Support

In addition to individuals and funding agencies, local businesses and industries are important sources of support and possible funding. Companies that sell products aimed primarily at children can be approached to support library activities through donations of materials or publicity. Toys or books for awards in summer reading programs may be obtained from booksellers, publishers, or distributors. Restaurants that want to attract families may provide publicity for the library on napkins, place mats, or containers. Many large corporations encourage their local branches to support community activities of this kind. Members of the school or library board are often good contacts to reach local businesspersons.

In arranging for publicity backed by business interests, there is some danger that the library could be seen as endorsing a particular product or company. This is not permissible for a public institution, and the library must be sure that sponsorship is free of commercialism. Businesses and industries can donate to public service organizations, such as libraries or schools, but they should view these donations as ways of promoting name recognition and goodwill, rather than using them to advertise their products or services. The librarian must maintain control over any material prepared, printed, or distributed by companies on its behalf.

In ensuring that requests are coordinated, a school or children's librarian who wants to approach a firm should follow the library's or school's rules for approaching outside groups and check with an administrator to be sure that another department is not asking the same company for support at the time. The children's librarian should state clearly but briefly the project that needs funding, the choice of the sponsor, and the rationale that will be given to the sponsor. The proposal may be made to the company by the administrative librarian, a member of the board, or the head of children's services, depending on the political climate and relationships within the community.

Grant Support

Grants from private foundations and government agencies are an important source of money for specific projects. The Laura Bush Foundation has given millions of dollars to support school library book collections, and the Bill and Melinda Gates Foundation has given millions to public libraries to support public computing in the United States and around the world. Grants can pay for the provision of computers in the children's department or school library, the establishment of a literacy program, or the development of a collection of multicultural materials. Grants are targeted funds; they cannot usually be obtained to pay ongoing library costs. Grant money allows the librarian to initiate a new program or service. After the project has been established, the librarian is responsible for its maintenance. Many granting agencies require a plan for continuing support of the project after grant funding ends. In applying for grant money, choose projects that are central to the library's mission so that they can be continued after the grant funding is ended.

The first step in preparing a grant proposal is to think through the project for which funding is being requested. Specific questions, such as the following, may be asked:

- Does the project fill an unmet need?
- What group of people will benefit from the project?
- What will be the result of the successful project? (e.g., more children prepared for school; better integration of an immigrant group into the community)
- Do the children's librarians have the expertise to carry out the project?
- Does the project duplicate or complement other social projects in the community?
- How will you know whether the project is successful? How will it be evaluated?
- How much will the project cost? What is the project's budget?
- How will the project activities continue in the future?
- Is there a specific time period during which the project must be undertaken?

Answering these questions will usually involve meeting with other staff members and perhaps outside experts in a planning session. Granting agencies want to see documentation for claims that a project is worthwhile. Locate facts concerning the number of individuals in the target group, related activities of other social agencies, and realistic cost estimates for equipment and personnel time. This careful planning makes a grant proposal more effective.

Locating Grant Opportunities

The first two steps in obtaining a grant are to identify an unmet need and to learn about available grant sources. For example, a librarian might recognize the need for internet access beyond what the library budget can provide and search for an agency to provide grant funding. Another librarian might learn that a large foundation is interested in funding literacy projects and recognize that the children's department could organize such a project locally. Whether the impetus comes from the library's need or from the foundation's funding interests is not as important as how well the two aspects match.

Many resources are available for locating funding agencies. The first sources of information to identify them are individuals within the region who have been successful in obtaining grants. State agencies and associations usually have listings of agencies that have given grants to libraries. Members of the library or school board and individuals from other community agencies are also good sources of leads to possible grants. The local United Way or community donors group may also have lists of funds available locally.

The sources of funding for many youth services in public libraries are Library Services and Technology Act (LSTA) grants. These funds come from the Institute for Museum and Library Services (IMLS) and are administered through state library agencies. Many state libraries use LSTA funds to provide summer reading programs and programs for teens and to support preschool programs. State libraries also have funding for individual library programs through a grant application process. State libraries may also have privately donated funds to distribute, such as the Gates Foundation funds to support electronic services or Target stores grant literacy funds. State departments of education vary considerably in support for grant funding.

There are other federal grant programs for public libraries and school libraries. The U.S. Department of Education has the Improving Literacy through School Libraries program that helps school librarians purchase up-to-date resources and technology. Another federal program that benefits school and public libraries is the E-Rate program that funds telecommunications and internet access. The E-Rate application is very demanding, so not all public libraries apply for it. Libraries serving low-income communities will be eligible for the most E-Rate funding as the purpose is to provide connectivity for people unable to pay for internet access. If the children's staff wants to expand or develop internet services, E-Rate can help reduce the communication costs.

The Foundation Center, a clearinghouse for information about foundation funding, has an informative website (http://foundationcenter.org) that provides a wide range of resources, including information on individual foundations, lists of the largest foundations, reports on trends in grants, articles on how to write a grant proposal, and names of individuals to contact for further information. In addition to the website, the Foundation Center maintains libraries in several U.S. locations, offers workshops, and publishes books to help nonprofit organizations to apply for grants. Another important internet location is the Chronicle of Philanthropy website (http://www.philanthropy.com). While this is not a library-specific site, it gives current information to nonprofits on fundraising techniques and opportunities.

Writing Proposals

Grant proposals normally follow a standard format. Librarians should always obtain information and guidelines from the specific foundation or granting agency that has been identified. If possible, obtain copies of grant proposals that led to project funding in the past. The standard format includes the following sections:

- Executive summary or project abstract
- Statement of need

- Goals, objectives, and outcomes
- Project description
- Budget
- Evaluation plan
- Information about the organization

Some grants also require a plan for dissemination of the results of the project, a description of staff who will work on the project, and/or letters of support from the community or cooperating agencies. Grants may also include a cover letter that states the importance of the grant project. Follow directions for who needs to sign the grant. This might be the lead staff person who will direct the grant, the library director, or the head of the library board.

Proposals for small projects, those for less than $1,000, often require only a two- or three-page letter rather than a formal proposal. This is especially true if the agency has previously funded library projects. No matter how brief the letter, it should include the elements of a proposal as outlined above. No matter the length, it is important to read the grant proposal guidelines carefully, follow the directions, and meet all deadlines.

Marketing and image building are often considered essential homework for successful fundraising. A good image is a necessary asset for success. "Libraries, like other not-for-profit institutions, base their successful fundraising culture on outstanding service, appropriate marketing and detailed attention to developing, cultivation and soliciting donors" (Holt, Holt, and Stratton, 2006, p. 13). Beyond asking specific donors for funds, the children's librarian should work to build a good image for the department and the library. Using a variety of marketing techniques (see chapter 12) and seeking good coverage in the press are prerequisites for successful fundraising. Individuals, corporations, and grant-giving agencies are more likely to give to libraries that have a positive image and to librarians who are known to be successful in serving the community. Having a good track record and projecting success is a key to successful fundraising.

Public and school libraries have not been aggressive fundraisers in the past, and many librarians find it difficult to ask for money. They are not alone. Many professionals working in hospitals, universities, museums, and the arts also dislike fundraising. Nonetheless, the majority of taxpayers in the United States have decided to cut back tax funding to nonprofit groups. The only way to maintain services is to obtain money from the private sector. Because most librarians believe strongly that the services they provide are valuable to the community, they should be willing to take on the task of asking for money. The discomfort of asking disappears when the funding arrives and the project is accomplished. The satisfaction of seeing the library live up to its potential makes the effort of fundraising worthwhile.

IF YOU WANT TO KNOW MORE ...

Burnett, Ken. 2006. *The Zen of Fundraising: 89 Timeless Ideas to Strengthen and Develop Your Donor Relationships.* San Francisco: Wiley.

Chronicle of Philanthropy. *Fund Raising.* Available at www.philanthropy.com/fund raising (accessed Aug. 29, 2012).

The Foundation Center. *Knowledge to Build On.* Available at http://foundationcenter.org (accessed Aug. 31, 2012).

Hennepin County Library. "Press Release." Hennepin Public Library. www.hclib.org/pub/info/support/whatsnew.cfm (accessed Sept. 2, 2007).

Holt, Leslie Edmonds, Glen E. Holt, and Lloyd Stratton. 2006. *Library Success: A Celebration of Library Innovation, Adaptation and Problem Solving.* Newton, MA: EBSCO Publishing.

Martin, Barbara Stein, and Marco Zannier. 2009. *Fundamentals of School Library Media Management.* New York: Neal-Schuman.

Mutz, John M., and Katherine Murray. 2010. *Fundraising for Dummies.* Hoboken, NJ: Wiley.

Smallwood, Carol, ed. 2011. *The Frugal Librarian: Thriving in Tough Economic Times.* Chicago: American Library Association.

Steele, Victoria, and Stephen D. Elder. 2000. *Becoming a Fundraiser: The Principles and Practice of Library Development.* Chicago: American Library Association.

Swan, James. 2002. *Fundraising for Libraries: 25 Proven Ways to Get More Money for Your Library.* New York: Neal-Schuman.

Woolls, Blanche. 2008. *The School Library Media Manager,* Fourth Edition. Westport, CT: Libraries Unlimited.

6

Facilities and Space Planning

"Why do we remember the places of our childhood so vividly? . . . Begin with a graceful floor plan, surfaces that are simple to maintain, hardworking furniture and space saving storage. Introduce fun details like toys and artworks to create a room that is easy to enjoy and, perhaps someday, a joy to remember." (Wills, 2005, p. 13)

Children's librarians need to create space that is inviting and useful to a variety of children. "In order for the child to thrive, the physical setting and the social interactions within that setting must be suitable for the age of the child and right for the particular individual. This premise is basic to the design of developmentally appropriate environments for children" (Feinberg, Kuchner, and Feldman, 1998, p. 4). In other words, the children's room should encourage use and positive activities for all the children who are served by the department or in the school library.

MAINTAINING LIBRARY SPACE

While new buildings or major renovation projects are infrequent, children's librarians will often spend time with modifications to space as technology is added and subtracted, as collections grow and change, and as service patterns alter. The look and feel of a school library says a lot about the library program. You need to arrange the school library for efficiency, but it is equally important that you create a welcoming environment (Stephens and Franklin, 2007, p. 59). If nothing else, school and children's librarians need to keep the space clean, safe, and attractive so children, families, and school groups *want* to visit the library.

Day-to-Day Issues

Most libraries have custodial service or employ workers to clean the entire library, and most libraries have contracts for repair of the library building, computer equipment, and furnishings. Some librarians even have preventive maintenance and cleaning programs that provide regular upkeep of machinery, carpet cleaning and ventilation, and lighting repair, for example. So why should the children's librarians have to worry about dealing with cleaning or repairs?

One reason is practical: at the very least children's librarians and school librarians have to let cleaners and repair workers know when there is a problem and make sure that problems are corrected in a timely fashion. The other is that children and children's activities in libraries may be messier than the adult counterpart or activities in the classroom. A reading art activity with glue and glitter will likely be messier that an adult book discussion or a math lesson in a classroom. The children's librarian should be prepared to clean minor messes or tidy up after kids have used the department for homework when necessary. It is also important to remove broken furniture and keep clutter off floors so kids won't trip, or make the problem worse. Young children can't read "out of order" signs, so hazards and frustrating malfunctions need to be removed and children supervised carefully.

Children's and school librarians should work closely with cleaners and others to keep the department space clean and in working order. Children are less knowledgeable about healthy behavior. Toddlers climb over all surfaces, teethers put everything in their mouths, and many older children believe in the "5 second" rule and will eat food off the floor if they pick it up fast. Cleaning staff may not have experience with children's behavior so they will need to work with the department to keep it healthy for the children who use it.

Looking Good

In addition to the basics of keeping the department clean and in repair, it is also important to keep the room looking attractive. This means that staff should display books, mount posters or other art on walls, and create bulletin boards that attract children to the department or the school library. Some children's departments also have stuffed animals or toys to use as decoration for the children's room. Staff also need to change displays and the art at least twice a year, to keep it fresh and to give children the message that there is always something new at the library. City Academy in St. Louis, Missouri, painted several walls in its library with magnetic paint, so that it was easy to maintain the wall-sized school calendar and add children's book reviews to themed wall displays. Paper is attached to these walls with small magnets and can be moved or removed easily with no damage to the walls. This paint is available at home improvement and paint stores.

Some school libraries or children's areas are big enough to divide by age group, so the use of art and displays helps all children feel welcome and helps them find the area that has material specifically for them. Younger children need to have at least one "cute" focal point in the department that will attract them and help them remember the library as a happy place. This could be stuffed animals or posters only a few inches off the floor. Older children need some part of the room that is not "babyish," so they feel comfortable. This could be as simple as having full-sized furniture, age-appropriate book displays, or bulletin boards with age-appropriate children's art. ImaginOn, the central children's library in Charlotte, North Carolina, installed chalkboards at the end of the book stacks, so kids, parents, and staff could write and draw book facts and ideas. Librarians write notes like "dinosaur books here" and kids add "LOL" by the joke section.

Adult Friendly

The school library and the children's department should also have adult-friendly features. If the department welcomes parents and teachers, it needs to have adult-sized furniture so adults will be comfortable. Some libraries have rocking chairs or reading nooks to encourage adults to read with children, or at least be comfortable while their children use the room. Some libraries have posters and book displays about children's literature and child development in the children's department to further attract parents and teachers to the children's area. School libraries may also include educational resources for teachers.

Both the school library and the children's room should also have comfortable and useable staff space. Staff need work areas that are ergonomically designed for adults, that are approachable by children and adults, and that provide good visual control of the children's area. While children's staff may be "on the move" most of the day, they need a reasonable work area. Children's staff need space out of the public eye where they can work on program planning, collection development, and displays and where they can store materials for outreach. Staff should keep work areas tidy and set up storage spaces so work and desk space can be shared by all staff. Secure storage is needed for coats, purses, and other personal items, and these areas need to be kept clean. Staff computers and machinery need to be kept in working order, stored out of the reach of children, and have secure storage when not being used.

CHANGING SPACES

> If the librarian's job is to provoke children's intellectual engage-
> ment, then perhaps the architect's job is to evoke their sensibilities.
> (Siddiqi, 2010, p. 23)

Whether your library is getting a new library building, a major interior make-over or just trying to update parts of the children's room, it is an opportunity to make the space more useable and more attractive. Changes in the children's room or school library are most often small and focused, but they can be a complete "gut" rehab or a whole new library building. No matter the size or scope of the change, careful research and planning can maximize the improvements to the children's department and to its appeal to children, families, and teachers.

A variety of changes can be made. If made to accommodate additional computers or technology, renovations may also include changes in shelving to accommodate more (or less) books, book display, and new media or for upkeep such as new floor covering, replacement of old and worn furniture, or new paint on the walls. Redecorating or renovation of the interior design gives the children's staff a chance to reevaluate their space and make changes to better serve the children who use the area. Or a library might go for a whole new look. For example, the Mount Laurel library in New Jersey decided on a cheerful environment for the children's room. Tall shelving was replaced by slat wall panels, colorful paint went on gray walls, and comfortable, colorful seating was added. Users asked, "When did you buy all these new books? When did you put in these new windows?" (same books, same windows) One mom said, "Now I come into the library and just shop the wall (book display)" (Bernstein and Schalk-Greene, 2006, p. 66).

Planning Interiors

Before making changes to the children's room, staff must know how the library will be used by staff, patrons, and the community. Perhaps the most effective way to assess this use is to keep a record of the patterns of current use over a period of weeks or months before formal planning starts. Use of the children's department or school library can be considered in terms of activities. Activities can be categorized as group activities and individual activities. By looking at this pattern of activity, a librarian can understand how the space and furniture is currently used in the children's department. For instance, library activities might require space for 65 patrons at one time. A school librarian may need to have space at tables for a class of 25 people. Seating is needed for adults reading to children, groups of students working together, children doing homework or individual research, and children using audiovisual materials. Study tables and probably carrels are needed, as well as chairs or cushions for leisure reading. How many computers are needed at one time? Make a list of all the activities that happen in the room to see how best to use the space.

As in assessing patron needs, the needs of staff must be judged on the basis of systematic observation of their activities over a period of time. Librarians may know, in general, the amount of space and equipment they need to do their work, but correcting a lack of space or facilities for one task can lead to the creation of new problems. Noting staff activities and needs for several weeks will provide a more accurate record of what is necessary than asking staff members to estimate needs.

When considering how to change the children's room or the school library it is also important to get staff input on what service and program space will be needed in the future. If a program room was available how would it be used? If display cases are added how would they be filled? Or, if a coatrack was added, would there be fewer coats on the floor?

It is also possible to get some good ideas from children, families, and teachers who use the children's room. Parents or teachers may have suggestions that would make them more likely to use the library, and children often see space differently than adults, so they may have some important suggestions to make. One librarian asked different aged children to sit on the floor of the children's room with a staff member and describe what they saw. Staff can ask older children to take them on a tour of the room and tell the staff what they like and don't like. Some librarians have focus groups with parents, teachers, or children before renovation to get more systematic input from them.

Knowing the way the library is likely to be used and the collections it will house are the first steps in planning facilities. After determining the needs, the planning committee should explore ways that these needs might be met. One way to do this is to visit other libraries, both locally and while attending conferences or workshops, or virtually by visiting new library websites. Touring other facilities allows the planners to observe both successful and unsuccessful arrangements. It is useful not only to look at the library but also to talk to staff members to learn about unseen aspects of the design. Do certain colors tend to soil easily? Does the attractive soft sculpture pose any dangers to toddlers? Librarians who have experience with various approaches can offer invaluable advice about their efficiency and practicality.

The goal of interior design for a school library or a children's department is to produce a space that is friendly, approachable, and welcoming for all users. The overall effect should be lively and appealing, with sections that visually indicate whether they are planned for toddlers playing with toys and boardbooks or for school-age children using computers and reference materials for school projects. School libraries need space for research projects, circulation, and reading enrichment activities, as well as being attractive to young children and older students. Teachers should be comfortable and be able to use the library in a variety of ways.

Informal seating should allow for a variety of postures while reading or taking notes but should somewhat limit conversational groups. For children, carpeting and cushions can take the place of chairs or carrels. However, study carrels are good for children who have a difficult time concentrating. The ideal room provides a variety of types of seating and work areas. Children, as a rule, like to sit closer to one another than do adults. Furniture should be scaled for children but should also allow for adult use as adults frequently accompany children. Comfortable seating arrangements should be available for parents that read to their children.

Usually the colors used in the children's department are brighter than those in other sections of the library. School libraries often can be brighter and more decorated than classrooms. The staff can gather ideas for effective color schemes by visiting other libraries. Some librarians are tempted to carry their personal color choices over into the library setting. This is unwise, because public spaces have different purposes than private spaces. It is better to look at public buildings—theaters, museums, and shopping malls, in addition to other libraries—for ideas about colors for walls, carpets, and furniture.

Artwork adds color and interest to a department and should be incorporated in the department's design. Permanent works of art, such as murals, add color and interest to walls. Some libraries have three-dimensional objects such as trains, story panels, or playhouses in the children's room. However, they limit the amount of display space available for temporary exhibits and may lose their charm over time. Many librarians have found that changeable displays and exhibits are preferable to permanent, built-in art. Glass-front display cases in which pictures, art objects, and books can be placed offer flexibility. Space for hanging posters, children's drawings, and seasonal decorations is also useful. Areas of corkboard or other soft surface make it possible to hang pictures and other items easily and safely. The decorator can suggest practical ways to achieve flexibility in the display of artwork.

Housing the Collection

The number of books in a collection is not the only factor to be considered in planning collection space for a children's department. Differences in format and in needs for access determine the type of shelving required. Some questions to be considered are:

- Will books be shelved in the traditional spine out fashion, or will books be displayed cover out? Or both?
- What is the most logical way, given the shelving space available, to divide types of materials? For example, put fiction on freestanding shelves and nonfiction on wall shelving to make it easier to keep books in order.
- What is the best way to divide the collection? Children's materials have traditionally been divided into preschool materials, primarily picture books, and materials for older children. Some librarians subdivide this further by having separate shelving for boardbooks and for early reading books. Audiovisual materials can be shelved separately from books. School librarians often divide books by reading or grade level.
- What special types of shelving are needed? Picture book shelving needs to have a different design than standard book shelving, face-out display shelves slant books toward the user, and magazine shelving usually allows for face-out display and storage of back issues.
- How should paperbacks be shelved? With hardbacks, or in spinners?
- How will audiovisual materials be shelved? Many choices exist.
- How high should shelving be? Children cannot reach high shelves, so books become inaccessible if adult shelving is used. Low shelving also makes it easier for the librarian to see what is happening in the department and to prevent discipline problems. The tops of such shelves can also be used for informal displays of new books or other items of seasonal or special interest.

Furnishings

Many librarians budget for changes in furnishings on a regular basis. Even if the children's department has the sturdiest of chairs and tables, day-to-day use wears out all furnishings. Nothing can do more to make a room more welcoming and comfortable than replacing damaged and worn furniture. *Library Journal* has an annual review of the best new furniture and display design (Spring Design Supplement), and this may a good place to start when looking to upgrade furnishings. Many library supply vendors exhibit at library or education conferences and have information on products both in catalogs and on their product websites.

New furniture should solve the immediate problem of replacing old or broken chairs, tables, desks, displayers, and other equipment. It also can be used to add color, update the look of the children's room, and make children more comfortable.

Staff should consider the following when evaluating the children's room furnishings:

- If you were a child, would you like this environment? If you were a four-year-old? An eight-year-old?

- Are shelves, furniture, and the convenience facilities scaled for children?
- Does staff have visual control over the area?
- Has space been provided for display of materials geared for children? (Murphy, 2007, p. 135).

Infrastructure

Occasionally libraries and schools get structural upgrades. Because of cost this does not happen often, but many buildings get infrastructure upgrades about every ten years. These upgrades may include electrical wiring; telecommunications/wireless installations; ventilation; repair of structural flaws; lighting; and changes needed to comply with changes in building codes.

Rarely do librarians deal directly with these issues, but the need for large changes gives the department an opportunity to make more significant changes to the space than can be done on an annual basis. Input into where electrical outlets are needed or where lighting or ventilation should be improved may be possible to insure that changes bring the greatest possible benefit.

Planning for Technology

Often wiring and the location of electrical outlets governs the number and placement of computer terminals and other equipment. As more libraries use wireless computer technology, there may be more flexibility as to how to plan space for computers and the need for more widely distributed electrical outlets. School libraries have been able to convert computer labs to other uses by teaching students computer skills with laptop computers stored on a cart. Students use tables in the library or their desks in the classroom for computer instruction or research, rather than a permanent computer workstation. Some public libraries check out laptops for in-library use or have enough outlets that children can use their personal laptops.

Since 85 percent of public libraries have wireless service (ALA, 2011), it is likely that the way librarians manage in-house technology will become more flexible. In addition, the actual computer hardware is changing with the availability of smartphones, notebook computers, and e-readers. Instead of workstations, libraries may have docking stations for kids to load materials on personal electronic devices.

Computer work areas should have good lighting and ventilation and be easy to supervise. Many libraries keep computer areas close to the information desk, so sign-up is easy and staff are available to answer questions. When planning the table area for computers, allow space for two or three children or a child and an adult to use a terminal together. Children often want help from friends or adults, and they often see computing as more fun when done together.

Other Considerations

Access to the collection is important not only for various age groups but also for users with disabilities. Government regulations, such as the Americans with Disabilities Act, require that all new and reconstructed public and school facilities must be readily accessible to and usable by individuals with disabilities

(Bryan, 2007, p. 31). Whenever possible, a new room should go beyond the minimum requirements to make use by persons with disabilities as convenient and pleasant as possible. Children with disabilities especially should not be segregated from other children who are using the library.

Objects such as fire extinguishers and wall lighting should not protrude into passageways or rooms. All other fire and safety codes should be followed. The children's room and school library should be as "childproof" as possible. Tables, desks, and shelving should have round edges to avoid injury to young children. Empty electrical sockets should be capped, and wiring should be hidden to prevent accidents.

NEW LIBRARIES

Although planning and building new libraries or new schools or making extensive renovations to existing structures are not done frequently, librarians may find themselves involved in such planning at some time during their career. Decisions made at the crucial early stages of planning will affect the working conditions of current staff and of a future succession of librarians. Careful planning requires hard work over a period of time, but the result can be a department that is both aesthetically pleasing and provides a setting for efficiently organized services.

A VIRTUAL TOUR OF CHILDREN'S LIBRARY SPACES

1. *ImaginOn* is the central children's library of the Charlotte Mecklenburg Public Library. It combines the Charlotte Children's Theater with a youth library and is worth an actual visit as well as a virtual one at http://www.imaginon.org/. Be sure to take the video tour.
2. In Rochester, New York, the *National Museum of Play* combines a branch of the Rochester Public Library and museum displays. Check out www.museumofplay.org to see how the museum integrates book displays into its exhibits. Take the virtual tour of Reading Adventureland. An in-person visit is wonderful fun as it has technology and the history of all things playful.
3. An excellent example of design for school libraries is the *L!brary Project* in New York City. The Robin Hood Foundation brought together several architects to help the city schools reconceptualize, redesign, and renovate school libraries. See slides of the new libraries at http://archleague.org/2010/05/the-library-initiative/.

Planning an effective facility requires that the librarians know the community or school in which the library is being built and the possible uses for the building. Librarians need to understand the demographics and think about which needs will change over time. Among the factors that affect planning are:

- the number of people expected to use the building
- the demographics (including age, education level, and income) and growth pattern of the community or school
- the presence of other libraries and information services
- what library services are provided offsite

- the availability of related institutions (e.g., museums, cultural institutions)
- the geographic location or location within the school
- the community's or school's social climate

Many libraries and schools built in recent years have had an open plan. In public libraries the children's section is visible and accessible from the adult circulation department, but clearly indicated by decor and signage as a special area for children. In schools the library is often an open area in the center of the building. The nature of the community can influence the desirable level of separation. If parents, children, and teenagers are the main users of a library branch, the traffic between adult and children's section is likely to be heavy, and noise from the children's department is unlikely to offend adult users. In a school library noise can disrupt classes, or hall traffic can disrupt the library. If, on the other hand, many adults are using the library for business or study, they may prefer to have the children's department out of sight and range of hearing.

Each school or library will have a planning team and process for a major building project. The school librarian or children's librarian should be willing to participate in this process and have the basic understanding of how the planning will be done. For the librarian who has no experience in building projects, it would be a good idea to read any of several books about the process that are now available (see the references at the end of this chapter) and/or attend a workshop or webinar on this topic.

Librarians should be ready to make suggestions that will make the children's space workable and pleasant. Every suggestion should be tested by asking such questions as the following:

- How will this suggestion help us provide better library services?
- Could this suggestion cause extra work for the staff?
- Could this suggestion cause a danger to children? (Attractive seating arrangements and sculptures, such as castles and dragons, have had to be dismantled in libraries because of their potential danger to young children.)
- Has this suggestion been tried in other libraries, and if so, how successful do the staff and patrons consider it to be?

Evaluating Space

Although few new facilities are systematically evaluated after they have been built or renovated, a strong case can be made for including evaluation as part of the children's department or school library's annual report. The first step in an evaluation is to collect observations and evidence about visible problems. Providing a notebook in which any staff member can record observations will facilitate the collection of information. A roof that leaks or a heating system that delivers uneven warmth are examples of obvious problems that should be recorded. Notable successes of space changes should also be noted. If time and resources are available, questionnaires may be administered to individuals using the children's department or school library to determine their satisfaction with the facility. Or the school library could put a survey on the library website or Facebook page.

All of these efforts will result in a collection of useful data to indicate directions for planning future changes.

IF YOU WANT TO KNOW MORE . . .

2011 State of America's Libraries Report. 2011. Chicago: American Library Association.

Bernstein, Joan E., and Kathy Schalk-Greene. 2006. "Extreme Library Makeover: One Year Later [April]." *American Libraries* 37: 66–69.

Brown, Carol R. 2002. *Interior Design for Libraries. Drawing on Function and Appeal.* Chicago: American Library Association.

Bryan, Cheryl. 2007. *Managing Facilities for Results: Optimizing Space for Services.* Chicago: Public Library Association/American Library Association.

Erikson, Rolf. 2009. *Designing a School Library Media Center.* Chicago: American Library Association.

Feinberg, Sandra, and James R. Keller. 2010. *Designing Space for Children and Teens in Libraries and Public Places.* Chicago: American Library Association.

Feinberg, Sandra, Joan Kuchner, and Sari Feldman. 1998. *Learning Environments for Young Children.* Chicago: American Library Association.

Murphy, Tish. 2007. *Library Furnishings: A Planning Guide.* Jefferson, NC: McFarland.

Siddiqi, Anooradha Iyer. 2010. *The L!brary Book: Design Collaborations in the Public Schools.* New York: Princeton Architectural Press.

Stephens, Claire Gatrell, and Patricia Franklin. 2007. *Library 101: A Handbook for the School Library Media Specialist.* Westport, CT: Libraries Unlimited.

Willis, Margaret Sabo. 2005. *Kid's Rooms.* Menlo Park, CA: Oxmoor House.

Section III

Developing and Managing Collections:
Challenges and Changes

Libraries are known for the collections they develop. Print books have traditionally been the core of library collections, but that is beginning to change. Today's librarian faces challenges in choosing materials in print and digital formats as well as in providing access to these collections to users within the library and other locations. Intellectual freedom issues and privacy issues remain important.

CHALLENGES

- While print formats remain an indispensable part of a children's collection, there is a growing demand from children, parents, and teachers for additional digital formats.
- Because of the fast-changing nature of devices for accessing digital formats, school and public librarians must make decisions about providing e-readers and other devices in the library.
- Changes in the publishing industry make it difficult for librarians to give their patrons access to recently published materials in e-formats.
- New cataloging rules first available in 2012 will require children's librarians to learn and apply the new rules to children's collections.
- Challenges to library materials continue to require explaining and defending the selection of library resources.
- Following professional guidelines for protecting the privacy of patrons and the security of library records has been made difficult by increasingly complex technology systems for recording and handling transactions.

CHANGES

Chapters in this section provide guidelines and tips for making changes to meet these challenges. We share strategies for selecting multimedia collections, choosing devices to allow better access to all formats, and keeping up with trends in publishing and technology. We give guidelines for developing policies to protect privacy and to respond to challenges to library collections.

7

Collection Development
in a Multimedia World

Children's collections have been changing dramatically during the last ten years or so. A 20th-century children's collection was usually contained within the department or school library, and users expected to visit the library to choose books and other tangible materials or to receive services such as reference or homework help.

The 21st-century children's collection more and more often includes a variety of formats both within and outside of the library. The books in the library are only part of the information the library makes available. Patrons are guided to information on websites and other electronic sources, databases access remote materials, and patrons are often able to access materials from home or school.

Developing a collection is one of the major tasks of a librarian, and it requires careful planning. Collection development is the overall program to build a collection of resources to meet the needs of library users. The selection of individual materials, whether books, databases, or digital materials, grows out of a master plan to ensure that the end product will be a balanced collection. The proliferation of different types of resources in recent years has increased the complexity of developing a balanced collection.

CHANGING NATURE OF LIBRARY COLLECTIONS

The shift in the nature of the library collection affects the process of collection management, but many of the basic tasks remain the same. Before addressing the details of developing a collection, it is important to make the philosophical

Figure 7.1
20th-Century Children's Library Collection

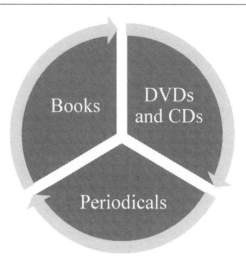

Figure 7.2
21st-Century Children's Library Collection

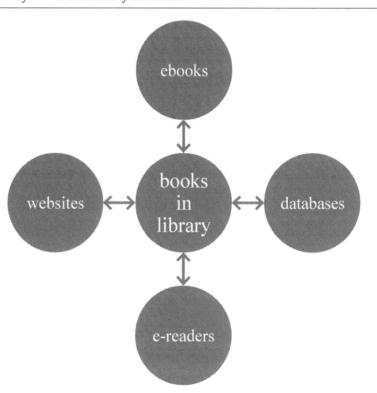

shift from defining the collection as a physical set of materials in the library to acknowledging the importance of less tangible sources of information throughout the community and the world. This change will affect the materials we choose, the equipment needed to use them, and the space in which we house them. Sometimes it is not the library staff who are slow to acknowledge changes, but the adults, parents, and administrators, who think of library collections as static book collections. Librarians should help the public understand the changing nature of the library by publicizing it through all their interactions with library users, in print, online, and in person.

What are some of the components of the library collection? Certainly a collection of books in the physical library remains a vital center, augmented perhaps by DVDs, periodicals, audiobooks, recorded music in various formats, and other materials. Additional resources that can be considered part of the library's collection are materials stored in other locations; these might include the adult section of a library, classrooms, and other institutions such as community colleges and universities. As budgets remain limited and books become more expensive, the amount of sharing between libraries is likely to increase.

In addition to these resources, there is the large body of material available online through websites, databases, and digital collections. These digital materials are valuable additions to the limited materials that any one library can purchase and store. A recent (2011) survey by *School Library Journal* reported that almost half (44%) of school libraries offer ebook collections.

The underlying purpose of any library collection is, of course, to meet the needs and potential needs of the users, and over the years traditional patterns of children's collections have developed. Both school library and public library children's department collections include fiction and nonfiction books, magazines, and digital materials. Unlike adult collections, children's collections are usually divided into age groups.

Figure 7.3
Materials for Different Age Groups

Age Group	Material
Toddlers	Boardbooks Picture books Apps
Preschoolers	Picture books Apps Recorded music
Beginning readers	Early reading books Apps Simple webpages
Fluent readers	Chapter books at many levels Apps Informational materials in many formats YA materials for older children

Many children's departments also collect materials of interest to parents and teachers, and some may provide textbooks, tutoring materials, and multimedia kits. Materials in formats for special needs children—large print, Braille, or audiobooks—may also be part of the collection. Many libraries have collections in languages other than English. Libraries may also have historical children's literature collections or special collections on local or regional history for children.

Although content is the major focus of collection development, differences in format cannot be ignored. Materials for children are now available not only in print, but also in several digital formats that can be read on computers or devices such as iPads, Kindles, Nooks, or variations of these. Whether the library should provide these devices or expect the borrowers to own them is an often-discussed issue. The traditional arrangements that libraries have had with publishers, under which they purchase a book and then lend it to one borrower at a time for as long as the book lasts, is being questioned by some publishers of ebooks. In 2011, Random House announced that the ebooks it sold to libraries would be limited to 26 circulations. Many librarians were outraged, and negotiations on this issue are likely to continue for a long time.

Selection of Print Materials

Whether a library has a large materials budget or a very small one, it is important to develop and use selection criteria, a selection policy that defines the scope of the collection, and selection procedures that describe the process used to select materials. That is, the children's librarian needs to make some decisions before looking at specific books or reading book reviews:

- selection criteria: what makes an individual book or item valuable
- selection policy: which categories of materials will be included in the collection
- selection procedures: how materials are ordered

Even in a small library, it is important to set up a system of selection. This ensures that a small budget is spent on the best and most useful materials, that the collection has strengths and is more than "books in a room," and that time spent selecting materials is used efficiently.

In medium or large libraries selection rules may be set for all selectors, including children's librarians. Even in this setting there will be some special issues to be included in collection planning. Children's librarians generally worry more about the ability of child users to read and understand materials than selectors for adults, and the attractiveness and durability of materials may be more important when selecting for children. Most librarians also consider the physical quality of materials, the attractiveness of covers, packaging and book layout, the quality of illustrations, and the literary merit of written works.

Selection of Digital Materials

The selection of electronic materials follows the same pattern as the selection of print materials, but there are some added complications. Because the packaging of electronic materials has changed so dramatically and so quickly in recent years, many librarians feel inadequately prepared for choosing materials. As a result, wholesalers have taken over the provision of ebooks in most libraries. This makes it easier for librarians, but letting the industry run selection rather than librarians leads to complications. Large companies prefer to deal with large, mainstream publishers, so works produced by smaller independent writers and independent publishers are often overlooked. Large public library systems with large budgets can influence wholesalers, but smaller libraries and school libraries often have less power.

If librarians want to keep control over their collections, and ultimately their libraries, they are going to have to develop the knowledge and confidence to pick and choose electronic materials. Probably the best way to do this is to attend conferences where librarians can interact with representatives of wholesalers and publishers and find out what is going on. Children's librarians often attend conferences and focus primarily on books and authors. While these are important, it is also necessary to learn the details of what is becoming available in electronic format, which formats are most useful for libraries, and the sources from which materials can be obtained.

In addition to the content of electronic materials, there are additional considerations in selection:

- Is the product available in a variety of formats?
- Does the library have the appropriate equipment?
- Does the community like and use the formats available?
- Is the format flexible or does it require proprietary equipment?
- Have the formats been available long enough for patrons to get used to them?
- Are the available formats gaining or losing popularity with users?
- For reference books, how does the publisher handle updates (through new editions or integrated changes in the text or supplements)?

Formats of electronic materials as well as the methods of distribution are changing rapidly, so it is important for schools and libraries to maintain contact with suppliers and evaluate changes. Most libraries and schools purchase or lease electronic materials from library wholesalers, often the same ones from which they get their print materials. Most companies provide subscription plans for online series of nonfiction books and reference materials. The pricing is often based on the size of the library (number of cardholders) and the circulation figures. Acquisition of these materials is often centralized in the library system or school district, but the children's services staff should take responsibility for reviewing these materials and making recommendations.

As more and more children's books are becoming available as apps for tablet and mobile devices, evaluation of individual products grows in importance. Often it is useful to ask one member of the children's staff to specialize in evaluating apps and suggestion criteria for them. Reviews are becoming available in professional journals and blogs. As a general rule, picture book apps should offer a reading experience comparable to reading the original print picture book but in addition give enhanced features such as video zooms, audio voices, or interactive features. Changes in technology will undoubtedly mean new features will become available, so this is an area in which it is essential for librarians to keep up with the professional literature and share insights with colleagues.

SHARING RESOURCES

Limited budgets and ever-more expensive materials make the sharing of resources between different institutions increasingly attractive. Not only are new materials expensive, but they are often time-limited as various formats become outdated and sometimes unusable. Some books keep their value for twenty years or more, but few electronic materials will be of value for so long. Sharing resources requires administrative flexibility, which is sometimes hard to achieve, but with goodwill on both sides, accommodations can be reached. Institutions can share resources in their collections in many ways:

- School and public libraries can share catalog information and some electronic resources through links on their websites.
- Public libraries can lend collections of materials to teachers for use in their classrooms.
- School libraries can lend similar collections of materials to public libraries for summer reading programs during times when the school library is closed.
- School and public libraries may be able to share non-English-language collections.
- Community college libraries can make their catalog information available through high school and public library webpages.
- Links to special collections in museums, hospitals, local businesses, or other institutions can provide access to reference materials for students.
- Links to community organizations that provide collections in languages other than English may be possible for both school and public libraries.

WEEDING THE COLLECTION

"Next to emptying the outdoor bookdrop on cold and snowy days, weeding is the most undesirable job in the library. It is also one of the most important. Collections that go unweeded tend to be cluttered, unattractive, and unreliable informational resources." (Manley, 1996)

Weeding is an unpopular task for many reasons. Not only do librarians hate to throw out books and other materials, but members of the public are frequently scandalized by the idea that any book is disposable. Nonetheless, we do our young patrons a disservice if we keep materials that are outdated and therefore might contain misinformation.

Weeding is the process used to withdraw materials from the collection. For most children's departments, weeding is an ongoing activity. Damaged and worn books need to be disposed of, and materials that are no longer useful need to be withdrawn to make room for newly purchased items. Because weeding is often considered a housekeeping issue, some librarians put off doing it as long as possible. Librarians don't like throwing materials away for fear that they may be useful "some day." The problem with not weeding is that children find it more difficult to find the "good" books in the forest of old, damaged, or unattractive books left in the collection. If the shelves are full, it may be more difficult to justify an adequate collection development budget to purchase new materials.

The concept of weeding is simple enough. Library staff set criteria for materials that are to be kept in the collection and systematically examine materials to see whether they meet the criteria. Some school librarians have developed a catchy list, known as MUSTY, as reminders of what needs to be discarded:

- **M** Misleading and/or factually inaccurate
- **U** Ugly and worn beyond mending or rebinding
- **S** Superseded by a newer edition or by a much better book (or other material)
- **T** Trivial with no discernible value
- **Y** Your collection has no use for this material, irrelevant to needs of your clients (Suffolk Public Library System, 2012).

Because even small libraries have a variety of materials in the collection, the criteria need to be tailored to each type of book or other material. For example, many libraries consider the following:

1. Weeding based on condition or appearance: torn pages, dirty covers or pages, dated and unappealing illustrations. For digital materials, the use of an outdated platform.
2. Weeding of duplicate volumes of once-popular materials.
3. Weeding based on poor content: information is dated, poorly written or incorrect, or cultural norms have changed so material is now considered biased or offensive. This is one of the most important criteria for weeding. Many children's departments and school libraries keep materials that offer children incorrect information—outdated names of countries or world leaders, discredited scientific findings, or unreliable statistics and maps.
4. Weeding based on low circulation or use. A time limit should be set for how long a book will be kept in the collection after its last use.
5. Weeding of materials for which hardware is no longer available or desired. Vinyl records and filmstrips were discarded from collections in the past. CDs and DVDs are formats that will probably be discarded in years to come. Community demands should determine when materials of this kind are no longer useful.

Disposing of materials that have been discarded can be a problem in some libraries. Members of the public have been known to complain loudly when any book, no matter how battered, is taken from the shelves. Many librarians put discarded books into book sales for the public. These can be useful for home use or for using pictures or pages for art projects. Books that are inaccurate or that promulgate unacceptable attitudes are better pulped and recycled. Many libraries try to have these materials removed quietly in the evening or during holiday periods.

Despite the difficulties of weeding materials, librarians owe it to their patrons to remove superfluous materials from their collection. This attracts greater usage because patrons can see the newer and more appealing items they might miss on overcrowded shelves. We owe it to our patrons to maintain a vital, attractive, and useful collection in our libraries.

SELECTION POLICIES

After setting criteria for selecting individual books or material, it is important to describe what the collection should be like. Selection policies often include procedures used in selecting, acquiring, and weeding materials, as well as selection principles. Because the library or school board should approve the basic selection policy, it is usually wise to keep the procedures in a separate statement for staff use. In this way, the entire document does not have to be brought to the board each time a change in procedures is made.

Whether contained in one or in several documents, selection policies and procedures for materials should cover such areas as:

- goals (meeting recreation and information needs)
- intellectual freedom statement
- balance of collection
- age of potential clientele
- type of service to adults
- relationship to school media center collections or public library collection
- provision for needs of special groups (e.g., special education students, immigrants)
- materials excluded (by format and content)
- gifts
- collection levels for various content areas
- method of selection
- selection tools used
- basis for evaluation (e.g., reviews, personal inspection)
- individuals involved in selection
- obtaining input from community
- special methods for specific materials (e.g., non-English-language)
- special procedures for particular formats (e.g., electronic resources, databases)
- method of acquisition
- dealers and other suppliers
- procedures (usually systemwide)
- weeding
- appropriate copyright date to discard (obsolete materials)
- appropriate length of time since last circulation to discard
- decision on mending materials
- procedure for systematic weeding

The first part of a selection policy describes the overall philosophy of the department. It sets the stage for the specific procedures by stating the audience for whom the collection is designed and the professional commitment to intellectual freedom and a balanced collection that guide the selection process. This part of the policy can be used as a defense against censorship attempts. If the library is officially committed to providing a balanced collection of information for all children in the school or community, the librarian is in a better position to defend the purchase of materials with subjects such as homosexuality, intelligent design, or witches.

General statements about the relationship of the public library to schools also make it possible to justify not buying materials that are adequately supplied by the schools. Although some overlap is always expected among collections, the differences in the aims of the two collections should be clearly stated in the policy. School library collections are based on the curriculum. Nonfiction selections in school libraries follow closely the subjects taught in school. Many schools use accelerated reading programs and expect school libraries to include these titles in their fiction collections. Lists of the accelerated reading levels may be posted on the school library website.

The gift policy is important as an explanation to would-be donors of unsuitable material. This section should state that any materials accepted as gifts should meet collection standards.

The development of standard collection levels for different content areas is a useful way to ensure that a balanced collection is acquired. The levels chosen should reflect:

- the composition of the community, for example, the predominant age level of the children, or the presence of specific language groups;
- the adequacy of the provision of school media resources;
- the strength or weakness of local interest in certain topics.

KEEPING UP WITH CHANGING NEEDS

A library collection is never a static object; it is an ever-changing body of materials in many formats. Books and other materials, once selected, are not necessarily a permanent part of the collection. Almost all children's library departments and school libraries have as their mission serving the needs of their patrons, not serving as depositories for print or nonprint material that is no longer used. There is a need, of course, for collections of historical children's materials, but these collections are special libraries that serve a purpose different from most libraries. One of the greatest challenges facing a children's librarian is to keep up with the changing needs of patrons. There are a number of steps that can be taken to do this.

- *Set up a system to monitor circulation records.* Most library materials are circulated and used outside of the library. There should be automatic signals sent when materials drop or increase sharply in circulation. Sometimes these changes are seasonal; sometimes they reflect changes in curriculum or school assignment; sometimes they are the result of a change in television programs or movies. Other changes reflect the natural seesaw of children's interests as vampires go out of fashion and zombies become more popular. Librarians should try to figure out the reasons for changes in circulation patterns and react by altering ordering of specific materials.
- *Monitor the usage of databases and other materials.* Vendors routinely provide figures for the usage of databases and other electronic materials. These figures should be examined closely and the trends in usage analyzed to find out whether the library is giving access to materials most needed by its patrons.
- *Observation.* Paying attention to what young people are talking about, which kinds of materials they are most often requesting and which they are ignoring, can give insight into their interests. It is useful to ask library clerks and pages to make a note if they notice particular interest in a certain area or type of material.

- *Surveys.* Periodic surveys on the library website can be used to discover what interests are growing—what kinds of books or other materials children would like to see in the library and which they can do without. Free survey tools such as Survey Monkey are easy to administer and can yield useful information.
- *Talk to teachers and other librarians.* Casual conversations with library colleagues from your own institution or neighboring ones will often alert you to the latest trends for children and teens.
- *Read the library literature.* Both print and electronic formats of library journals give news about changing trends. The blogs of the major professional organizations—ALSC (Association for Library Service to Children), YALSA (Young Adult Library Services Association), AASL (American Association of School Librarians)—provide valuable ideas about what other librarians are doing and how they perceive the needs of children.
- *Attend library and educational conferences.* Attendance at conferences is often very beneficial to collection development. Not only do you have a chance to go to programs to hear about new trends and activities, but the exhibits show the latest books and other materials available. Vendors are very willing to talk to librarians about materials that might strengthen their collections.

It is important to remember that not only the materials but also the formats in which they are presented will be changing over time. Trends in use of mobile devices, laptops, types of media, and other changes that are still unknown will affect what library collections offer their patrons. After a collection has been developed, a plan for collection growth has been adopted (and funded!), and materials are in place, it is important to let library users know what the collections hold and how to use them. Traditionally, children's librarians have encouraged reading through topical and seasonal book displays and created booklists on topics of interest to library users. As materials shift in format and content, it is more important than ever that librarians find new ways of engaging young people's attention. They must encourage reading and media use by keeping abreast of developments in both print and digital media and helping their patrons find and use the information and recreational materials on offer at the library.

IF YOU WANT TO KNOW MORE . . .

Baumbach, Donna J., and Linda L. Miller. 2006. *Less Is More: A Practical Guide to Weeding School Library Collections.* Chicago: American Library Association.

Gregory, Vicki L. 2011. *Collection Development and Management for 21st Century Libraries.* New York: Neal-Schuman.

Hughes-Hassell, Sandra, and Jacqueline Mancall. 2005. *Collection Management for Youth: Responding to the Needs of Learners.* Chicago: American Library Association.

Johnson, Peggy. 2004. *Fundamentals of Collection Development & Management.* Chicago: American Library Association.

Manley, Will. 1996. "The Manley Arts." *Booklist*, March 1, 1108.

Polanka, Sue. 2010. *No Shelf Required: E-Books in Libraries.* Chicago: American Library Association.

School Library Journal. *The Digital Shift. LJ/SLJ Ebook Summit: More School Libraries Offer Ebooks; Increased Demand, Rise in Circulation.* Available at http://www.thedigital shift.com/2011/10/ebooks/ljslj-ebook-summit-more-school-libraries-offer-ebooks -increased-demand-rise-in-circulation (accessed Aug. 27, 2012).

Suffolk Public Library System. http://www.suffolk.lib.va.us/ldnd_template/youth -services/library-tip-sheets/weeding.html (accessed Aug. 27, 2012).

8

Acquisition, Automated Systems, and Access

Technology plays a large role in Jeannine's job. She maintains the automated circulation system, creates PowerPoint presentations, does podcast of books, communicates via e mail, maintains the library website that is used by teachers, students and parents. She is familiar with various websites for use by students working on homework and research projects. She also teaches an Internet safety curriculum as dictated by the school district. (Kane, 2011, p. 96)

While many school and children's librarians work in institutions that centralize the nuts and bolts functions of acquisitions, automation, and cataloging, it is important to understand how the systems work and how to advocate for policies and practices that best serve the children who use the library. Some school and children's librarians have little direct control of these technical functions because they are centralized for the system or district, and policies and procedures have been established and used for a long time. If this is the case, it is still important to understand the functions and be able to comment on them when appropriate. In medium and small libraries, acquisitions might be handled by one staff person and cataloging provided by a vendor or consortium, so the children's librarian has more responsibility to oversee the work and provide quality control. In small schools, children's collections in museums, or other organizations the children's librarian may have to "do it all" and have the knowledge and skills to purchase, catalog, and circulate all materials.

Librarianship has always been about building collections, providing ways of finding things in a given collection, and keeping track of where items are when not on the library shelf. Fifty years ago this was all done "by hand," that is, librarians ordered books from paper catalogs or bought them from salespeople who called at the library in person to show the books to the librarian. There was standard cataloging practice, but books were cataloged by each library and clerks typed card sets and manually filed them. Circulation was done by signing a card for each item taken out (or printing the user's card number on the book card).

Twenty-five years ago all these functions had been automated in most public and school libraries. Most libraries ordered a wide variety of materials online from a handful of vendors. Cataloging was supplied for copy cataloging online, and most libraries, including school libraries, had an automated system that provided both the catalog and a circulation system.

Today, technical functions are all electronic, but because of the variety of materials formats and the growth of e-materials, rules and practices are changing. There are more vendors and licensing agreements in addition to purchase contacts. Standard cataloging is giving way to new rules and open source systems. Providing for access and circulation includes use of databases, downloading ebooks and subscriptions to electronic magazines in addition to print materials.

Whether the children's or school librarian is the sole provider of technical services or the person who interacts with other library departments to get the work done, it is important to understand how systems work and make sure that the systems work well for the children and adults served.

MATERIALS ACQUISITION

Once materials are selected for the collection, they must be purchased or, in the case of electronic media, contracted for. Acquisition is the process of ordering and obtaining materials after they have been selected (Intner, Fountain, and Weihs, 2011, p. 111). Acquisition also can include the considerable financial bookkeeping needed to account for money spent on materials purchased. In many medium and large libraries, acquisitions is centralized or at least done by a single person rather than by the staff who select materials. This makes the process of ordering and receiving materials more efficient and problem solving more effective. Because of this practice of centralizing acquisitions, procedures are the same for the children's department as for the rest of the library.

The majority of materials are purchased from vendors or materials wholesalers. Often the library negotiates standard discounts or contracts (usually based on the size of the book or materials budget) and sets terms of service that include rules for back-ordered materials (books or other items that are out of stock), material returns, processing standards, and other terms of service. Libraries might pick one vendor to supply books, another to supply music and digital materials, and another to supply all the library's periodicals and full text databases. Most vendor orders are placed and tracked electronically, so order forms and billing practices are also set with each vendor. Using these vendors simplifies the order process and makes the billing easier than dealing directly with each publisher or producer.

Many school and public libraries are required to bid out contracts with major vendors at regular intervals of time. Usually contracts last several years, and the same vendors are used again and again. This bidding allows librarians to negotiate better discounts and better service. Most libraries have two or three materials vendors with which they do the majority of the library's materials purchasing. It is important for the children's librarian to be sure that at least one of these vendors has a good selection of children's materials.

Another type of purchasing done by the children's department includes specialty companies that sell children's music, DVDs, ebooks, software, puppets, games and toys, and other items that are unique to children's work. Often the contract arrangements are similar to those with larger vendors, but discounts are less likely to be given, and a standard library purchase order is used to track purchases. Often the children's librarian has to identify these specialty companies and then work with the acquisitions staff to conduct business with them. Other specialty companies used by the children's department include alternative and diversity publishers. These include small presses that sell foreign-language materials for children and cultural, religious, and political groups that publish materials for children. It is important to seek out these publishers if the community has immigrants, cultural and ethnic groups, or if the library has requests for alternative political viewpoints.

Another type of acquisitions is the use of approval or standing order plans. These plans allow the librarian to set a profile for the vendor to use to send titles to the library. The librarian does not order individual titles under the plan, and there is usually a restriction on how many approval plan books can be returned. Librarians often use an approval plan if there is no children's librarian to select books or to get books that are sure to be selected (Newbery and Caldecott winners for example). Librarians also may buy access to children's music, ebooks, or electronic magazines with blanket licenses that provide access to a collection of items, rather than one title at a time.

Most publishers and vendors offer similar services that allow local librarians more opportunities for selecting or tailoring group orders to the libraries' specific needs. Vendors will generate lists on topics (mysteries for middle school, materials for parents, books about the Olympics, etc.) and allow the children's librarians to select and order books as a group. Vendors also allow libraries to have standard orders for types of materials (books on the *New York Times* best sellers list, top 20 music albums, or book-award winners). These orders allow the library to get materials in a timely manner and to avoid having to order individually materials that library users will be sure to enjoy.

The last kind of acquisitions is purchasing materials from retail stores and retail online companies. The advantage of using local stores is that the school or children's librarian gets to see the actual item before purchase, and it is a way to get materials needed immediately and support the local economy. It is also time consuming to shop for individual books, the selection of even good retail stores is limited when compared to national vendors, and often the discount is less than using library vendors. Some libraries set up accounts with local stores and allow librarians to purchase from them. Children's librarians need to know how and when to use retail outlets to buy materials for their collections.

Many libraries also set up online accounts with national retail companies rather than use local book, music, or video stores. Such companies as Amazon and Barnes & Noble allow libraries to set up accounts and offer discounts and free or reduced-rate shipping. Smaller libraries may find the discounts of these companies similar to those offered by library vendors and that the selection of materials is very broad. This provides a good alternative to the bookstore, a wider selection, and generally good customer service. For children's librarians these companies offer customer reviews that might help them understand which books are really popular with children and why.

When acquiring databases and other electronic materials the process is not purchase but rather licensing agreements. In essence the library "rents" access for library users rather than purchasing a database. Databases can be licensed from the company that produces them, or they may be sold in packages that combine products. For example, many encyclopedias sell both the print version and electronic access for one price. There may also be fees to access internet sites that are especially useful or interesting to children. Prices are often determined by how many potential users of the site the library has, whether the site can be accessed from home or school, and how many simultaneous users of the site the library can support.

School and children's librarians need to understand and follow their library's acquisitions policies and procedures and work to get the most for the least amount of time and money. Most libraries need several ways to purchase materials to get the collections they need, so children's librarians need to research companies that can be used to purchase materials for children.

AUTOMATED SYSTEMS

A collection of materials is of little value unless users can find the specific items they want or browse books and materials of interest to them. The services for making resources accessible include cataloging and classification of materials to ensure that individual items can be located within a collection and that the school or public library has an accurate inventory of what it owns. Librarians also need a way to circulate materials and keep track of users, use, overdue materials, and fines. Most libraries also benefit from systems that can generate use statistics so selectors have a better, more accurate idea of what materials get used and what doesn't. A new challenge is how to make sure children know what is available electronically and how to actually download or check out items they cannot touch or see.

Cataloging and Classification

Electronic catalogs provide access to information about where and in what format materials are housed and if materials are on the shelf and available for circulation. Electronic catalogs facilitate resource sharing among locations by allowing reciprocal borrowing between branches in a single system or between separate library systems. Electronic catalogs also facilitate requests through interlibrary loan. Online catalogs may include access to electronic information such as full-text magazine articles, specific internet sites, or specific databases. Another important access point is the library's webpage. This allows users to access the catalog and other electronic information from home or school as well as within the library or from the classroom.

Most public libraries provide an electronic catalog, available at the library as well as accessed online from remote locations. Schools provide catalogs that are available from any computer in the school building and sometimes by remote access outside the school. These catalogs are maintained by at least one professional staff member with specific training in cataloging rules and standards. Some libraries are part of a system of independent libraries that have joined together to provide a catalog. Some libraries purchase cataloging from the jobber or book wholesaler that sells the materials the libraries buy. Publishers and the Library of Congress have cooperated for decades to provide cataloging for each title sold through the Cataloging in Publication (CIP) that provides classification (assigning location) and cataloging (identifying and describing the item) for titles before publication so it can appear in the material when it is published.

In a library that has a specific staff person responsible for cataloging and classification, or one that buys these services from a vendor or cooperative regional system, what is the role of the children's librarian in providing a useful catalog for children? The first role is to help set specifications for cataloging and classification that best serve children who use the library. Cataloging and classification are rule-based using a classification schedule—Dewey Decimal or Library of Congress system; the Anglo-American Cataloging Rules (AACR2 and updates, RDA); machine readable cataloging (MARC format)—and subject heading rules—Library of Congress or *Sears List of Subject Headings*. Even with all these rules, there are decisions to be made that will make the library's catalog more useful to the children it serves. The children's services manager should be involved in setting and reviewing cataloging specifications.

Some decisions are basic. Should cataloging be in English only, or should other languages be included? Should the catalog include icons or pictures to help children find what they are looking for? In figure 8.1, Pamela Newberg and Jennifer Allen suggest specific concerns for children's catalogs.

While catalogs need to be governed by rules to be consistent, children's and school librarians also have to use common sense. They must develop a sense of their students and the community so they know to bend to rules in order to help students access information (Stephens and Franklin, 2007, p. 170). It makes more sense for most schools and children's departments to use "car racing" as a heading than "automobile racing."

Once catalog specifications are developed, the children's librarian needs to be sure there is a system to check that these specifications are followed and that the specifications create the catalog that is needed. Also, remember that as publishing trends change, so does cataloging. For example, should graphic novels be classified separately from traditional books? If so, a separate classification will need to be created. While the children's librarian may not control cataloging decisions, oversight of the catalog and participation in library-wide or systemwide cataloging discussions are important to get the best catalog possible for the children served.

A second responsibility of children's librarians is to develop services that help children, parents, and teachers understand and use the library's catalog. No matter how user-friendly a library's catalog is, catalogs are difficult to read and understand. Young readers need staff help to use the catalog, and older

Figure 8.1
Cataloging Specification Decisions

Call Numbers

Questions regarding call numbers involve policies covering the assignment of classification numbers and the addition of book numbers. If Dewey is used

- Should the source be the abridged edition or the unabridged edition?
- Are the numbers carried to the first slash? Two digits past the decimal? Four digits past the decimal?
- Are author letters or Cutter numbers used? If so, how many characters or digits will be assigned?
- Where are the biographies? 921? B? Will they be shelved in a separate section or mixed with other nonfiction?
- Where are easy books? Are they marked E or P, or something else?
- Are there special collections that require a prefix (Reference, Professional collection, Foreign language, Story collections)?

If automated, in which tag and subfield divisions do the call numbers belong?

Subject Headings

Questions about subject headings include the following:

- What subject authority will be used: LC adult headings, AC headings (LC children's headings), or Sears?
- Are the numbers of subject headings used limited in some way?

Reading Programs

Special treatments to facilitate reading programs require asking the following:

- If a reading program is used, how are the books identified? If automated, are there special requirements for this tag?

Physical Processing

Choices about physical processing include decisions about the following:

- Covers or not?
- Cards and pockets?
- Bar codes? If so, where will they be placed on the materials?

Armed with this information, vendors can be selected who meet most of these needs.

Source: Intner, 2011, pp. 190, 191.

children and adults often do not understand the catalog and also need assistance. Library staff should be available to help all users find what they need in the catalog and then on the shelf. Staff should be trained to give individual catalog instruction as needed and explain how to do advanced catalog searches to help users find everything they need.

Many public libraries offer group catalog instruction to schools or other groups of users. Most school librarians have a set of lessons for use of the library for each grade level. This is particularly helpful for students doing research for reports if the instruction is tailored to the specific needs of the students. It is also important to respect the developmental level of students so as not to provide information beyond their learning level. It is useful to explain how to access the online catalog from school or home and to describe library procedures needed to access the computer as well as to use it. Most instruction includes helping students understand catalog vocabulary (what is a call number?), techniques for searching, understanding the catalog entry, and how to locate the actual material found in the catalog. If the local school teaches information literacy in its library, it is helpful to coordinate catalog instruction at the public library with this instruction.

Changes in Automated Systems

With the advent of electronic media including databases, ebooks, e-tunes, and evideo products, catalogs and catalogers have been challenged to find ways to integrate these new products into the traditional catalog. Catalogers have long struggled to adapt current cataloging rules and practice to include new materials and changes in programming for catalogs. As a response to criticism that cataloging had become too complicated and that even the best MARC (machine readable cataloging) records didn't make our OPAC (Online Public Access Catalog) records work as well as we would like, catalogers decided to create new rules for cataloging. In 2005 work on Resources Description and Access (RDA) was begun (Intner, Fountain, and Weihs, 2011, pp. 74–75). Testing, training, and evaluation are due to begin in 2012, so the switch to RDA will not be immediate. The promise of RDA to make cataloging easier and the catalog easier to understand and use and to be better integrated to include social media and e-resources is attractive, but it will be several years before we will know if the promise is met.

Another attempt to simplify finding and describing items in a collection is "LibraryThing.com." It provides a free or low-cost way for small libraries to catalog and inventory items in the collection (Bisson, 2007, p. 5). It is an "open" social network that allows users to add subject headings and links to book information on Amazon.com. For small schools or child-serving organizations that don't have funds or expertise to do cataloging, LibraryThing would provide an inventory and subject access. With a little work, shelf location can be added. Circulation would need to be done separately, and because the system is open someone would need to monitor changes made by users. The positives are that it is easy to use and provides a lot of information about items in the collection.

Another major change in automated systems may eventually allow children's librarians (with technical services help) to provide a more flexible, simpler catalog for young users. In traditional automated systems, the library adds local holdings, patron information, and circulation specifications but can't make changes to format or the functioning of the system. The vendor owns the code and doesn't allow an individual library to make system changes. Since most libraries don't have the expertise or funds to make changes, vendors have felt no pressure to change. In the past several years open-source automated systems have been developed, so that librarians can make changes to the system. The idea is that librarians can fix errors and make changes that better serve their users than relying on a vendor to do this (Breeding, 2008, p. 7). This would mean that if a library wished to circulate toys, for instance, they could change the cataloging format to better describe the items in the collection, or could even add a picture of the item without permission from the system vendor.

CIRCULATION

While some small schools and special libraries use a hand circulation system, most libraries have an integrated automation system that provides both the catalog and an electronic circulation system. The main function of the school or children's librarian is to manage the system, that is, to keep user information up to date, send out overdue notices, and solve problems for individual users as they arise. In larger libraries most of these functions will be handled by a circulation department, but it is important to understand the system and the rules and be prepared to intervene for individual children.

Librarians should review circulation rules regularly to be sure they cover all issues fairly and clearly. School and children's librarians should be actively involved in this review. Issues that may need to be addressed are:

- Can homeless children get a library card with no address? Can they get a "day pass" to use computers and books at the library?
- Does the circulation system sort non-English names correctly?
- Does the circulation system contain a student's room number and home address?
- Does the circulation system list the custodial parent or guardian?
- Can teachers access information on student reading?
- Are fines reasonable and effective?

ACCESS

As well as having systems in place to catalog and circulate materials there is important work to be done to make sure children can find what they want whether or not they can use the catalog. Teachers, parents, and other adults also may need help to make full use of the collection of materials available at your library. How materials are shelved, what finding aids and displays are provided, and how electronic communication is used to market the collection can be crucial to help users be successful in finding what they want at the library.

SHELVING MATERIALS

Most school and children's librarians work in libraries where the shelving pattern is set and with signage that is uniform throughout the library. Some children's room managers or school librarians may get the opportunity to design new interior schemes as part of renovation or new building projects. Whatever the situation, it is the responsibility of the children's librarian to evaluate how well the shelving plan works for child users and whether the directional signs are effective in helping children find what they want. If shelving is confused or signage inadequate, the children's librarian should suggest changes that will make the best use of the space available for the children's collection; display the collection in an attractive manner; and make it easy for children, parents, and teachers to find materials of interest.

The number of books in a collection is not the only factor to be considered in planning collection space for a children's department or school library. Differences in format and in needs for access determine the type of shelving required.

Children's materials have traditionally been divided into preschool materials, primarily picture books, and materials for older children. Some librarians subdivide this further by having separate shelving for boardbooks and for early reading books. Audiovisual materials are often shelved separately from books, and so are Braille, large print, and other formats designed for special needs children. Some school libraries shelve books by grade or reading level. Award-winning books may be shelved together as a collection. Although this arrangement may help the librarian choose books for a child by going to the most appropriate shelf, it can make it more difficult for patrons to choose books on their own. The goal of most libraries is to enable young patrons and their parents to select materials for themselves, rather than having to ask library staff for help. Unless a clear need for segregated collections is apparent, the simplest system is usually the best: picture books in one visible area, fiction in alphabetical order, and nonfiction in one sequence of Dewey decimal order.

Both fairy tales and graphic novels can cause special problems in shelving. While collections of fairy tales are shelved by Dewey number, some librarians choose to shelve fairy tales in picture book format that are appropriate for young children with the picture books to make them more available to the intended audience. Often children want to read graphic novels because they like the format, so it is easier for them if the library has a separate section for them rather than integrating them into the fiction section. Whatever shelving scheme used will need good, clear signage and helpful staff to direct library users to the materials they want.

Special types of shelving are needed for picture books. Because most of these books are oversized and thin, with little information on the spine, the most effective shelving is face-outward. Slanting shelves, which allow browsers to see the front cover of the books and to open them easily, are highly desirable, but most collections are too large to allow all books to be displayed this way. One solution is to have most of the books shelved spine-outward on a set of low shelves and to have one row of slanted shelving above these to display a constantly changing selection of books. Some librarians have experimented with keeping picture books in large baskets, in bins, or on book trucks for easy browsing. Although these methods make it difficult to find a particular book, most children choose their books by browsing. Some libraries have tried integrating nonfiction picture books with other nonfiction books on the same topic. Whatever shelving is used, estimate the number of picture books that are likely to be collected and housed separately from other materials.

Periodicals are similar in format to paperback books. Because most libraries do not bind children's periodicals, back issues soon become tattered and unsightly. The most frequently used system allows current issues to be shown face-outward and provides shelf space to stack back issues. Most periodicals are used in-house, so the shelving should be placed near comfortable seating for easy browsing.

Paperback materials are usually stored separately from hardcover books. Many libraries use spinners, revolving book racks, which allow books to be displayed face-outward. Spinners tend to attract several children at a time and may cause congestion if not allotted sufficient space.

The standard collection of children's fiction and nonfiction takes up more space than an adult collection of similar size because usually only low shelving is used. Children cannot reach high shelves, so books become inaccessible if adult shelving is used. The tops of such shelves can also be used for informal displays of new books or other items of seasonal or special interest. When predicting an increase in the size of the collection, the children's department's need for easy access should be taken into account.

Nonprint materials require special types of storage: trays or spinners for CDs and DVDs, shelving for games, cabinets for toys, and files for pamphlets. Placement of computers should also be thoughtfully done and labeled. Having OPAC placed conveniently by the collection as well as close to librarian help is a good idea. Label these as catalogs so students don't try to surf the net from the catalog. Many librarians find grouping computers together with clear labels of what use is appropriate makes it easy for children to sign up for them, use them, and ask questions of staff.

Marketing the Collection

After a collection has been developed, a plan for collection growth has been adopted (and funded!), and materials are shelved, it is important to let library users know what the collections hold and how to use them. Traditionally, children's and school librarians have done topical and seasonal book displays and created bibliographies on topics of interest to library users. Some librarians do bibliographies "on demand" from teachers or other childcare workers to help the users find books or materials that meet their needs. With the development of nonprint materials and electronic media, bibliographies now include books (print and electronic), audio materials, magazines, websites, and other electronic sources on a topic.

Beyond these basic recommendations, librarians often have the opportunity to "sell" materials that have value but may be overlooked by users. It is also good to remember that even if the collection does not change, many parts of it will be new to children as they grow and mature. Preschool children will find it exciting to be able to use beginning reading books and third and fourth graders need to be introduced to chapter books as they gain the ability to read books of more than 100 pages. Children need recommendations of nonfiction books as they broaden their personal interests and as they have more complex homework assignments.

Children with special needs and their parents and teachers need to know what materials the library has for them and how to find them in the library's collection. Special lists or information on the library's website will help attract these users who might not think of the library as having materials they will find useful. If the library has foreign-language collections, it is also important to find ways of highlighting non-English materials and by providing foreign-language cataloging and getting library materials translated into languages spoken by immigrants.

As well as including reader's advisory services as part of children's reference, librarians can plan displays, programs, and book talks to help children move through the collection as their needs grow. Many children's librarians also provide specific transition from the children's collection to the young adult and adult collections, so young teens will feel comfortable with the library's entire collection. School librarians need to find ways to help elementary students transition to using larger more sophisticated middle school collections. It is also fun to figure out ways to attract children to all parts of the collection. Whether it is providing ways for children to review and recommend books to their peers, designating a star book of the week or website of the month, or book talking good books about Italy to a fourth-grade class working on an Italian festival for parents' night, librarians should always be aware of the potential for marketing the collection to the community of users.

Promoting Electronic Media

For elementary school students it may be difficult to find and use electronic media. Young children learn about books and other print media by touching the physical item and by manually manipulating it. While even very young children may be comfortable using computers, pads, smartphones, and other devices, they may not be able to understand how to access and use a database or find a list of ebook holdings on the library's catalog. Electronic resources can offer a great deal of variation in skill and interest. According to Harris, we need to have an "accurate and nuanced approach to young peoples' needs and digital knowledge than to simply assume all young people can (and will) use all media" (Harris, 2011, p. 70).

The first task for the librarian then is to assess or help the student assess which media fits the student's need. Librarians need to make a habit of reminding children of their choices, both print and nonprint. The next step is to make sure the students know how to use the resources at hand. School librarians have the opportunity to systematically teach media use through a planned curriculum of library instruction. Public librarians should develop short (less than three minutes) lessons to get individual students started on use of each digital media available or provide short videos of this presentation on the library website.

Librarians should feature or display electronic resources in a way similar to the way print materials are displayed. Feature an ebook of the week on the library webpage. Make a bulletin board display of images printed from various databases including the appropriate web address. Keep a whiteboard in the computer lab and list seasonal websites for children to try. When you recommend a book, mention an associated electronic resource. When demonstrating an electronic resource, mention an interesting print resource.

A good collection meets the needs of users and will attract children to the library by providing both a good collection *and* services to expand children's knowledge of what is in the collection.

IF YOU WANT TO KNOW MORE . . .

Bisson, Casey, 2007. "Open-Source Software for Libraries." *Library Technology Reports.* Vol. 43:3. Chicago: American Library Association.

Breeding, Marshall. 2008. "Open Source Integrated Library Systems." *Library Technology Reports*, Vol. 44:8. Chicago: American Library Association.

Harris, Frances Jacobson. 2011. *I Found It on the Internet: Coming of Age Online.* 2nd ed. Chicago: American Library Association.

Intner, Sheila S., Joanna F. Fountain, and Jean Weihs. 2011. *Cataloging Correctly for Kids: An Introduction to the Tools.* 5th ed. Chicago: American Library Association.

Kane, Laura Townsend. 2011. *Working in the Virtual Stacks: The New Library & Information Science.* Chicago: American Library Association.

Stephens, Claire Gatrell, and Patricia Franklin. 2007. *Library 101: A Handbook for the School Media Specialist.* Westport, CT: Libraries Unlimited.

9

Intellectual Freedom and Privacy

Both school and public libraries are dedicated to the idea of making available a range of information and entertainment on a variety of topics. Intellectual freedom is a basic philosophic underpinning for libraries. When it comes to serving children and young people, however, librarians, parents, and many other adults are also dedicated to shielding them from excessive violence, unacceptable ideas, and inappropriate sexual materials. The struggle between intellectual freedom and the protection of children has caused tensions ever since libraries were first developed.

ISSUES IN INTELLECTUAL FREEDOM

A child is often pictured as being subjected to a barrage of ideas and media, as shown in figure 9.1.

What responsibility does the library have to protect children from perceived dangers as well as protecting their right to freely access information and entertainment? The American Library Association's Library Bill of Rights describes its importance to libraries:

I. Books and other library resources should be provided for the interest, information, and enlightenment of all people of the community the library serves. Materials should not be excluded because of the origin, background, or views of those contributing to their creation.

II. Libraries should provide materials and information presenting all points of view on current and historical issues. Materials should not be proscribed or removed because of partisan or doctrinal disapproval (Library Bill of Rights, available at http://www .ala.org/advocacy/intfreedom/librarybill; accessed Aug. 30, 2012).

Figure 9.1
Ideas and Media Aimed at Children

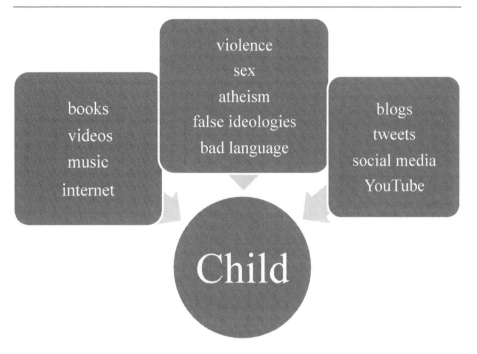

This is in accord with the United Nations' Universal Declaration of Human Rights, which defines intellectual freedom in Article 19:

Everyone has the right to freedom of opinion and expression; this right includes freedom to hold opinions without interference and to seek, receive and impart information and ideas through any media and regardless of frontiers. (Universal Declaration of Human Rights UN, available at http://www.un.org/en/documents/udhr/index.shtml#a19; accessed Aug. 30, 2012)

Furthermore, the ALA policy is that minors are entitled to free access to libraries and all the materials and services provided there. Article V of the Library Bill of Rights states,

A person's right to use a library should not be denied or abridged because of origin, age, background, or views. The "right to use a library" includes free access to, and unrestricted use of, all the services, materials, and facilities the library has to offer. Every restriction on access to, and use of, library resources, based solely on the chronological age, educational level, literacy skills, or legal emancipation of users violates Article V. (http://www.ala.org/advocacy/intfreedom/librarybill/interpretations/freeaccesslibraries; accessed Aug. 30, 2012)

Despite these clear declarations of principle, many questions still arise about which specific materials are suitable for children and teenagers, and many parents complain about books and other resources they consider harmful to children.

THE ALA'S TOP TEN MOST FREQUENTLY CHALLENGED BOOKS OF 2011

1. *ttyl; ttfn; l8r, g8r* (series), by Lauren Myracle
   Offensive language; religious viewpoint; sexually explicit; unsuited to age group
2. *The Color of Earth* (series), by Kim Dong Hwa
   Nudity; sex education; sexually explicit; unsuited to age group
3. *The Hunger Games* trilogy, by Suzanne Collins
   Anti-ethnic; antifamily; insensitivity; offensive language; occult/satanic; violence
4. *My Mom's Having a Baby! A Kid's Month-by-Month Guide to Pregnancy*, by Dori Hillestad Butler
   Nudity; sex education; sexually explicit; unsuited to age group
5. *The Absolutely True Diary of a Part-Time Indian*, by Sherman Alexie
   Offensive language; racism; sex education; sexually explicit; unsuited to age group; violence
6. *Alice* (series), by Phyllis Reynolds Naylor
   Nudity; offensive language; religious viewpoint
7. *Brave New World*, by Aldous Huxley
   Insensitivity; offensive language; racism; sexually explicit
8. *What My Mother Doesn't Know*, by Sonya Sones
   Sexism; sexually explicit; unsuited to age group
9. *Gossip Girl* (series), by Cecily Von Ziegesar
   Drugs; offensive language; sexually explicit
10. *To Kill a Mockingbird*, by Harper Lee
    Offensive language; racism

Source: American Libraries. http://www.americanlibrariesmagazine.org/censorship-watch/top-10-challenged-books-2011 (accessed Aug. 30, 2012).

As the reasons mentioned in the list show, explicit sex, drug use, homosexuality, and offensive language are often the reasons given for asking that a book be removed from the library shelves. Sometimes the complaint is that the book is unsuitable for a particular age group and should be limited to use by teens or adults. Librarians themselves struggle with deciding in which section of the library a book should be located. Many subjects that are appropriate for tweens and teens would be incomprehensible or frightening to preschool children. In recent years librarians and others have raised questions such as these:

- Should we purchase a book that includes stories about witches or vampires even though some parents object?
- Should filters on the computers in school libraries and the children's department of public libraries prevent access to websites that provide information about gay/lesbian/transgender youth issues?
- Will the religious context of this story make children of other religions or no religion feel marginalized?
- Should an explicit sex education book in picture book format be available in a K–6 school library?

- Are words like "penis" and "vagina" appropriate in a picture book?
- Do children who read books that include profanity learn to use this language in the classroom or at home?

Most librarians select materials based on reviews and recommendations from trusted sources about the value of each item, but this does not guarantee that parents will not object to some of them. Shared community values ensure that some language and some content will not be provided for young people; graphic descriptions of violence or sexual activities are generally omitted from materials for children. In recent years, some topics that were previously taboo, including divorce, single-parent families, premarital sex, and gay and lesbian characters have appeared in many materials designed for children and young adults. These changes are accepted by individuals and communities at different rates. Problems arise at the margins where books and other materials are probing situations previously unmentioned in children's books and including language that may be common in some communities but shunned in others. These materials are sometimes challenged by parents and other adults, so librarians should be prepared to address their concerns.

Both school and public libraries have as a goal the provision of balanced collections of material representing different viewpoints. In religious schools, there may be limitations placed on the selection of resources that fit into the belief system of the religion. Within the parameters of the belief system, most libraries try to represent a range of opinions. The collection development policy of the library should clarify the range of materials included.

In some states, school personnel act in loco parentis (in place of parents) on some aspects of their care. Occasionally the question of whether or not libraries should act in loco parentis when deciding which materials a child may access arises. Most libraries and schools specify that they do not act in place of parents and that parents who wish their children not to read or view certain materials should discuss these rules with the child, not expect the librarian to monitor use. It is the responsibility of a parent or guardian to limit access for their child.

SPECIFIC ISSUES WITH DIGITAL RESOURCES

Information in electronic format is not immune to challenges. In fact, many of the most publicized controversies in recent years have been over internet access for children. Almost as soon as public libraries began offering internet access to patrons, debate started over what kind of access was appropriate for children (Minow, 1997). In 2000, Congress passed the Children's Internet Protection Act (CIPA) designed to prevent children from having access to inappropriate online materials. This act requires all libraries receiving federal funding for electronic services to "adopt a policy and employ technological protections that block or filter certain visual depictions deemed obscene, pornographic or harmful to minors" (CIPA). In 2003, the Supreme Court upheld this law, although some libraries protest that it infringes the intellectual freedom rights of patrons. State and local laws may also restrict access to certain types of materials in school and public libraries. These laws have spurred many libraries to develop an "Acceptable Use of the Internet" policy to clarify the ways in which both children and adults are allowed to use library computers.

The American Library Association and its divisions have developed resources to help librarians deal with these policy issues. The ALA section on the Children's Internet Protection Act (http://www.ala.org/advocacy/advleg/ federallegislation/cipa; accessed Aug. 30, 2012) provides a wealth of resources for libraries seeking guidance on how to comply with the act and provide services for their patrons.

An important part of an internet policy is distinguishing between adult use and children's permissible use and defining who falls into each category. Some libraries have written policies clarifying appropriate age levels.

Public Internet computers are equipped with commercial filtering software. The library's filtering policy upholds the principles of intellectual freedom, allowing adults to make their own choices regarding filtering. The policy also aims to ensure that our libraries are safe and welcoming places for children, and it affirms the right and responsibility of parents to make choices for their own children and teens.

- Adults (18 years and older) may choose filtered or unfiltered searching at each login.
- Teens (13–17) have the choice of filtered or unfiltered Internet access unless their parent or guardian designates filtered access.
- Children (12 years and younger) have filtered Internet access unless a parent or guardian designates they can choose between filtered and unfiltered access (Multnomah County Public Library. Parent's Guide to Filters and the Internet, available at http:// www.multcolib.org/parents/parents_filter.html; accessed Aug. 30, 2012).

Because parents have differing views on how much freedom children and teenagers should have on the internet, there are likely to be complaints about too much or too little filtering. Librarians should be prepared to defend the library's policy and adhere to it.

Libraries do not monitor patrons' use of the internet, but they have a legitimate interest in encouraging responsible use. An approach taken by many librarians is to provide lists of appropriate websites where children can find information relevant to school assignments or other interests. If the time a child can spend on the internet is limited by library policy, as it is in many libraries, children can locate useful sites for their assignments, but do not have time to aimlessly surf and find objectionable materials. Librarians can also provide copies of guidelines for children's use of the online resources to help parents set limits for home use of this medium.

Websites are accessed in a more public way than other library materials, and this sometimes leads to complaints about the sites other people are viewing. To protect privacy, some librarians place terminals close to a wall or provide screens that make it difficult for others to observe what is being viewed. Computers used by adults can often be placed far away from the children's room, so children do not see the sites adults are visiting.

In school libraries the issues are somewhat different because all of the patrons are students. Many schools have Internet User Agreements signed by both students and parents that outline acceptable use of school computers and the internet. An example of such a policy is one used at the Hannibal, Missouri, School District, available at http://www.hannibal.k12.mo.us/agreemen.html (accessed Aug. 30, 2012).

The most recent area of concern about use of the internet is access to social media. The ALA Intellectual Freedom Manual has a section on Minors and Internet Interactivity, which includes this statement: "The rights of minors to retrieve, interact with, and create information posted on the Internet are extensions of their First Amendment rights" (Morgan, 2010, p. 172).

BASIC STEPS FOR PRESERVING INTELLECTUAL FREEDOM IN YOUTH SERVICES

Step One: Know the Documents Supported by the American Library Association

The American Library Association has prepared a number of documents explaining the professional attitude toward aspects of intellectual freedom. These offer useful information to help the media and the general public to understand the reasons for the library's choices of material and policies. The basic position on Intellectual Freedom is stated in the Library Bill of Rights (ALA, 2010, 49).

Figure 9.2
Library Bill of Rights

The American Library Association affirms that all libraries are forums for information and ideas, and that the following basic policies should guide their services.

I. Books and other library resources should be provided for the interest, information, and enlightenment of all people of the community the library serves. Materials should not be excluded because of the origin, background, or views of those contributing to their creation.

II. Libraries should provide materials and information presenting all points of view on current and historical issues. Materials should not be proscribed or removed because of partisan or doctrinal disapproval.

III. Libraries should challenge censorship in the fulfillment of their responsibility to provide information and enlightenment.

IV. Libraries should cooperate with all persons and groups concerned with resisting abridgment of free expression and free access to ideas.

V. A person's right to use a library should not be denied or abridged because of origin, age, background, or views.

VI. Libraries that make exhibit spaces and meeting rooms available to the public they serve should make such facilities available on an equitable basis, regardless of the beliefs or affiliations of individuals or groups requesting their use.

Adopted June 19, 1939, by the ALA Council; amended October 14, 1944; June 18, 1948; February 2, 1961; June 27, 1967; January 23, 1980; inclusion of "age" reaffirmed January 23, 1996. Reprinted with permission from the American Library Association. Available at http://www.ala.org/advocacy/intfreedom/librarybill (accessed Aug. 30, 2012).

This document has been updated several times in the years since its initial approval. One of the interpretations especially relevant to children's librarians is that on allowing children and teenagers free access to libraries.

When the ALA took the position that children should be allowed to use materials in any part of the library, some adults thought that special children's departments would no longer be allowed. The interpretation does not go that far. Librarians may set up specialized collections for any group of people provided those people (including children) can also obtain materials from the whole collection. Not all libraries have embraced the idea of setting no age limits on access to materials. Many parents have complained to libraries that their child borrowed unsuitable material. The professional response has been that "parents—and only parents—have the right and the responsibility to restrict the access of their children—and only their children—to library resources" (see figure 9.3). This position includes nonprint as well as print materials.

Figure 9.3
Free Access to Libraries for Minors

An Interpretation of the Library Bill of Rights

Library policies and procedures that effectively deny minors equal and equitable access to all library resources and services available to other users violate the Library Bill of Rights. The American Library Association opposes all attempts to restrict access to library services, materials, and facilities based on the age of library users.

Article V of the Library Bill of Rights states, "A person's right to use a library should not be denied or abridged because of origin, age, background, or views." The "right to use a library" includes free access to, and unrestricted use of, all the services, materials, and facilities the library has to offer. Every restriction on access to, and use of, library resources, based solely on the chronological age, educational level, literacy skills, or legal emancipation of users violates Article V.

Libraries are charged with the mission of providing services and developing resources to meet the diverse information needs and interests of the communities they serve. Services, materials, and facilities that fulfill the needs and interests of library users at different stages in their personal development are a necessary part of library resources. The needs and interests of each library user, and resources appropriate to meet those needs and interests, must be determined on an individual basis. Librarians cannot predict what resources will best fulfill the needs and interests of any individual user based on a single criterion such as chronological age, educational level, literacy skills, or legal emancipation. Equitable access to all library resources and services shall not be abridged through restrictive scheduling or use policies.

Libraries should not limit the selection and development of library resources simply because minors will have access to them. Institutional self-censorship

(*continued*)

Figure 9.3
(Continued)

diminishes the credibility of the library in the community, and restricts access for all library users.

Children and young adults unquestionably possess First Amendment rights, including the right to receive information through the library in print, non-print, or digital format. Constitutionally protected speech cannot be suppressed solely to protect children or young adults from ideas or images a legislative body believes to be unsuitable for them.[1] Librarians and library governing bodies should not resort to age restrictions in an effort to avoid actual or anticipated objections, because only a court of law can determine whether material is not constitutionally protected.

The mission, goals, and objectives of libraries cannot authorize librarians or library governing bodies to assume, abrogate, or overrule the rights and responsibilities of parents and guardians. As Libraries: An American Value states, "We affirm the responsibility and the right of all parents and guardians to guide their own children's use of the library and its resources and services." Librarians and library governing bodies cannot assume the role of parents or the functions of parental authority in the private relationship between parent and child. Librarians and governing bodies should maintain that only parents and guardians have the right and the responsibility to determine their children's—and only their children's—access to library resources. Parents and guardians who do not want their children to have access to specific library services, materials, or facilities should so advise their children.

Lack of access to information can be harmful to minors. Librarians and library governing bodies have a public and professional obligation to ensure that all members of the community they serve have free, equal, and equitable access to the entire range of library resources regardless of content, approach, format, or amount of detail. This principle of library service applies equally to all users, minors as well as adults. Librarians and library governing bodies must uphold this principle in order to provide adequate and effective service to minors.

See also Access to Resources and Services in the School Library Media Program and Access to Children and Young Adults to Nonprint Materials.

---

[1] See *Erznoznik v. City of Jacksonville,* 422 U.S. 205 (1975), "Speech that is neither obscene as to youths nor subject to some other legitimate proscription cannot be suppressed solely to protect the young from ideas or images that a legislative body thinks unsuitable for them. In most circumstances, the values protected by the First Amendment are no less applicable when government seeks to control the flow of information to minors." See also *Tinker v. Des Moines School Dist.,* 393 U.S. 503 (1969); *West Virginia Bd. of Ed. v. Barnette,* 319 U.S. 624 (1943); AAMA v. Kendrick, 244 F.3d 572 (7th Cir. 2001).

Adopted June 30, 1972, by the ALA Council; amended July 1, 1981; July 3, 1991; June 30, 2004; and July 2, 2008. Reprinted with permission from the American Library Association. Available at http://www.ala.org/advocacy/intfreedom/librarybill/interpretations/freeaccesslibraries (accessed Aug. 30, 2012).

A document of special importance in school libraries is the Access to Resources and Services in the School Library Media Program (http://www.ala .org/advocacy/intfreedom/librarybill/interpretations/accessresources; accessed Sept. 5, 2012).

Figure 9.4
Access to Resources and Services in the School Library Media Program

---

An Interpretation of the LIBRARY BILL OF RIGHTS

The school library media program plays a unique role in promoting intellectual freedom. It serves as a point of voluntary access to information and ideas and as a learning laboratory for students as they acquire critical thinking and problem-solving skills needed in a pluralistic society. Although the educational level and program of the school necessarily shape the resources and services of a school library media program, the principles of the Library Bill of Rights apply equally to all libraries, including school library media programs. Under these principles, all students have equitable access to library facilities, resources, and instructional programs.

School library media specialists assume a leadership role in promoting the principles of intellectual freedom within the school by providing resources and services that create and sustain an atmosphere of free inquiry. School library media specialists work closely with teachers to integrate instructional activities in classroom units designed to equip students to locate, evaluate, and use a broad range of ideas effectively. Intellectual freedom is fostered by educating students in the use of critical thinking skills to empower them to pursue free inquiry responsibly and independently. Through resources, programming, and educational processes, students and teachers experience the free and robust debate characteristic of a democratic society.

School library media specialists cooperate with other individuals in building collections of resources that meet the needs as well as the developmental and maturity levels of students. These collections provide resources that support the mission of the school district and are consistent with its philosophy, goals, and objectives. Resources in school library media collections are an integral component of the curriculum and represent diverse points of view on both current and historical issues. These resources include materials that support the intellectual growth, personal development, individual interests, and recreational needs of students.

While English is, by history and tradition, the customary language of the United States, the languages in use in any given community may vary. Schools serving communities in which other languages are used make efforts to accommodate the needs of students for whom English is a second language. To support these efforts, and to ensure equitable access to resources and services, the school library media program provides resources that reflect the linguistic pluralism of the community.

(continued)

Figure 9.4
(*Continued*)

Members of the school community involved in the collection development process employ educational criteria to select resources unfettered by their personal, political, social, or religious views. Students and educators served by the school library media program have access to resources and services free of constraints resulting from personal, partisan, or doctrinal disapproval. School library media specialists resist efforts by individuals or groups to define what is appropriate for all students or teachers to read, view, hear, or access via electronic means.

Major barriers between students and resources include but are not limited to imposing age, grade-level, or reading-level restrictions on the use of resources; limiting the use of interlibrary loan and access to electronic information; charging fees for information in specific formats; requiring permission from parents or teachers; establishing restricted shelves or closed collections; and labeling. Policies, procedures, and rules related to the use of resources and services support free and open access to information.

It is the responsibility of the governing board to adopt policies that guarantee students access to a broad range of ideas. These include policies on collection development and procedures for the review of resources about which concerns have been raised. Such policies, developed by persons in the school community, provide for a timely and fair hearing and assure that procedures are applied equitably to all expressions of concern. It is the responsibility of school library media specialists to implement district policies and procedures in the school to ensure equitable access to resources and services for all students.

Adopted July 2, 1986, by the ALA Council; amended January 10, 1990; July 12, 2000; January 19, 2005; July 2, 2008. Reprinted with permission from the American Library Association. Available at http://www.ala.org/advocacy/intfreedom/librarybill/interpretations/accessresources (accessed Aug. 30, 2012).

Step Two: Have a Selection Policy in Place

Policy should include:

1. Objectives of library service
2. Selection procedures
   a. Person responsible for selection
   b. Sources of recommendations for materials
3. Requests for reconsideration procedure

Step Three: Be Prepared to Deal with Challenges

The first responsibility in reacting to any challenge to library materials is for the librarian to handle these complaints respectfully and fairly. Most complaints come from concerned local residents who care about the welfare of children, their own and others. The librarian's job is to explain the library's philosophy and procedures.

As normal operating procedure, each library should maintain:

- a materials selection policy
- a library service policy
- a clearly defined method for handling complaints
- inservice training
- lines of communication with civic, religious, educational, and political bodies of the community
- a vigorous public information program on behalf of intellectual freedom
- familiarity with any local municipal and state legislation pertaining to intellectual freedom

Following these practices provides a base from which to operate when concerns are expressed. When a complaint is made, the librarian should listen calmly and courteously. Good communication skills can help the librarian explain the need for diversity in library collections and the use of library resources.

If, after discussion, the person is not satisfied, advise the complainant of the library procedures for handling statements of concern and provide a form for requesting a reconsideration of the materials. Figure 9.5 shows an example of the type of form used.

Figure 9.5
Sample Request for Reconsideration of Library Resources

[This is where you identify who in your own structure has authorized use of this form—Director, Board of Trustees, Board of Education, etc.—and to whom to return the form.]

Example: The school board of Mainstream County, U.S.A., has delegated the responsibility for selection and evaluation of library/educational resources to the school library media specialist/curriculum committee, and has established reconsideration procedures to address concerns about those resources. Completion of this form is the first step in those procedures. If you wish to request reconsideration of school or library resources, please return the completed form to the Coordinator of Library Media Resources, Mainstream School Dist., 1 Mainstream Plaza, Anytown, U.S.A.

Name _____

Date _____

Address _____

City _____

State _____

Zip _____

Phone _____

(*continued*)

Figure 9.5
(*Continued*)

1. Do you represent self? _____ Organization? _____

   Resource on which you are commenting:

   _____ Book   _____ Textbook   _____ Video   _____ Display

   _____ Magazine   _____ Library Program   _____ Audio Recording

   _____ Newspaper   _____ Electronic information/network (please specify)

   _____ Other _____

   Title _____

   Author/Producer _____

2. What brought this resource to your attention?
3. Have you examined the entire resource?
4. What concerns you about the resource? (use other side or additional pages if necessary)
5. Are there resource(s) you suggest to provide additional information and/or other viewpoints on this topic?

Revised by the American Library Association Intellectual Freedom Committee June 27, 1995.

Reprinted with permission from the American Library Association. Available at http://www.ala.org/advocacy/banned/challengeslibrarymaterials/copingwithchallenges/samplereconsideration (accessed Sept. 5, 2012).

This form is also available at http://www.ala.org/advocacy/banned/challengeslibrarymaterials/copingwithchallenges/samplereconsideration (accessed Aug. 30, 2012).

If the individual submits a written complaint, make sure a written reply is sent promptly. Inform the administrator (school principal or public library chief librarian) and/or the governing authority (usually the library board or school board) of the complaint. Send full, written information about the nature and source of the complaint to the immediate supervisor promptly so appropriate individuals can be briefed without delay.

If the complaint becomes a public issue, the librarian should inform local media and civic organizations of the facts and enlist their support. The person or group making the complaint should not be allowed to dominate community information sources. Contact the ALA's Office for Intellectual Freedom and the state or provincial intellectual freedom committee to inform them of the complaint and to enlist their support and the assistance of other agencies.

CHILDREN'S RIGHT TO PRIVACY IN PUBLIC AND SCHOOL LIBRARIES

In a world where students often post details of their ideas, their likes and dislikes, and the parties they attend on Facebook or other social media and share them with a hundred "friends," it sometimes seems as though privacy is no longer important. If you talk to tweens or teens, however, you usually find that however much they share, there is a core of concerns and questions that they want to keep to themselves. Libraries offer information on many topics that students feel uncomfortable discussing with peers or adults. Sexuality is one of the first subjects people think of as being private, but questions about religion, medical issues, adoption, divorce, and other topics may also be areas students want to keep to themselves. As librarians, we must respect the right of our patrons to access the information and materials that serve their needs, and our professional organizations provide the tools to guide our policies. One of the basic principles of the American Library Association is the protection of the privacy of library patrons. The statement on the importance of individual privacy says clearly:

Privacy is essential to the exercise of free speech, free thought, and free association. In libraries, the right to privacy is the right to open inquiry without having the subject of one's interest examined or scrutinized by others. Confidentiality exists when a library is in possession of personally identifiable information (PII) about users and keeps that information private on their behalf. (ALA, 2003, available at http://www.ala.org/ala/ aboutala/offices/oif/iftoolkits/toolkitsprivacy/libraryprivacy.cfm#youthservices; accessed Aug. 30, 2012)

This policy applies to minors as well as to adults. The ALA explains: "The rights of minors to privacy regarding their choice of library materials should be respected and protected." One of the tasks of a children's librarian in a public or school library is to ensure that library procedures do not infringe on the individual's right to privacy.

The American Association of School Librarians has a comparable position when they affirm that "The library community recognizes that children and youth have the same rights to privacy as adults" (AASL "Position Statement on the Confidentiality of Library Records," available at http://www.ala.org/aasl/ aaslissues/positionstatements/conflibrecds; accessed Aug. 31, 2012). Several federal laws protect the confidentiality of students' educational records, and a variety of state laws deal with educational records and sometimes specifically library records. For a more detailed account of the range of laws on this issue, see Adams (2008, pp. 79–87). State laws about who has the right to access student records and whether library circulation records are included under "educational records" vary widely. Librarians should be familiar with both federal and state laws in setting their policies. Several of the online data management and catalog services used by school librarians to collect circulation records can be searched for records of particular schools, classes, teachers, and students. It is important to examine the privacy policies of these companies to be sure that the systems do not infringe on a student's right to privacy about the materials accessed in the library.

BASIC STEPS FOR PRESERVING THE PRIVACY OF LIBRARY USERS

Step One: Develop a Privacy Policy

Library records should be used only to keep track of library materials and should be preserved only as long as they are needed for that purpose. A privacy policy should state clearly who has the authority to access student records. Any record that links the name of an individual patron to a particular library item should be accessible only to the librarians, not to student assistants, volunteers, or parents. The American Library Association has a number of documents relating to patron privacy, including "Guidelines for Developing a Library Privacy Policy" (http://www.ala.org/ala/aboutala/offices/oif/iftoolkits/toolkitsprivacy/guidelinesfordevelopingalibraryprivacypolicy/guidelinesprivacypolicy.cfm #special; accessed Aug. 30, 2012).

Sample library privacy policies are available at many public and school library websites, and it is useful to look at these before attempting to develop a policy. Some examples of privacy policies include those of the New York Public Library (http://www.nypl.org/help/about-nypl/legal-notices/privacy-policy; accessed Aug. 30, 2012), Berkeley Public Library (www.berkeleypubliclibrary .org/about_the_library/privacy_policy.php; accessed Aug. 30, 2012), Boston Public Library (www.bpl.org/general/policies/privacy.htm; accessed Aug. 30, 2012), and Ontario High School Privacy Policy (http://www.ohslibrary.org/ privacy.htm; accessed Aug. 30, 2012). Privacy policies should include several basic points:

- Statement about minor's right to access information
- List of personal information the library will collect
- Who is allowed access to personal information from a minor
- Length of time circulation records are kept
- Procedures for deleting personal information from online resources

Step Two: Review Your Privacy Practices

The American Library Association recommends that librarians conduct privacy audits periodically to review whether their practices follow the guidelines of their policies. These audits should include questions such as the following:

1. Has the staff (including volunteers) been instructed both verbally and in writing about policies for protecting patron privacy?
2. Are circulation and registration records password protected so that only authorized staff has access to them?
3. Are circulation records destroyed within a specified, limited time after materials are returned? (The reason for not destroying them immediately is to allow time to ensure that the item has not been damaged.)
4. Are registration records deleted within a limited time after the registration has expired?
5. Are computers set so that users can access most information without having to log in?
6. Does signage warn computer users to be sure to sign out of email accounts or other personal accounts when they leave the computer?
7. Are overdue messages sent out to individuals in such a way that the titles of materials are not easily seen?

Step Three: Protecting Children from Social Media Misuse

Social media, which include any computer program that allows users to share information, pictures, or files, are becoming increasingly important in young people's lives and in libraries. Facebook and Twitter are probably the two most popular and most talked about forms of social media, but blogs are also interactive; so are many smaller programs tailored to young users. Other chapters in this book will cover the use of social media by libraries themselves and the use of professional social media by library staff. This section deals with how children can benefit from the use of these tools without losing their privacy or compromising their safety.

Fear about the lack of concern for privacy many youngsters exhibit when using social media dominates much of the coverage of these new tools. Ever since Web 2.0 developed, there have been news stories about how social media have been used for bullying, for harassment by predators, and for the posting of sexual material, often called sexting. It is important for librarians to keep in mind that most use of social media does not involve misbehavior. It can be used by teachers and students to interact with young people in many parts of the world and can help teens develop social skills dealing with their peers. Interactive media has become an important part of our society and seems unlikely to disappear anytime soon. Trying to prevent children and teens from using it will not help them to grow up capable of managing their lives in the world they live in. The important point is to set guidelines for the use of social media in the library and let young people know what kind of behavior is acceptable and what is not. Here are some useful tips for making young people's experiences on social media safe in your library.

1. Prepare guidelines for internet use for your library and post them near the workstations for library computers.
2. Post your library's internet use policy on the library's webpage and also prepare booklets for parents and children about responsible internet use. Suggestions for preparing this and other policies are available at the Office for Intellectual Freedom of the American Library Association.
3. On your homepage, link to internet safety sites such as the Boston Public Schools Cyber Safety Campaign (http://www.bpscybersafety.org/studentresources.html; accessed Aug. 30, 2012) and the Connect Safely site (http://www.connectsafely.org; accessed Aug. 30, 2012).
4. Organize programs for various age groups (children under 10 and their parents; tweens; and teens) to learn how to use the internet and how to interact safely with social media. Speakers from a school, college, business, or community group are often available to speak to library groups on this issue.
5. In all interactions with young people concerning internet use, emphasize the basic rules about how to handle online interactions:

   - Do not post personal information such as last names, address, or phone number.
   - Learn the privacy settings of social media sites such as Facebook and allow only friends to see pictures and comments that you post.
   - Tell an adult immediately if anyone bothers you online or if you see pictures or messages that make you feel uncomfortable.
   - Never agree to meet with anyone you know only online. Tell an adult if anyone asks you to meet them offline.
   - Remember that videos, pictures, and information you post now will be available for many years and may be seen by teachers and other adults, including future employers.

TALKING POINTS FOR EXPLAINING LIBRARY POLICY

The freedom to read and access information and recreational materials is a basic right of all individuals. Library patrons, whether adults or minors, should have free access to a balanced collection of information in a variety of formats. It is the responsibility of the library to collect and make available appropriate materials; it is the responsibility of parents to guide their children's choice of materials and to restrict access to those they deem inappropriate.

A fundamental step for ensuring that children's intellectual freedom rights are not infringed is to have appropriate policies based on the professional documents prepared by library organizations such as the American Library Association. Each library should also have policies on materials selection and on handling any challenges to materials that arise. Every policy document should be approved by the library's governing body.

Children and other patrons also have the right to privacy about the materials they access. Libraries should not keep records of materials consulted and borrowed except for those needed to keep track of registration and circulation. When records are no longer needed, they should be destroyed. Only authorized library staff members should have access to users' personal information.

Librarians should have policies to inform children and their parents about how to safely access online media. They have a responsibility to guide young people in their use of social media.

IF YOU WANT TO KNOW MORE . . .

Adams, Helen R. 2008. *Ensuring Intellectual Freedom and Access to Information in the School Library Media Program*. Westport, CT: Libraries Unlimited.

American Association of School Librarians. "Position Statement on the Confidentiality of Library Records." Available at http://www.ala.org/aasl/aaslissues/position statements/conflibrecds (accessed Aug. 30, 2012).

American Library Association. 2010. *Intellectual Freedom Manual*. 8th ed. Chicago: American Library Association.

Electronic Frontier Foundation. www.eff.org (accessed March 7, 2012).

Minow, Mary. 1997. *Library Law Blog*. http://blog.librarylaw.com/librarylaw/ (accessed Aug. 30, 2012).

Morgan, Candace D. 2010. "Challenges and Issues Today." In *Intellectual Freedom Manual*. 8th ed., 37–46. Chicago: American Library Association.

Scales, Pat R. 2009. *Protecting Intellectual Freedom in Your School Library: Scenarios from the Front Lines*. Chicago: American Library Association.

Section IV

Managing Services: Challenges and Changes

Building collections is only a part of providing services to children. Librarians also forge links between the collections and the children for whom they are intended. Library services are designed to help children learn to read effectively; to seek and find information in print and digital formats; and to enjoy the social and cultural activities that draw them to the school or public library. Library services also inform parents, teachers. and the community about library activities and collections.

CHALLENGES

- Libraries now serve a diverse student base or community. Programs and services need to meet the needs of various ages, ethnicities, learning abilities, and language groups. School libraries need to offer programs that help students succeed and schools meet state standards. Public libraries need to offer engaging and various programs for children of all ages and their families.
- The rapid growth of digital books, apps, and information has convinced some young people and their families that all their needs for recreation and information can be met through online sources and libraries are unnecessary.
- Public library programs may provide excellent service to children who come to the library, but libraries are also being asked to reach out to those who find it difficult to get to the library because of distance, cultural factors, or lack of transportation. School librarians have to find ways to serve teachers and students who don't visit the library regularly. Both these groups may prefer programs that can be accessed online and in non-library settings.
- Community members may not be aware that libraries now offer more than just collections of print materials.

CHANGES

Chapters in this section will help you to develop services and programs that appeal to the entire range of children in your school or community. They suggest ideas for making homework help and information services available through home and school computers and mobile devices. Guidelines for increasing the library's visibility in your community will help you design programs that build awareness of what your library has to offer.

10

Programs and Services for Children

Providing a collection of materials for children, whether in a building or online, is only part of the reason for having a library. The librarian serves a vital function as the bridge between the collection and the child. Sometimes this bridging function is provided individually, as in helping a child select a book to read or to find information, and sometimes the bridging is done through a program presented to a group of children. These programs and services serve different goals: some develop reading skills and help children use the library collection; some enrich children's experience in various ways; some market the library and increase its visibility in the community. In all of these, the librarian is the intermediary between the collection and the audience.

READING ENHANCEMENT PROGRAMS

Helping children achieve literacy is one of the most important goals of both public and school library programs. In public libraries, these efforts often take the form of supporting family literacy programs; in school libraries they involve working with reading teachers, especially those in the primary grades. Librarians do not teach reading themselves—that is the job of teachers—but literacy programs help young children learn pre-reading skills and introduce children to books and the conventions of reading. Many children grow up in homes without books, so just being introduced to the physical format of the book is a step toward literacy. Children are often familiar with stories on television or mobile phones, but these stories are told through pictures and sound, so children do not necessarily connect them with books or printed pages.

Reading stories to children has been a traditional activity in public libraries and in school libraries, especially for children in the primary grades. In recent years, storytime programs, as they are usually called, are presented for

Figure 10.1
Types of Library Services for Children

children from infancy through the early grades of school. Often the programs are designed for specific age groups:

- Lapsit programs for infants with caregivers
- Toddler storytimes for children 18 to 36 months old, often with a caregiver present
- Preschool storytimes for children ages 3 to 5 years of age

Because these programs are aimed at developing early literacy, the focus should be on books, but other materials may be used to enrich the program. Recorded music often introduces a program, and group songs are interspersed with the stories. Short videos may be used in between the reading of picture books. Because young children cannot sit still for very long, an activity such as a finger play or game is often used after each picture book read. This gives the children a chance to change their positions and release some energy. The length of each program should be tailored to the age of the child. Lapsit programs generally last only twenty minutes; toddler programs may be approximately half an hour long; programs for preschool children may run up to 45 minutes and sometimes are followed by a craft activity.

Steps in Planning a Storytime

The first step in designing a storytime program is to define the goals and choose the audience. There is a series of questions to be answered:

- Which are the most important target groups in the community—infants, toddlers, preschoolers (3–5), or parent groups?
- Should programs be offered in other languages? Do we have staff or volunteers to support this?
- How much staff time should the library dedicate to planning and giving programs?
- Will the programs be on a registration basis or a drop-in basis?
- How frequently should programs be offered? (Weekly is the most common pattern.)
- What time of day should the programs be offered—morning, after school, early evening, weekends?
- Will each session of programs have an overall theme, or will each be a separate event?
- How will the storytimes be made available to offsite library patrons?

The answers to these questions depend on knowing the community as well as understanding the financial strength of the department. In many communities there are nonlibrary organizations offering story-reading programs, so perhaps some groups do not need programs at the library. Bookstore and community organizations most often offer story programs for preschoolers, children three and older, so perhaps the library should concentrate on the infants and toddlers. Or perhaps non-English-speaking families are not being served by other groups. When resources are limited, it is important to use them to serve those who will benefit most. In some communities the most effective way to present stories to children is to hold programs for groups in preschool facilities or after school programs. (See chapter 11 for additional suggestions.)

Once you have established the target groups for your story programs, decisions about the timing and methods of registration can be made. Programming for preschoolers is often provided during morning hours, but this may not be convenient for many families. In some communities most young children are in some kind of group care or are at home with caregivers who do not have access to a car. This may make it impossible for them to visit the library during the morning. Alternative times such as early evening after parents have returned from work or Saturday morning may make library visits more convenient. Registration for a series of storytime programs makes it possible to carry themes over several weeks and provides a richer experience for many young children, but this may not be possible in communities where parents are not accustomed to planning schedules in advance. Drop-in storytimes meet the needs of parents whose uncertain schedules do not allow them to commit to specific days and hours.

Most programs for young children are scheduled weekly because most children don't remember clearly experiences separated by longer time periods. It's also easier for parents to remember a weekly schedule such as "every Thursday at 10:30" rather than "the second Thursday of each month at 10:30." Even with reminder notices, many people find it confusing to try to recall schedules that are not simple and clear.

Making Preschool Programs Available to Offsite Children

Traditional preschool programs have been offered in a library setting. This serves the double purpose of introducing the library and its services as well as providing the program. Today's families, however, are often unable to attend in-library programs, and technological advances make it possible to serve their needs, too. Storytimes can be captured on video, which can then be made available through streaming on the library website. If any children are shown in the video, permission must be obtained from a parent or guardian. Many parents are happy to have their child photographed in a library setting. An audio recording of the storytime can also be made for a podcast.

Reading Development Programs for School-Age Children

Many school-age children can benefit from library programs, although fewer are offered for them than for preschoolers. These programs can help children learn reading skills and practice reading and can also introduce important children's authors, various genres of literature, and stories that embody the cultural heritage of various groups.

Many school-age children need help in strengthening their reading skills and in practicing reading. Libraries can be venues for developing reading skills through programs such as providing reading buddies or more formal tutoring. Reading buddies are usually volunteers who come to a library and share listening and reading books to children. Sometimes the child and adult take turns reading a book, or the adult listens while the child reads, depending on the child's level of reading skill. Often an individual adult is paired with the same child for a series of meetings over six to eight weeks. In other libraries, a more informal session of reading buddies can be developed with a new pairing every week or two. School librarians may pair students in upper grades with buddies in the primary grades.

A recent development in reading buddies has been the use of pets, usually dogs, as buddies to listen to a child reading. Many children feel less self-conscious reading to an animal than they do to an adult. The volunteer dogs and their owners have to be vetted, of course, to be sure that the animal is well-trained and has a suitable temperament for this work. An added bonus in offering this kind of program is that besides helping children with their reading, the scheme gives an opportunity for much favorable publicity about the library and lots of photo ops.

Some librarians arrange for more formal tutoring sessions for school-age children. These are generally staffed by trained teachers, on either a voluntary or paid basis. Public librarians can sometimes obtain grant funds to pay for these programs, especially for branches in neighborhoods where many children are reading below grade level. Tutoring sessions can be scheduled during the school year or over the summer to prevent loss of reading skills during the long vacation.

Reading stories aloud offers enrichment possibilities for children who have mastered the basics of reading. School-age children also enjoy sharing the stories they have read or heard with others in a social setting. Reading groups that meet over a period of time to talk about a particular book or author, or perhaps a specific genre, enhance children's enjoyment of reading. Storytimes and experiences with stories should not end just because a child has learned to read.

HELPING CHILDREN FIND INFORMATION

Children often use libraries to find information, either for schoolwork or for their personal interest. In providing information, or reference services, librarians can now draw upon resources in various media both within and outside of the library. The traditional reference books, including print encyclopedias, dictionaries, atlases, and almanacs, are disappearing in many children's collections in both public and school libraries. They have been replaced by online sources that can more easily be updated and are frequently less expensive than their print counterparts.

Information Services in Libraries

Helping children find the information they need has become more complex with the increasing availability of different media. When asked to find information on a subject for a school project, for example, an endangered mammal, a child has several options:

- Go online and query Google or another search engine
- Check the library's website and use one of their linked sources
- Use the library catalog to search for a print source
- Ask a librarian for help

As librarians and teachers know, going first to Google has become the most popular way to search for information. When querying Google, children seldom go beyond the first page of results. This often means linking to Wikipedia, which has become the encyclopedia of choice for many children as well as adults. Teachers and librarians often encourage children to use a variety of sources by arbitrarily restricting the number of electronic sources acceptable. This leads to a number of questions. Should we focus mainly on print sources when we know that children will often need to search for information when they are outside of the library? Is the objective of teaching information literacy to help children learn how to use the library? These are questions that 21st-century librarians will have to answer.

Many public and some school libraries have cut back sharply on the number of print reference sources they buy. Keeping up to date on print encyclopedias is very expensive. More and more information books for children are being published as part of a series of digital books, and these are likely to eventually replace most print information books in library collections. The advantage of having ebooks for information sources is that interactive graphics, videos, and audio clips can be included, making the books more readable and the information more accessible. One effect of having more information available online is that it will be easier for children to move from an ebook to an online source such as a website or search engine page. Helping children navigate between different digital media will be the key to teaching information literacy.

Managing information services in children's departments or school libraries can be made more difficult because the same search is often made by many individuals. When a teacher assigns a topic, or a group of topics, several students are apt to flock to the library to search for the same basic information. Sometimes the first one who comes monopolizes the best print material available, and others are left with very little. This difficulty can be minimized by forging links with teachers and asking them to inform the library of upcoming assignments. It takes time and effort to set up communication channels, but the rewards are great. A key principle is to make the task as easy as possible for the teacher: provide forms online and on paper; accept assignment information by email; encourage telephone contact in the hour before and after school; use instant messaging or chat sessions to interact with teachers. Once the library has been notified about an assignment, try to set aside relevant material, write a list of resources, both in print and online, and post it on the library webpage, and limit the circulation period for important sources.

In a public library, having a clearly identified reference librarian available during the after school hours and on the weekend is helpful. Many children are reluctant to approach a librarian, so providing staff with a large button saying "Looking for information? Ask me" or a similar slogan can help. The important focus is to make it clear that the library wants to help in information searches and that asking library staff is not an imposition but rather a sensible use of time for any patron. Needless to say, whenever a child (or any library user) asks a question, no matter how elementary, the librarian should treat it as a serious inquiry and not suggest that the answer is so obvious the individual should have known it without asking.

Alternative Delivery Programs

Many people, including children, find it difficult to go to the physical library for information services, and they often feel it is unnecessary to do so. Online searching has replaced going to the library as the most frequently used means of finding information. Librarians are aware of the weaknesses of online search engines and the frequency with which they turn up incorrect or insufficient information. It's important for librarians to help patrons find the most useful information for their needs; therefore, it makes sense for them to offer information to offsite patrons.

Telephone reference service has been offered by librarians for decades, although some public and school libraries do not allow children to use this service. A policy like this often leads to a parent calling in a question for the child, making it hard to know whether the prohibition is worthwhile. In a time when the majority of middle school students have cell phones, it is only natural that they want to use the phone to get reference service. The logistics of handling telephone reference can be difficult, because patrons who are in the library often resent having staff tied up on phone messages. Unless a library can assign specific staff members for telephone duty, the hours for telephone reference may need to be limited. Public or school libraries can offer district-wide telephone reference service if they have the facilities and staff to handle the volume of calls.

Texting, instant messaging (IM), or online chatting are text-based formats for offering reference service in real time. Because texting is so popular with young people, this format is a natural for librarians to adopt. Implementing this kind of service usually requires setting certain hours when a librarian will be available to interact with patrons. Using text-based messaging gives the librarian an opportunity to clarify the question and assist a child in deciding what specific information is needed. Often there will be gaps in the response, however, as the librarian goes to the shelves to check print resources in the library.

Email reference service is offered by most public libraries, although children's departments have lagged behind adult services. Questions can be emailed to the library at any time, but they are often answered only during the library's slow periods. Some departments set up specific hours for responding to these questions. The problem with receiving email queries from children is the difficulty of clarifying queries. Many reference interviews with children take a long time because children have little experience in formulating questions. It is difficult to refine a question sent by email because of the gap in time between sending and answering the question. Unless an email question is for a specific fact, for example, "Who is the Chief Justice of the United States?" it may be difficult for the librarian to respond. Nonetheless, the service is popular and helps many families who could not easily visit the library.

Librarians need to assess what technologies are widely used in the school or community, how many children have access to these technologies, and what it will cost the library to provide each e-service. Not all children will feel comfortable with electronics or have the skills or access to use them, so traditional services should also be available. The library will probably have to consider offering a variety of e-services as the market produces more and different technologies.

Homework Help

Helping children cope with their homework assignments is an important part of library service. Many of the reference questions asked in school libraries and public library children's departments are related to completing homework assignments. Besides giving individual help with questions, many librarians have set up special homework help programs.

- Specific homework help sessions can be offered in the library during after school or weekend hours. This requires assigning library staff or volunteers to be available to guide students during this time. Sometimes a room can be set aside for the homework help so that a group of children can be served at once and conversation can take place without bothering other patrons.
- Offsite homework help sessions by telephone or online chatting can be offered following the same principles as the in-house sessions. In some cities teachers have volunteered to act as guides during these sessions; in others the library has received a grant to pay for hiring helpers.

ENRICHMENT PROGRAMS FOR CHILDREN

Reading clubs are popular in many public libraries, and some school librarians also organize them for groups of children. Joining a reading club requires some commitment on the part of the child (and often the parent), so most members are drawn from families who already use the library. Clubs can be formed for specific pairings—for example, mother-daughter or father-son reading groups—or they can be built around a specific type of reading such as graphic novels, adventure, or mystery stories. Many reading groups are gender-specific with a woman leading an all-girl group and a man moderating an all-boy group.

The optimal size for a reading group is generally not more than ten or twelve individuals, and many clubs are smaller than that. Most traditional reading clubs meet in the library once or twice a month, but an increasing number interact through blog postings or social media.

The purpose of a reading group, besides being enjoyable, is to develop reading skills and to help children to discuss issues and ideas that do not often come up in everyday conversation. Because the groups are small, the library cannot directly offer this service to a large number of patrons. Adults outside the library, volunteers from community groups, churches, or other organizations, can be encouraged to form their own groups with librarians available to suggest appropriate materials and topics. Some publishers and vendors sponsor online book groups that children can join through their library.

Craft and activity programs are often tied to the library's collection and used to stimulate reading and learning. Programs focused around an activity, such as producing a video or website on community history or local attractions, not only offer fun and companionship but can also be active learning experiences. Programs that focus on holidays, such as Halloween and Thanksgiving, are often popular. Before setting up a craft or activity program, librarians should determine the need in the community. Many organizations offer programs for children, and cooperation is usually better than competition between nonprofit groups. Many craft and activity programs can be run by volunteers, so invite people with special skills to help the library set up programs. Friends of the Library groups are often helpful in finding volunteers.

CHECKLIST FOR PLANNING
CRAFT AND ACTIVITY PROGRAMS

- Investigate other community youth organizations and avoid offering programs that conflict in time or content with what is being offered elsewhere.
- Allow school-age children to give input into the type of programs they want.
- Encourage participation by nonprofessional staff in implementing programs.
- Publicize ongoing programs outside as well as inside the library.
- Use the library website, blogs, and social media as means of publicizing programs.
- Use activity programs to encourage additional reading and to get feedback from patrons.

PROGRAMS TO INCREASE LIBRARY VISIBILITY

While basic library programs and services are designed to further the library's goal of serving patrons, it is also beneficial to have special events and programs designed especially to publicize the library and its collections and services. These events often include:

- the opening of a new branch or department
- a visit by an author, illustrator, or performer
- the opening of a special collection
- the inauguration of a new service
- a special library assembly program

Any event not foreseen in the normal program planning of a library department is to some extent a special event. To take advantage of the public relations value of events, librarians must plan carefully. Well-organized events run smoothly and appear effortless, but they are usually the result of careful planning on someone's part. Special events generate excitement among patrons and staff; but because they take considerable time and planning, as well as costing money, no library department can expect to handle a great many of them. A realistic goal would be for a department to have two events each year.

Preparing for an Event

The first question to ask is, "What do we want to gain from this event?" It is usually foolish to invest time and money with only the vague hope that the public will notice and appreciate the event. While thinking about the objectives for an event, librarians should also devise evaluation measures to see whether the objectives are achieved. Some possible reasons for special events include:

- obtaining favorable publicity
- attracting a large audience
- bringing nonusers into the library
- presenting a quality experience for committed library users
- serving a particular target audience, ethnic group, or age category
- offering civic information or voter education

Each of these objectives requires a different approach.

Attracting a Large Audience

If the objective of an event is to attract as large an audience as possible including people who do not currently use the library, librarians should try to find community partners who will help in providing publicity. This can be done by

- Finding partners to cosponsor an event—local civic groups, parent-teacher associations, ethnic and religious groups can publicize the event through their membership and encourage participation
- Enlisting the aid of prominent media figures—a local television personality or sports figure will attract community members simply by attending an event
- Working with community leaders—members of the city council, executives of local businesses, and prominent supporters of local charities have wide networks of friends and colleagues who will be influenced by their support of an event
- Finding a large local business or national corporation with a local branch to sponsor the event in exchange for advertising privileges
- Using as many channels of publicity as possible—flyers and posters in the library, news releases for newspapers, television and radio stations, notices on the library websites, messages on and mailing lists, news items posted on social media, ads in buses—each channel will reach a different audience.
- Providing publicity in appropriate languages for the community

Planning an Author Visit

Some events, such as the visit of a children's author or illustrator, aim to provide a more intensive but smaller program. If the author writes difficult books for older children, you don't want to send out invitations to preschools. Preschool children might be disruptive, whereas children who have read the author's books would be able to have an exciting, reasonably intimate inter-action with the author. The steps to providing a rich experience include

- Identify the appropriate audience. Talk to the author or illustrator in person or on the phone to find out what kind of program will be offered and decide on age limits
- Contact teachers in public and private schools and invite their students to attend
- If you have a local bookstore, be sure to send them information about the visit
- Invite youth groups from community centers or churches
- Post notices on the library website and link to school websites

The first step in arranging a visit from an author or illustrator or other nota-ble person is to brainstorm about the choices. Staff members and the children themselves can be asked which author or illustrator they would most like to have visit the library. Choosing a visitor whose books are popular with your clientele ensures a large audience, but widely popular authors are difficult to schedule and are often expensive. Sometimes an interactive video session or a Skype call can be set up rather than an in-person visit. Ask your tech staff about this possibility.

Authors and illustrators who live in the community or close by are easier to attract than national figures, and the costs are usually lower. People with ties to the community may be interested in returning. Other attractions are a regional interest or a relationship to an ethnic group within the community. Try to think of why the visitor would want to come to your community as well as why you want to have him or her come.

If after considering the possibilities you and your staff decide you want a nationally known figure, try to find other groups in the community to cospon-sor a visit. This not only limits the cost that each participating group incurs, but also gives the visitor a wider audience and greater potential sales. You can contact schools, universities, bookstores, community or religious groups, and museums as potential partners. You may also be able to write a grant proposal to finance an appearance by an author or illustrator if the event is a workshop that offers an educational opportunity for children.

After you have drawn up a pool of potential candidates, try to find out whether they are dynamic speakers. Colleagues may have heard some of them speak at conferences. Visit the author or illustrator's website to get an idea about their style and what they offer on school and library visits.

CHECKLIST FOR AUTHOR AND ILLUSTRATOR VISITS

- Does the library have the individual's books? Do they circulate frequently? Be sure to buy copies and publicize them.

- Where does the speaker live? Long distances and inaccessible locations make transportation more expensive.
- Has the speaker appeared at other local institutions recently? Has he/she appeared on television?
- Is there a new book coming out that the publisher would like to publicize?
- Has the speaker won an award recently?
- Are there any connections between your chosen author/illustrator and a specific community ethnic or interest group?

Armed with this information, a department head can approach the chief librarian for permission to implement the visit and provide funding. Authors and illustrators can be contacted through their publisher. A preliminary letter should lead to a telephone call in which the proposed dates, the type of presentation the library would like, the honoraria, and expenses can be discussed. It is important to be realistic and honest with the speaker and the publisher about the amount of publicity to be given to the event, the size of the anticipated audience, and the number of the author or illustrator's books that are likely to be sold. Some authors have regular fees for school and library visits; others are negotiable. Their publisher can often tell you what is expected.

CHECKLIST FOR A BUDGET

- Preparatory costs include publicity, printing, fees for extra staff, if any.
- Direct costs include speaker's fee, transportation, hotel, meals.
- Event costs include refreshments, extra security and janitorial services, technology costs.
- Staff costs include the time spent in preparation and follow-up for the event, arranging for volunteers, interacting with the speaker. These costs are often greater than expected but should be planned in advance.

Special events of any type require careful planning and marketing (see chapter 12). They should also be carefully evaluated after they occur. If done right they build support for the library within the community. After each event the department head should prepare a written report even if this is not required. Reports are useful for planning future events and in documenting activities for annual reports or grant applications. Reports usually describe the event and how it was planned, estimate the time commitment required, describe any problems that arose, and suggest ways of improving future events.

Other Programs to Increase Library Visibility

Visits from children's authors and illustrators are not the only events that increase the library's impact on the community, although they are perhaps the most common. Parent education programs also attract many community members. Programs for expectant parents and the parents of young children can bring in speakers and films on a variety of relevant topics. Library staff can tie the speaker's remarks more closely to the library program by providing a list of available resources for parents to take away from the meeting. A staff member might also give a short talk on books and other materials available at the library that complement the speaker's remarks.

IF YOU WANT TO KNOW MORE . . .

Brown, Anita. 2004. "Reference Services for Children: Information Needs and Wants in the Public Library." *Australian Library Journal* 53 (3): 261–274.

Coleman, Tina, and Peggy Llanes. 2009. *The Hipster Librarian's Guide to Teen Crafts*. Chicago: American Library Association.

Dresang, Eliza. 2005. "The Information-Seeking Behavior of Youth in the Digital Environment." *Library Trends* 54 (2): 178–196.

East, Kathy. 1995. *Inviting Children's Authors and Illustrators: A How-to-Do-It Manual for School and Public Librarians*. New York: Neal-Schuman.

Eisenberg, Michael B., Carrie A. Lowe, and Kathleen L. Spitzer. 2004. *Information Literacy: Essential Skills for the Information Age*. 2nd ed. Westport, CT: Libraries Unlimited.

Ghoting, Saroj Nadkami, and Pamela Martin-Diaz. 2011. *Early Literacy Storytimes @ your library®: Partnering with Caregivers for Success*. Chicago: American Library Association.

Intner, Carol F. 2011. *Homework Help from the Library: In Person and Online*. Chicago: American Library Association.

Silverstein, J. 2005. "Just Curious: Children's Use of Digital Reference for Unimposed Queries, and Its Importance in Informal Education." *Library Trends* 54 (2): 228–244.

Thomas, Nancy Pickering, Sherry R. Crow, and Lori Franklin. 2011. *Information Literacy and Information Skills Instruction*. Santa Barbara, CA: Libraries Unlimited.

11

Outreach and Cooperative Programs

> In 1888 Melvil Dewey, a founder of modern librarianship, said that the school is the "chisel" and the public library the "marble" and without both there can be no "statues." (Bostwick, 1914, p. 73)

The two major community institutions designed to help children learn and succeed should be the school and the public library. Often the public library has resources and staff that can supplement the resources the school has, and schools offer access to children that the library does not always have. By working together school and public librarians can help children be better students, readers, and independent learners. Cooperation and partnerships also serve the mission of both the school and the public library.

SCHOOL AND PUBLIC LIBRARY COOPERATION

In most communities the school library and the public library serve the same people. Students, teachers, and parents who live close to the school are, at least some of the time, public library users. Both libraries "promote reading and literacy and often benefit from a state or regional consortium for electronic databases. Given these commonalities, it is foolish not to work together to achieve similar purposes" (Toor and Weisburg, 2011, p. 71).

The benefits of public librarians cooperating with schools are:

- Reaching children who live a long way from the library or have no way to get to the library facility.
- Helping teachers and other school workers to use library services and resources that in turn help them work with children more effectively.
- Recruiting more users and stimulating more use of the library.

- Helping the school achieve success in meeting its goals.
- Accessing teacher and school librarian knowledge of students and the curriculum.

The benefits of school librarians cooperating with the public library:

- Access to more print and electronic resources.
- Promoting reading and learning during nonschool hours.
- Added reading enrichment programs.
- Helping the public library achieve success in meeting its goals.
- Access to public librarian and state library expertise.

The biggest liability for cooperation between schools and the public library is that it takes time, energy, and resources that may be needed to provide services to individuals. In addition, some people in the community may see service to the school as unnecessarily duplicating services. School librarians, teachers, and youth workers may have some conflicts about how to use time within the school day or program.

The essential elements of successful outreach are:

- Personal contact with teachers, administrators, school librarians, and public librarians. Face-to-face contact helps outsiders focus on the benefits of each type of library. Contact also helps library staff know what happens at school, the pressures and issues faced by teachers and workers, and builds empathy for the work done by others working with children at the public library.
- A careful plan for the services offered. These should relate directly to the goals of the school as well as to the goals of the library.
- Patience and persistence in developing a relationship between schools and the public library. Teachers and others may not "drop everything" at the first opportunity and begin using the library's services. Public librarians may not be available at a time when the school asks for help.
- A flexible work schedule that allows librarians to visit schools and flexibility of teachers to be available at times convenient to public librarians and, in general, an openness to make cooperation work.

Public libraries often grew out of the need for schools to provide materials that support student learning. Many public libraries were, indeed, part of a school system in the early part of the 20th century, so the practice of serving students and teachers was one of the first reasons to create libraries. While most public libraries are now separate from the local school district, this symbiotic relationship still exists. To best educate students, schools and libraries need to work together. In most communities there is more than one school, and some school districts are served by more than one public library. While there is a lot of uniformity in what schools and public libraries do, not all schools or libraries are alike in mission, staffing, hours, or budget. These differences need to be explored and taken into account when planning for cooperative services.

This work can include sharing materials both print and electronic, staff communication, planning, librarian visits to schools and class visits to the public library, and sharing facilities as well as joint programs like writing, art, and student performance projects. Most libraries offer services to students, teachers, school librarians, and school administrators who work in public, private, and charter schools located in the library's service area. While public schools outnumber private schools in most communities, librarians should make a special effort to communicate with private schools. Some independent, parochial, and charter schools have fewer resources than the public schools and will be especially receptive to overtures from the public library.

Resource Sharing

Public librarians should become familiar with the general curriculum of each of the schools in the community. School librarians should actively share school and curricular information with public librarians. Although the public library does not usually build its collection around curricular needs, subjects covered in the school will undoubtedly be reflected in requests for materials. Information about the public school curricula is usually available online from local or state boards of education. Librarians should be alert to major shifts in topics covered or the introduction of new subjects. If the schools in a community begin instruction in a new language, for example, the public library will want to strengthen its collection in this language. Similarly, a new health education curriculum stressing the role of nutrition in childhood obesity will lead to heavy demand for this type of material in the public library. Information about extracurricular school activities—theatrical productions, sports, extended trips—are often reported in local newspapers. Public librarians can capitalize on this information by displaying materials related to, for example, a school trip to Hawaii or a school production of *Aladdin*.

Similarly, the public library should promote the use of fiction, graphic novels, audiobooks, magazines, DVDs, and other materials that schools may not collect, but which support student learning and help to foster a love of reading. School library budgets rarely are adequate to keep collections broad or current. Some agreement about what will be collected by the school and by the public library will help maximize the financial support of each institution. A part of any formal or even informal collection development cooperation should be an agreement about how public library resources will be made available to teachers and students at the school. Libraries can offer courtesy cards to teachers and tailor loan periods to meet their needs, or transport books to and from schools on public library trucks.

Another possibility for resource sharing is sharing database access. Most libraries offer cardholder internet access to databases; offering this service to teachers would be easy. Schools can provide a direct link to the public library's webpage from the school library computer and classroom workstations. The public library might also offer staff and student training on using electronic resources.

Communication

School library personnel can be a first line of communication for public librarians. If there are no school library employees or no school library, communication can start with the principal, a vice principal, or an instructional coordinator who has responsibility for community relations. When dealing with large single or consolidated school districts, the children's librarian should communicate with the district library coordinator or the superintendent's office as well as with the individual schools. By visiting with various levels of school staff and asking who is the person to contact or who has authority to cooperate with the library, the children's librarian can create a reasonable and effective list of contacts. The list will need to be updated at least annually as school staff may be reassigned or leave the school.

Regular meetings with personnel from the schools served by a branch library should help avoid problems associated with heavy school-oriented use and streamline activities that involve the school and the library. The public library can take the initiative in contacting school personnel. A coffee hour or other informal annual meeting may be scheduled at the beginning of the school year or some other convenient time. Or the school librarian can invite the public librarians to meet at school. At this meeting, mutual concerns can be discussed before they become problems. The meeting should focus on finding solutions. Many school librarians have the same problem as public librarians with unexpected assignments, for example. The more that each institution knows about the resources of the other, the more likely it is that appropriate referrals will be made.

Continuing contact maintains strong relations between the school and the public library. Information about relevant new acquisitions or services can supplement the annual meetings. Include the school library person in the electronic mailing list for library press releases and other publicity. An informal email message sent every few weeks provides an excellent format for efficient communication between the public library and the schools.

In addition to the school library staff, librarians will want to keep local teachers informed about the library's collections and services, as well as problems with students. Letting teachers know why the public library cannot provide some materials for school assignments is important, but negative feedback should not be the only type of communication. The library should send information about library services to schools at the beginning of each school year. This information is particularly useful for new teachers but can also remind all teachers about the hours, services, and limitations of the public library. Brief, clear information presented with a touch of humor is most effective. In the mailing, teachers can also be invited to schedule class visits to the library. Also, information about school assignments, science fair projects, and other activities that may affect the public library should be requested. Set up a feedback section on the library website to make it easy for teachers to keep the library informed. If possible, a library staff member should monitor the school library website to find information about changes, projects, and activities at the school that may affect the public library.

Not all teachers will respond to the invitations and requests. Teachers are often overwhelmed with paperwork in addition to their teaching duties, and a request from the public library adds to the burden. Many teachers will be willing to email assignment alerts, requests for materials, or requests for librarian visits, so the children's department may want to assign staff to read and respond quickly to teacher inquiries. Email is usually the quickest and easiest way to communicate efficiently, but librarians should not deluge teachers with more messages than they want. Teachers who realize that the library can make their jobs easier are likely to make their satisfaction known to other teachers. Gradually, the library may build up a solid core of teachers who keep the library informed about activities that require materials beyond the resources of the school libraries. While no public library can hope to have enough materials and staff to supply the needs of all students for all assignments, cooperation with the schools can help both agencies provide the best service possible with their limited resources.

School Programs and Services

In many communities, class visits to the public library are the principal form of interaction between schools and libraries. Sometimes these visits are formalized so all the children in a certain grade visit the library once during the year. In other communities, individual teachers or schools arrange for class visits, which may involve any grade level. Either the public librarian or the schools can make the initial contact. Once a routine is established, the practice may continue without much further input.

The purposes of class visits may include:

- A general introduction to the library
- Library registration
- A lesson in how to use the library
- A demonstration of internet resources
- Introduction of materials for a specific school project
- Encouragement of recreational reading and book talks
- A recreational program of story reading, films, etc.
- Introduction of a summer reading program

The teacher and the librarian should understand and agree on the purpose of a particular visit. If a teacher expects the librarian to teach the Dewey decimal system, while the librarian plans to read the latest Caldecott Medal–winning book, both may be disappointed, and the relationship between the school and the library strained. To avoid this problem, the librarian should always ask the teacher what he or she expects from the visit and inform the teacher about the library's plans. If the library plans to give the children library cards, the librarian should inform the teacher about any necessary documentation. If the teacher wants the children to be introduced to materials on a particular topic, the librarian should try to obtain a copy of the assignment or lesson plan for that topic. This makes it easier to gather and present appropriate material. Librarians should also ask about any special needs. Children with special needs, non-English-speaking children, and those with behavioral problems may require particular care.

Librarians who are organizing a program of school visits to the library will want to consider overall department goals in deciding the objectives of these visits. If schools in the area have adequate school libraries, public library visits will probably not involve library instruction or an introduction to materials for class assignments. In such situations, visits are more likely to focus on the public library as a source of recreational reading, programs, and other services. In rural areas, where most children are bused to school, and even in urban areas, where children's parents do not use the library, many children may be unaware of the public library unless they are introduced to it during school visits. In these situations, the librarian should use the class visit to introduce a range of materials and services that the child and other family members may wish to use. Storytelling, puppet shows, film programs, and crafts are appropriate ways to introduce the library as a pleasant place to visit. The emphasis on recreational activities clearly differentiates the public library from the school library, with its mandate to support the curricular needs of the school.

Time spent preparing for a class visit helps to make it go well. Librarians often ask the teacher to send a class list so name tags can be made for the children. This is particularly useful for kindergarten and primary grade children, who like to feel the librarian is interested in knowing them as individuals. Book lists or bookmarks (personalized with the child's name) make good souvenirs and will remind the children and their parents of the services and materials available. Be sure to include the URL for the library's website and invite parents to "like" the library's Facebook page, so they can keep up with library events. Brochures and newsletters aimed at parents and older siblings make useful handouts because they encourage the use of the library as a family resource. Depending on the season, information about holiday or summer programs should be available as well.

As an alternative to class visits to the library, a public librarian may visit schools. Having one person travel to a school to visit three or four classes is more economical than having dozens of children and several teachers traveling to the library. The disadvantage is that children do not have an opportunity to see the library building and the range of materials available. If children have never been inside the library, it is important for them to have a chance to visit and see it for themselves. In classrooms with appropriate connectivity, the librarian can demonstrate the public library website, which gives children a glimpse of what the library looks like and information about its resources.

Despite their limitations, visits to the schools can publicize library services and introduce programs. Some librarians schedule visits to the schools at the end of the school year to encourage children to register for summer programs at the library. Most teachers enthusiastically support summer reading programs and welcome the opportunity to inform children about the opportunity to continue their reading during the summer. Visits at the beginning of the school year can focus on the public library as a source of recreational reading and information for school projects; visits during the year can be tied to holiday programs, science fairs, or other seasonal activities.

During the class visit, most librarians give a book talk on materials chosen to match the grade level and interests of the group. Use attractive and appealing materials and present them in an enticing way. (For suggestions about book talks and other ways to introduce children to books, check the webpage www .scholastic.com/librarians/ab/booktalks.htm; accessed Sept. 5, 2012.) Children in a classroom are a captive audience and can be difficult unless the librarian quickly establishes a rapport. Primary-grade children are usually receptive to a visitor talking about books and reading, but those in the junior or intermediate grades may require skillful handling. An honest, informal presentation usually makes a better impression than one that strains at humor or relevance. The best approach is to emphasize how the library can help students without gushing or overselling library resources.

Attractive handouts help to make the librarian's visit memorable. If each child receives a personalized packet of materials to take home, the library's public image may be enhanced throughout the community. Sometimes the librarian can leave books as a long-term loan for the classroom. This allows the children to read the materials they are interested in and may increase their desire to visit the public library.

The teacher should not be forgotten during a visit, but should receive a packet of materials about the library and its services and a list of all titles mentioned during the book talk. The librarian should discuss the teacher's perceptions of the library and ask about possible future needs for library services. If any problems have surfaced in regard to unannounced assignments, this can be an unthreatening time to raise the issue. Be sure to ask for an email address, so the teacher can be added to a mailing list to receive library news.

Sharing Space

The most dramatic form of cooperation is sharing space. Many communities have considered having the public library located in a school building so one facility can serve the needs of the school and the public more efficiently. The appeal of this solution lies in reducing library costs, eliminating duplication of services, and getting wider use of library materials and services. Communities that have tried the system have met with varied success.

A school's location can be an asset when it is one of the few public buildings in a rural community or an isolated urban neighborhood, but often schools are not located on main streets with ample parking that would make them attractive for a public library site. Many members of the public do not consider schools to be welcoming institutions, and adult use of the public library often drops when it is housed in a school. School security may make it difficult to open the library to the public.

In spite of these problems, some communities have found school-housed public libraries a desirable alternative to the provision of two separate collections aimed at the same clientele. The pressure on local governments to reduce spending levels has influenced this trend, and this pressure is likely to continue. The role public librarians can play is to document how joint-use facilities have worked elsewhere, to work with schools to clarify the goals of each institution, and to develop clear guidelines for continuing the public library's programs and services if a joint-use facility is developed.

Whatever pattern of cooperation evolves between schools and public libraries, attempts to create closer cooperation will undoubtedly continue. Information technology has made it easier for services to be provided regardless of their physical location. As this technology becomes available to everyone, schools and libraries will have to work together to ensure that every member of the community has access to the widest possible range of information.

For more information on cooperation between the public library and schools go to the ALA website at www.ala.org/aasl/aaslpubsandjournals/slmrb/slmr contents/volume32000/relationships (accessed Sept. 5, 2012). This site includes a database of model programs, a bibliography, and a list of websites about cooperation.

WORKING WITH CHILD-SERVING AGENCIES

Most communities have additional agencies that also serve children. Both school and public librarians may have an opportunity to offer them service. These include out of school programs for grade-school children, YMCAs (YWCA, YMHA, YWHA, etc.), boys and girls clubs, 4-H, and a myriad of programs that have specific audiences or missions like scouts, juvenile correction agencies, homeless shelters, and summer camps. Each child-serving agency offers the opportunity to expand the library's influence and accomplish its mission and to attract new library users by developing services to agencies. Generally, school libraries serve agencies and programs that occur in the school building, while public libraries serve agencies that operate in the community.

These services recognize the organization or agency as deserving of library services because helping youth workers helps the children they serve *and* uses the agency as an effective intermediary to serve children directly.

While homeschooling families normally visit the library or take some classes at school, some libraries offer outreach services to homeschool associations or groups where the librarian might provide stories, parent training, book talks, or technical training and computing services to homeschoolers and their parents that meet away from the library.

Libraries have often served groups and organizations that are not traditionally educational. Scouts and other youth organizations visit the library or meet in the school building. They need help with badges and other projects or simply explore books or websites of interest. Librarians, particularly if they have other affiliations with these programs, may visit meetings, provide leader training, or even develop libraries at scouting headquarters.

To build on this tradition, many public librarians seek out youth-serving agencies and provide them with programs and services. Librarians do this to support youth in the community and to reach a bigger audience. These agencies have even more variety than in education, so finding the organizations and making lasting contact is the first challenge in providing service.

- Many libraries offer services to children in homeless shelters. Multnomah County Library in Oregon opened a small reading room for homeless people and then used donations and withdrawn books to place book collections in 30 homeless shelters in its service area (Osborne, 2004, pp. 12–13).
- The Memphis Public Library serves its immigrant community with a bookmobile and a multilingual staff, including a children's librarian who works with ESL (English as a Second Language) students (Osborne, 2004, pp. 9–10).
- Many libraries provide outreach to after school programs for students ages 6 to 12. These programs may be run by school districts, churches, boys and girls clubs, libraries themselves, or other service organizations. Services include providing library

collections, storytelling, age-appropriate programs at the centers, bus trips to the library, and space for tutoring and homework help.

- Many school libraries are used for special testing by social workers or speech therapists, and librarians take the opportunity to use web searches and other resources to support students, their families, and youth counselors.

Finding an agency with which to work may happen naturally. Agencies may request services of librarians and find out about a program, but a more systematic approach may be useful. Some communities have a youth commission or children's advocate as part of city or county government. These agencies may keep a current list of youth-serving agencies and be willing to share access to it. States may offer similar lists of social service agencies. The local United Way organization should have a list of organizations it funds and the nature of the services offered. Again, listening to children, families, and teachers may help you identify agencies with which to work.

In developing programs, it is important to listen carefully to what each agency is trying to do. One program or service does not fit every agency. Be creative. Be flexible. Try to begin with very focused programs that relate directly to the mission of the organization and expand as possible to include more library-oriented activities. If a local museum or zoo wants the library to provide storytelling for a family day event, start there and then explore other ways the library can do outreach to users of the museum or zoo. Be aware that you may also be able to cooperate to let other organizations present programs at the library. While you might tell stories at the zoo, zoo staff may do animal programs at the library. Or when you provide a list of books about conflict resolution for children to a group of local social workers who counsel children, these social workers may provide library staff training in dealing with troubled children. These outreach partnerships can be very beneficial to both organizations.

PUBLIC LIBRARY OUTREACH

Many public libraries have community outreach as part of their mission. This is unique among libraries. School, academic, and special libraries almost always serve only those who visit their location and are not expected to work in the larger community. While special, school, and public libraries may provide online resources available to those outside the building, they don't usually physically go outside the building to serve the community. For the public library outreach is a powerful tool to help children's librarians to reach new or infrequent users and to meet the library's mission of helping children learn and grow. Having a good sense of what will make outreach activities successful, what fits the library's mission, and how to schedule and support outreach activities is essential to providing ongoing, valuable programs. Set goals; ask for honest evaluation from outreach partners; and be open to finding new, better, and easier ways to provide service outside the library building.

Successful outreach programs should:

- Help each participant meet their service mission. Visiting a homeless shelter helps reach the underserved in the community. Operating a homeless shelter is not the mission of most public libraries.

- Have a staff member from each participant assigned to coordinate the program. Each staff person has the time and support to work on the program.
- Be clear about what resources each participant will provide (money, space, staff time, publicity, etc.) before the program begins.
- Identify program goals and outcomes at the beginning of the program and evaluate on a regular basis.

The best partnerships are ones that create something that the partners cannot do well by themselves. Often personal connections lead to good partnerships, but children's librarians should always be looking for new agencies with which to work to better serve children and families.

Outreach to Daycare

Preschool storytime has become a staple of public library service to children. Many libraries offer several sessions a week to three- and four-year-olds who are brought by a parent, relative, or caregiver. Kids enjoy the experience; benefit from time with other children; and begin to develop skills, knowledge, and attitudes that will help them become readers. Many libraries also find it useful to offer story programs at daycares, Head Start, nursery schools, and other programs in their community. According to Kids Count 2009, 60 percent of children under age six attend childcare. This means more and more young children are not home during the day and do not necessarily have individual caregivers to take them to the library. To reach the young children who are likely in daycare, the library needs to offer outreach services.

If the library has a goal to introduce books, reading, and the library to young children, librarians may have to take their programs to daycares as well as offering services in the library. Many of the issues and techniques described above relating to outreach to schools hold true for outreach to preschools. Personal contact, willingness to be flexible, and tailoring services to the needs of children and care providers are essential for success.

A few key differences between schools and daycares that children's librarians should realize and acknowledge are:

- Daycares are often independent small businesses with no district management, or unified program. This means each must be contacted individually, and each program may be different from others in the community. School districts may have an early education program, and Head Start and other federal and state programs are often run regionally, but communication and oversight will vary considerably from community to community.
- Daycares and nursery schools are subject to licensing by the state. Most libraries only visit licensed centers as they are likely to have a program and staff who can work with the library to arrange visits. Each state's regulation is different, so children's librarians need to understand the rules of each local community.
- Many children are cared for at home. Most states license homecare providers and keep a list by community of these licensed homes. Children are often cared for by unlicensed babysitters and relatives. Many libraries try to create a mailing list for homecare providers, so they can invite them to library programs.

- Unlike schools, most daycares and preschool programs have no library or only a small collection of books. Some states are beginning to certify early education teachers, but many childcare workers, who may have good practical skills, have limited formal education in child development and program planning.
- Daycares and preschool personnel change often, and independent daycares and homecare providers move or go out of business frequently. Keeping an accurate list of early education contacts is an ongoing task.

Children's librarians need to acknowledge that keeping track of daycares will require constant effort, but there are some ways to get help in locating early education programs.

- Check state lists of licensed daycares and home providers. These can be sorted by zip code. Some states provide this information free online; some charge a small fee.
- Check daycare associations. They may have a newsletter, mailing list, or meetings where library information can be shared.
- Look at online listings of daycare facilities in your community.
- If all else fails, checking the phone book and community website and asking young families and kindergarten teachers who may know where their students were cared for before coming to school are ways to make contacts with early education programs in the library's community.

Outreach services at daycares are similar to those in schools. Many libraries offer loans of books and other library materials as well as visiting daycares with story programs. Some libraries have special materials like puzzles, toys, or picture sets that are particularly useful for young children. Libraries may also make books about young children available to childcare providers. Children's librarians may, in addition to offering programs for children, offer programs for early education staff on how to use the library, how to share books with young children, new books for young children, and other topics of librarian expertise. Librarians may also be able to offer similar programs to preschool parents at daycare meetings, or use daycares to publicize child and parent programs offered at the library.

Though it may be time-consuming and be an additional job, serving daycares furthers the library's mission to reach the whole community and provide library service tailored to the needs of the user. Giving young children a good start on their way to becoming readers and learners is satisfying and essential to their education. One study showed that as many as 40 percent of children entering kindergarten are as much as three years behind in their language development (Fielding, 2006, p. 32). Offering language experiences and training teachers and parents to use books with young children are meeting an important educational need. Reading aloud builds language and sharpens thought even for the youngest children (Fox, 2001, p. 17).

IF YOU WANT TO KNOW MORE . . .

Bostwick, Arthur. 1914. *Library and School: The Relationship between the Library and the Public Schools.* New York: HW Wilson.

Bromann, Jennifer. 2005. *More Booktalking That Works*. New York: Neal-Schuman.

Fielding, Lynn. 2006. "Kindergarten Learning Gap" [April]. *American School Board Journal* 193 (4): 31–35.

Fox, Mem. 2001. *Reading Magic: Why Reading Aloud to Our Children Will Change Their Lives Forever*. New York: Harcourt.

Irving, Jan. 2004. *Stories NeverEnding; a Program Guide for Schools and Libraries*. Englewood, CO: Libraries Unlimited.

Norfolk, Sherry, Jane Stenson, and Diane Williams. 2006. *The Storytelling Classroom: Applications across the Curriculum*. Englewood, CO: Libraries Unlimited.

Osborne, Robin, ed. 2004. *From Outreach to Equity: Innovative Models of Library Policy and Practice*. Chicago: American Library Association.

Pfeil, Angela B. 2005. *Going Places with Youth Outreach: Smart Marketing Strategies*. Chicago: American Library Association.

Toor, Ruth, and Hilda K. Weisburg. 2011. *Being Indispensable: A School Librarian's Guide to Becoming an Invaluable Leader*. Chicago: American Library Association.

12

Marketing and Maintaining a Public Profile

> With a few clicks, you can create a flyer, bookmark, email blast, press release; post it to social media sites; and even send a few letters to invite local stakeholders—all with a cohesive look and feel and your library's branding. (Circle, 2012, p. 31)

Sometimes library services for children and families, particularly new services or programs, are a very well-kept secret. Only children who are already regular visitors to the library know about what goes on there. This kind of secret can leave program attendance low and dim visibility of the library as a vital youth-serving organization in its community. The library may be well known and well regarded as a place for young children because preschool storytime is so popular, but not seen as a place for older children. Or it may be seen as a "book place" by children, because kids are unaware of the availability of online or electronic resources. An effective librarian tries to ensure that all members of the community know about library resources and services through a carefully designed marketing and public relations program.

Marketing generally refers to the overreaching activities that promote the library to the community. Many libraries have a marketing plan that identifies needs of the community, including children and families, and how the library can inform the community about how it meets these needs.

Public relations usually refers to the specific activities librarians undertake to inform the community about specific services and activities.

Branding Your "brand" is defined by what your users and prospects think about you, good or bad. You create or change your brand by using a term, design, symbol, or slogan that identifies the library as distinct from other educational or recreational organizations, or other school services ("Brand," Wikipedia).

Many libraries use public relations to promote specific programs and services, but librarians should also give some thought to an overall, ongoing departmental marketing plan. Having a cohesive marketing plan will keep library staff "focused on key audiences and messages, tactics for engaging them, and available resources" (Hill, 2009, p. 69).

Larger libraries or school districts may have a marketing department or a staff member or part-time consultant to direct marketing and public relations. In this case, the school or children's librarian should work closely with these professionals to craft the children's department or school library's marketing message and to execute public relations activities. Often marketing professionals have a background in promoting activities to adults and will need the help and expertise of children's staff who know about children in general and the school or community's children specifically.

In smaller libraries the library director or other administrative staff may coordinate marketing and public relations, or the library director and the children's librarian will work together to get the library's message out to the community. In schools, the principal may be responsible for marketing to parents, the larger community, or within the school. In some libraries, there is no formal marketing program, and the children's staff can take the lead by informing the public of all that is happening at the library.

Whether working as a group or as the one staff member who markets the library, the school or children's librarian should seek help by attending marketing workshops, working with other government or profit agencies such as the local United Way to learn more about marketing, and developing a basic library message as well as a marketing plan. Some advertising or marketing firms may offer free or low-cost help to the library as a donation. It is helpful to seek outside help from time to time to get a fresh perspective and to augment the knowledge and skills of library staff.

BRANDING

After you have a marketing plan for your library or school it is important to sort out how to apply the marketing plan to the school library or the children's department. The school library and the children's department marketing activities have to be consistent with the institutional plan, but what works for promoting the school in general or the public library to adults in the community may not be particularly attractive to children. By segmenting the market—identifying discrete groups of children, parents, and teachers—school and children's librarians can tailor the institutional message to the people they need to reach.

A way of organizing the specialized marketing is by using branding. You target your audience, preschool families and caregivers, or students with reading problems, for instance, and define your library's story for that audience. Through branding, librarians distill the library story to a sentence or tag line and visually convey the story with a logo, mascots, and other marketing elements (Doucett, 2008, p. 3). Branding provides a way to have a uniform and recognizable "look" and a consistent message to target particular users or services.

For example, the St. Louis Public Library developed a logo and color palette for all its publications. This improved the appearance of materials and helped identify the library in the community. But the logo (the St. Louis Arch and the Mississippi River stylized in teal) was not interesting to children. Through some donated help from a local advertising firm, the children's department developed two mascots, a logo, and brighter colors to use to promote the library for younger users. Theo Thesaurus (big, furry, purple) and his cousin Dina Dictionary (big, fashionable, lime green) appeared on flyers, stationery, and pencils; and the costumed characters marched in parades and attended library events.

DEVELOPING A MARKETING PLAN

The library, library district, or school may have a formal marketing plan or an informal understanding of how it wants to project its image and convey information on specific programs and services to the community; or the children's department or school library may be expected to market itself independently. In either case, the school or children's librarian should have a sense of how all the various promotional activities for the department fit together. Having a written marketing plan for the school library or children's department or a children's section in the library's marketing plan will help coordinate all the individual promotional activities, keep them on target, and make promotional activities more efficient and effective.

An effective marketing program will:

- Identify what effect marketing will have on library users (what you want your users to do or think)
- Describe how your library services benefit your users better than other services available
- Identify your target audiences (preschoolers are different from ten-year-olds and different from their teachers or parents)
- List marketing strategies that will best impact your audiences
- Set priorities as to which niche markets are the most important
- Influence attitudes toward the library as the "best" service for children in town
- Create a marketing budget
- Create a marketing evaluation plan (based on Levinson, Adkins, and Forbes, 2010, pp. 319–321)

Marketing plans describe target markets, identify needs and concerns of users and non-users of libraries, and suggest effective ways to convey library information to each target audience. A marketing plan may also identify a theme and catch phrases to use in talking and writing about the library, effective timing of media messages, and the expected cost of promoting the library as well as the expected results of library promotion. Having the "big picture" plan in place will make individual public relations activities easier to manage and evaluate.

No matter how much or how little promotion the library does for adults, there needs to be a marketing plan that addresses marketing to kids. James McNeal, an expert in business marketing to kids, points out that the kids' market is different from the adult market and has three distinct targets. They are:

- Kids are the primary market. They spend their own money [and time] on their own wants and needs.

- Kids influence the market. They determine much of the spending [and use of time] of parents.
- Kids are a future market. Eventually they will be a potential market of all goods and services. (McNeal, 1999, p. 16)

While McNeal uses business language, it is good to understand that kids influence their own library use; they also bring parents, teachers, and other adults into the library; and they will continue to use and support libraries for a lifetime. Or they can decide not to use the library; they can discourage parents' use of the library; and they may never be library supporters. How kids decide often depends on the library's ability to market itself successfully.

PUBLIC RELATIONS

Once the school library or the children's department has a marketing plan or strategy, specific public relations techniques can be used to communicate library information to the public. The ongoing public relations program includes all of the contacts librarians make with the community both inside and outside the library and through websites, social media networking or print announcements, displays, radio or television spots, and news stories. An effective public relations program provides an honest and persuasive account of what the library offers and its value to the community. Because the children's department is an important and highly visible part of library service, children's librarians should make an effort to publicize the department's services.

The goals, objectives, and role of the department (discussed in chapters 1 and 2) suggest ideas for the types of information given to library users and potential users. Many adults have the idea that a children's collection consists of picture books and literary classics and services are limited to story programs for young children, or that it is the detention center of the school. Sometimes this image is perpetuated by newspaper or television stories that feature traditional library programs but do not mention parenting books, homework help, and electronic and print-based reference services. In recent years, the availability of computers in children's departments and school libraries has caught media attention, but they are often presented as an alternative to traditional books, not as an integral part of an overall service program. Children's librarians should encourage the media to present a balanced picture of the department's services.

Just as many adults think of the children's department or school library in limited ways, they often think of children's librarians as women who love books and are more at home with *Peter Rabbit* than with science fair projects and databases. While children's librarians are knowledgeable about picture books and children's classics, they also know a great deal about other subjects. The objective of a public relations program is to ensure that librarians determine the message that will be conveyed to the public by consciously choosing factors to be publicized rather than relying on the media or others to decide what to share with the public.

Librarians also have to overcome the belief that libraries are boring and the "Marian the Librarian" image. This special marketing concern has been described this way:

The library, tradition says, must be perceived as a center for serious thought and contemplation. . . . The librarians and staff who work in the libraries must be perceived as serious scholars. . . . Herein lies the problem for a marketing person: how to bring customers into an environment that often chooses to present itself as a place where even life insurance salesmen would look like party animals (McGinn, 2006).

The task is to respect our serious side, portray the breadth and depth of children's services, and make the library attractive and fun for young users.

A variety of ways are available to publicize both the school library and children's department in general as well as specific programs and services. Few libraries have enough time, staff, and finances to use all the techniques available all the time to inform the community about the library. Not all public relations activities are available to all libraries, and not all techniques work equally well in all locations. It is the job of the children's librarian to figure out how to create the best combination of public relations activities that meet the specific needs of the department. Good public relations activities should:

- Attract users to the children's department or school library (attendance or visitation or website hits).
- Promote an accurate, positive, and informed public attitude toward the school library or children's department.
- Be cost effective in its use of funds and staff time.
- Be lively, attention getting, fun, and fresh.

Quality Library Services

A public relations program is often thought to be aimed at people outside of the library, but encounters within the library, the way users are treated by staff and what services are offered, affect the public's perception more than anything else. Every time a librarian helps a child or parent to find a book, explains the way the catalog works, or fails to locate information, he or she is affecting the way the user thinks about the library. No amount of external publicity will make up for the rudeness or neglect of a staff member in the library, an inadequate collection, or unnecessary rules. Publicizing library resources raises expectations, which the library staff must be prepared to meet. Otherwise, publicity will have a negative effect.

Often, a particular challenge to school and children's librarians is to make people aware of what the library does and why using the library is a good thing. For instance, if the school librarian has a list of teachers who never use the school library, a marketing plan might include several things. First, make these teachers aware you exist by offering personal invitations to meet for coffee. Get to know what interests teachers have. Find out a unit that is coming up and pull books and list database resources that are on the topic and deliver this to the teacher. Answer questions and give the teacher time to look over the books and databases. If the teacher responds by asking for more or different information, the school librarian knows the "campaign" has been successful (Toor and Weisburg, 2011, pp. 123–124).

A cheerful, knowledgeable, and willing staff or volunteer is the greatest asset of any school library or children's department. Any publicity efforts to bring more users into the library should be made in cooperation with staff members whose work will be affected by the additional traffic. If new services, such as gaming stations or a homework hotline, are to be established, the librarians should ensure that staff members can efficiently handle these services. Premature publicity about services can give a bad impression about the ability of the library to help patrons.

Meeting the Public

The library staff is the public's chief source of information about library activities, and talks to teacher, parent, or community groups about this topic can be effective. Most librarians are not practiced public speakers or entertainers, but almost anyone can learn to give a successful speech about a topic of interest. The keys are planning, enthusiasm, and clarity. Nothing is more discouraging than a rambling talk that attempts to cover the entire field of children's literature or to mention all of the good picture books for children. Since most talks to community groups will be limited to about a half an hour, the librarian should try to make only two or three points, but make them effectively.

PowerPoints and handouts help focus attention during the talk and act later as a reminder to the listeners of a particular book or author. The handout can also include information about library hours and services. Anecdotes about children's reactions to books bring life to a talk and emphasize the importance of books in children's lives. Showing books and having them available for browsing demonstrates their attractiveness. Lists of materials developed for a specific program can be mounted on the library website, where they create additional publicity and demonstrate the library's activities.

Presenters should:

- Speak clearly and informally
- Make good eye contact with each member of the audience
- Solicit questions from the audience
- Make three or four main points during a half-hour presentation
- Practice
- Stay after the program for individual questions

In addition to parent or teacher groups, librarians should try to speak to business, civic, or service groups whenever possible. Discussions about the library's efforts to increase literacy or to help persons with disabilities may interest these groups and raise their awareness of the importance of children's services in libraries.

Outreach services as described in chapter 11 also bring goodwill to the library and will attract users. Finding a way to make sure parents know that the library visits their child's preschool or classroom will help encourage family visits to the library. Some librarians ask daycares or schools to inform parents of library visits or give out library stickers when they visit, so parents will know their child heard library stories. Teachers, too, may be encouraged to make more use of the library for their class if the school librarian presents regularly at teachers' meetings or meets individually with each grade level. Always leave the library newsletter, flyers about upcoming programs, information about how to get a library card, and a business card with the teacher to encourage further use of the library's services.

Handouts: Flyers, Posters, Bookmarks, and Brochures

Almost all children's departments and many school libraries find a way to create print handouts about upcoming events, specific services, and general library information. With the advent of computer programs that include graphic design, clip art, and high-resolution printing, creating professional-quality handouts is relatively easy. While not every children's librarian has fine-tuned graphic design skills, handouts should:

- Be accurate: times and dates correct, books and websites listed up to date
- Have attractive, appropriate illustrations
- Not be cluttered
- Include the library's name, address, phone number, web address, and logo (Brand "look")
- Have correct spelling and grammar
- Use color if possible

As well as producing print materials, some thought needs to be given to distribution of these materials. Some libraries have mailing (email or snail mail) lists and send announcements directly to users, teachers, or parents. Many libraries mount print materials on their website and broadcast images on social networks. Most libraries make print materials available at the library or hand them to children who attend programs. Make sure that each handout is timely and needed and that there is a distribution plan before it is produced. Too many handouts at one time can overwhelm users, and not enough can leave users unsure of what events are coming up. Program budgets should include funds for handouts such as flyers, booklists, or posters.

Electronic Media Promotion Services

A website offers a public library the chance to give current information about its location, services, programs, and collections, as well as access to its catalog, community and regional information, and other electronic resources. Because many users of the internet are young, the youth services department should make sure that it has a highly visible presence on the library's website. School libraries should be part of the school's website. Many libraries are on Facebook, Twitter, and YouTube or other social networking sites.

The most basic use of electronic communication to promote the school library or children's department's services is by using the library's own website. The children's department should be listed on the homepage of the library, not two or more mouse clicks away, through a "public services" heading. An attractive graphic next to the spot where children should click will better entice the audience to go to the children's department page than a text-only entry. School library services should also be easy to find and visually attractive. Some types of information included by most children's departments or school libraries on the web are the following:

- Location
- Contact information
- Library events
- Programs, including registration
- Reading lists and reading activities/games
- Homework help and other services
- Links to library catalog, databases, and other sources of information
- How to get a library account and other simple rules

In addition to using the library's website, youth librarians may also post library information on other websites that are aimed at children and families. This might include a community bulletin board run by city government, a recreation website run by the park district, or the websites of other profit groups like the local scouting councils, the Y, or a daycare site. Using these sites will get the word out to new audiences about specific programs as well as raise the profile of the library's children's programs to the community in general.

Some libraries have set up email lists for individual children or families. Librarians ask users if they would like to receive announcements sent directly to them at their email address, then the library can send or broadcast messages about programs and new books, or highlight services without the cost of mailing. Some libraries offer the library's newsletter by email. Teachers may also be willing to receive library announcements through their email. Care should be taken not to overuse this form of communication. No user wants library spam, and users should be able to "unsubscribe" from the list easily.

Some libraries have also used the internet to communicate information about the library by participating in blogs, chat rooms, or live discussion groups; offering virtual library tours to school groups; or participating in youth-oriented websites. Younger and younger children are socializing online, using online help sites, and shopping online. If there are ways for the library to be a legitimate presence on these popular sites, they can attract young users to more conventional library services, including the library's website. Some librarians or libraries have their own Facebook pages or "friend" other people to promote the use of the library.

Social networks are a useful, if a bit limited, way to communicate with users and non-users. Communications are short and invite comment. In fact, the initial message can easily get lost in the comments, and comments can be negative, inaccurate, or unintelligible; but as more and more people use social networks for the bulk of their communication, it is important for librarians to gain networking skills to promote children's services. Also be aware that though the communications are short and pictures and video shine in the networker environment, it takes time, skill, and concentration to keep the messages fresh and up-to-date. As with websites, the information must change frequently to keep people coming back.

News Releases

Many local newspapers, electronic sites, and television and radio stations depend heavily on information sent to them by community groups and are always looking for interesting local stories. The library should keep a file of contact information for local newspapers (including foreign-language papers), electronic bulletin boards, and radio and television stations, as well as the person at each source who is responsible for library coverage. Follow each news outlet's directions for submitting press releases. Most news outlets want releases sent electronically, or program information entered electronically in a specific format at the reporter's address. Electronically transmitted announcements may also include digital photos, but again, each news agency will have its own rules for technical quality and content of photos.

News releases should be sent for any special event or change of policy in the library. News releases can also:

- Announce new programs or services at the library
- Provide new information about existing programs and services offered
- Announce special events, seasonal programs, or meetings
- Inform the public about positions or policies adopted
- Introduce new library staff to the community
- Describe library successes

News releases should be written clearly and concisely in newspaper style, that is, with the most important information presented in the first paragraph. The short paragraphs that follow give additional information that the newspaper may print or cut depending on the amount of space available. Releases for radio and television must be even more concise than those for newspapers; broadcast news releases should use short, easily understood words.

Often the story will be rewritten for presentation, so the librarian should concentrate on giving facts that will be useful in preparing the story. The name, telephone, email address, and fax number of a contact person should be included with each release.

Devising news connections for library events requires imagination. A successful summer reading program may warrant a story in the local paper if it can be tied in with a national issue, such as literacy. Media personnel may not think of the library as a source for stories, so it is up to the librarians to provide the connections. A community plan to encourage recycling might suggest a story about the library's books and films on environmental issues; a special exhibit at a local art or historical museum might lead to a story about the library's holdings in these areas.

A library event that warrants coverage by a newspaper photographer or a television station offers a department an opportunity to make a strong impact on the community. More people look at pictures in the newspaper than read the stories, and more people get their news from television than from newspapers. Some thought should be given to the impression of the department presented by pictorial coverage. Pictures that show or imply action generally catch the viewer's attention better than static images.

The librarian should provide the photographer with the names of the individuals shown. Names must be spelled correctly. If individual children are to be featured in a picture and their names given to a newspaper, obtain their parents' consent in writing. Just as with a news release, the photographer should be given the name of a contact person in the event that further information should be needed.

Public Service Announcements

Radio and television stations are required to carry public service announcements (PSAs), brief messages about profit organizations. Some websites also carry them. Messages to be broadcast on the radio are the easiest to prepare. They can be read live by the station announcer or prerecorded. Because they are designed to be heard, rather than read, the sentence structure must be simple and the message clear. The pronunciation for difficult words or names should be included.

Check with local radio stations or media outlets to obtain the length of PSA that they require. Usual lengths are 10, 20, 30, or 60 seconds. If the radio station prefers a specific length, the PSA should not exceed that time. Only about 25 words can be said in 10 seconds. If a telephone number is included, each number counts as a word.

A sample 10-second message:
Have any questions?
The Beaverton Public Library can send the answers to your home computer.
Call three-four-two . . . one-four-six-eight for information.

PSAs are sent to radio stations in much the same format as news releases. The library should be clearly identified and a contact person's name included.

Local cable television stations or webcast outlets can be contacted for information about how much access they give to community groups. Some stations will give the use of a studio and perhaps some staff assistance to prepare PSA messages for television use. Professional help can make a library's message more effective than an amateur effort. If the television station cannot provide expertise, volunteers may be found at a community college media program or among the Friends of the Library. Remember that if resources are limited, the time and expense of preparing releases for television might not be worth the effort. More people can be reached by brief PSAs on radio at much less cost in time and money. Radio stations are also effective in reaching non-English speakers, so PSAs in several languages can be very useful.

Media Interviews

Interviews with the media can be an important way to publicize the services of a department. Sometimes a journalist seeks an interview because of a sudden news development: a library user has demanded the removal of a book from the library, someone has been charged with stealing library materials, or there has been a change in internet regulations. Most reporters will try to call the chief librarian or school principal, but occasionally one may contact someone at the department level. It is usually wise to suggest that questions be directed to the chief executive or to the library board as any information given to reporters may be made public. Such referrals are essential if a legal case is being brought against the library.

Even if the issue is less formal—for example, someone has written to the local newspaper complaining about the availability of "immoral, sexually explicit" internet sites in the children's department or at the school library, and the reporter wants a department head or staff member's point of view—follow your library's guidelines for who can speak for the library. Reporters may be friendly and imply that they understand the library's side of the story, but care should be taken in what is said. Casual or joking comments that sound innocuous in conversation may appear foolish or insulting in print. Reporters look for good stories. Drama and conflict are emphasized, and remarks may be quoted out of context, either through error or deliberate distortion. The interview should be handled carefully, and nothing unnecessary should be stated.

If you are busy or distracted when a media contact calls, ask the reporter to call you back in a few minutes. To avoid the risk of giving inaccurate information if questions are asked about dates, facts, or specific holdings, the interviewer should be told that time is needed to check these details. Most reporters try to present the news in a clear and unbiased way, but they do not have library backgrounds and often do not understand the problems of running a public institution or the reasons for many library regulations. Give the background of library practice whenever relevant, rather than dealing solely with the immediate conflict.

Most library interviews are not conducted in the rush of a news story but are planned as general-interest items for newspapers or for radio and television talk shows. If the library maintains contact with the media through news releases and publicity, it may be easy to suggest that an interview about children's books or reading might be of interest to readers and listeners. Sometimes the reporter or talk show host will suggest an interview on a library-related topic. Given time to prepare, a librarian should become familiar with the work of the journalist conducting the interview. What kinds of stories does this individual do? Do they prefer a folksy, neighborly tone or a more formal, professional one? The more that can be discovered about the interviewer's expectations, the more likely the interview will be successful.

In preparing for the interview, librarians should think of one or two points to be made. These points can be worked into the interview and, if repeated several times, will usually be reported in the story. Questions that the interviewer is likely to ask should be considered, and answers prepared for them. Specific facts and statistics can be written down to be given to the interviewer or consulted when questions are raised. A librarian who is not accustomed to being interviewed may stage a mock interview with a friend or colleague to practice responding to questions.

Paid Advertising

Larger libraries or schools may have funds to pay for advertising, or grants may allow smaller libraries to pay for advertising to support use of the library. This could include paying to put program announcements in the local paper or on a popular news website. The advantage is that the library controls the message; that is, the librarian writes the ad, and the information is placed on a page where readers are more likely to see it. For example, a local paper might run a special section on things kids can do in the community during the summer. While the library's summer reading program may be reported as one program among many, placing an ad on the page may highlight the library's program in an effective way.

Libraries may buy ads in magazines, on websites, or in profit newsletters or place ads on local movie theater screens. Often the library's ad can run for a month or more on the screen as the audience settles into their seats. Librarians can also pay to have PSAs played at particular times of day and on particular television or radio stations. Stations are required as part of their licensing regulations to run PSAs, but they often run them at times when they have the fewest listeners. By paying a fee the library can have these messages run at times while commuters are in their cars listening to the radio rather than at 2 AM when there are fewer, and possibly less alert listeners.

Librarians can also place ads on municipal buses and commuter trains. Ads on the inside will be read by passengers, and ads on the outside will be viewed by both passengers and people in the community; these become moving billboards. Libraries may also pay for billboards along highways or major streets. These boards can get the library's messages to people who do not go to the library. They may highlight a new library service or how the school library helps students succeed.

Libraries or schools may also pay for direct mail to the community. This can be a newsletter mailed to each user household, a postcard to teen cardholders asking them to join a specific program, or a letter to teachers telling them how to get a library card. Some librarians buy or share mailing lists from other community institutions like museums or zoos and write letters to people on these lists in an effort to reach nonlibrary users. Most states will sell lists of licensed daycare providers by zip code. The children's department could use this list to contact these providers about preschool services.

Marketing and public relations may seem like an extra burden to the children's or school librarian, adding work to program planning, or it may seem hopeless to have the library's message compete with mainstream advertising; but it is vitally important that children, their parents, and teachers know about library services. It gives every child in the community fair access to all library services and keeps the library in the forefront as a child serving agency. As Angela Pfeil says, "marketing is an essential tool for building successful relationships with the community. Marketing services to children may be the most powerful but underused part of a library's marketing plan" (Pfeil, 2005, p. 2). Used correctly and done regularly, marketing is essential to the success of the children's department. It can be fun and once started should become fully integrated into the work of the children's librarian.

EVALUATING MARKETING AND PUBLIC RELATIONS

The simplest way to evaluate your marketing and public relations program is to see if library use is increased and to count the number of positive mentions the children's department gets in the press and other media as well as the number of hits the library webpage receives and the number of people who "friend" the Facebook page. In the marketing plan you have stated the results you expect. When a particular public relations technique is used, there is an expectation of what will happen. Ask the questions "Did we succeed?" and "How will we measure success?" When you have the answers, you will have an idea of what is working (and what is not). Part of the marketing plan should be stating goals and how progress toward these goals will be measured.

For example, a school librarian may want to increase teacher use of electronic databases. It would be important to know what the baseline use is, how much and what kind of use is desired, and what would induce teachers to change their behavior. If the school librarian publicized three important databases with presentations, demonstrations, flyers, and mails, and teacher use increased, it would be helpful to ask teachers which PR technique induced them to change. Or a librarian may want parents to believe that the library computers are safe for their children to use. In this case, the children's librarian will need to survey parents initially to find out their attitudes, develop marketing to meet parent concerns, and do another survey after the marketing campaign to see if attitudes have changed.

It is important to find systematic ways to evaluate both the overall marketing program and the individual techniques used. Several useful tools, such as Google's Analytics, can help measure online success. As with any library evaluation, planning ahead, gathering relevant information from users, thinking about the results of evaluation, and adapting the next evaluation to improve library use and reputation should be an integrated part of marketing children's services.

IF YOU WANT TO KNOW MORE . . .

"Brand," Wikipedia. http://www.wikipedia.org/wiki/brand (accessed Sept. 5, 2012).

Circle, Alison. 2012. "A New Player in Marketing." *Library Journal* 137 (2): 30–31.

Doucett, Elisabeth. 2008. *Creating Your Library Brand: Communicating Your Relevance and Value to Your Patrons*. Chicago: American Library Association.

Fasick, Adele M. 2011. *From Boardbook to Facebook: Children's Services in an Interactive Age*. Santa Barbara, CA: Libraries Unlimited.

Gould, Mark R., ed. 2009. *The Library PR Handbook: High Impact Communications*. Chicago: American Library Association.

Hill, Chrystie. 2009. *Inside, Outside, and Online*. Chicago: American Library Association.

Holt, Leslie Edmonds, Glen Holt, and Lloyd Stratton. 2006. *Library Success: A Celebration of Library Innovation, Adaption and Problem Solving*. Ipswich, MA: EBSCO Publishing.

Landis, Cliff. 2010. *A Social Networking Primer for Librarians*. New York: Neal-Schuman.

Levinson, Jay Conrad, Frank Adkins, and Chris Forbes. 2010. *Guerrilla Marketing for Nonprofits*. Irvine, CA: Entrepreneur Press.

McGinn, Howard F. 2006. "Getting Started: Case Histories. Carlson Library, Clarion University." In *ALA (American Library Association). Public Information Office, Campaign for American Libraries.* Available at http://www.ala.org/advocacy/advleg/publicawareness/campaign@yourlibrary/prtools/academicresearch/successful academic (accessed Sept. 1, 2012).

McNeal, James U. 1999. *The Kids Market: Myths and Realities.* Ithaca, NY: Paramount Market Publishing.

Pfeil, Angela B. 2005. *Going Places with Youth Outreach: Smart Marketing Strategies.* Chicago: American Library Association.

Toor, Ruth, and Hilda K. Weisburg. 2011. *Being Indispensable: A School Librarian's Guide to Becoming an Invaluable Leader.* Chicago: American Library Association.

Section V

Creating a Productive Work Environment: Challenges and Changes

The key to any library's success is an effective staff attuned to the needs of the community or school and knowledgeable about trends in library collections and services. Recruiting and retaining staff is an important part of any manager's job, whether the staff members are professional librarians, clerical assistants, shelvers, or volunteers. Leading a diverse staff and establishing appropriate communication channels that elevate staff morale help ensure that the library will serve its public well.

CHALLENGES

- Librarians function in bureaucratic organizations that require strict adherence to regulations governing the hiring, retention, and firing of staff.
- Public funding for schools and libraries is often uncertain and may cause abrupt changes in staffing plans.
- Traditional patterns of communication such as face-to-face meetings and paper newsletters may be ineffective as not all staff or volunteers work the same hours, always work in the same room or building, or are attuned to paper communication. Library staff members of different generations may prefer different communication formats.

CHANGES

Chapters in this section offer guidelines for dealing with the responsibility of hiring and retaining staff while meeting institutional and union requirements. We provide suggestions for best practice in human resource management. You will also find tips for being a good leader in a school or public library by maintaining effective communication with staff at all levels and with volunteers.

13

Recruiting and Retaining Staff and Volunteers

Children using library services today may be at home, at school, in the library, on a cell or tablet, or accessing a wireless network in a coffee shop. No matter where they are or how they contact the library, they deserve staff members who understand their needs, have the skill to serve them well, and are enthusiastic about children. Most libraries spend at least half of their budgets on staff salaries because staff is the key element in providing services.

STAFFING PLAN

Even children's departments with few staff or one-person school libraries need a staffing plan in place to get the right people doing the work set out in the library's mission and service plan. For multibuilding school districts and public libraries, the children's library staffing plan will be part of the larger plan of the whole institution. Because hiring (and firing) staff can be governed by labor laws and union contracts, often the school or library's human resources department takes the lead in writing the plan and coordinating staff hiring, training, evaluation, and termination. Department heads, the children's librarian, or the district school library director should take an active role in developing the plan and all other aspects of staff recruitment and retention.

A staffing plan should include expected staffing levels (number of MLS staff, technical assistants, clerks, pages) as well as a statement of how volunteers will and will not be used. For instance, some libraries will not let volunteers work with user records because of privacy concerns or prohibit using volunteers to replace paid staff.

The staffing plan should also include a budget for staff and define salary levels. Schools often have defined salary steps based on staff education and longevity on the job. This is often negotiated at regular intervals with the unions operating in the school district. Public libraries may also have salary negotiations with unions on a regular basis. Schools have annual contracts with employees, but usually public libraries do not. The staffing plan should include all the standard terms of employment in addition to salary information. Many staffing plans include projections of staffing cost over a three- to five-year period. All this basic information makes it more clear how many staff at what levels are available to serve children.

Once the plan defines the basics, the next task is to have up-to-date job descriptions for each level of job. As the name suggests, job descriptions give a brief overview of what work will be done, hours worked, skills and education needed, and the requirements needed to do the job. See the sample in figure 13.1 below.

Figure 13.1
Sample Job Description

Position: Page

Hours per week: 12

Supervisor: Circulation Librarian, Children's Dept. Supervisor

General Description:

Sorting and shelving library materials and performing other tasks as assigned

Duties include:

- Sorting and shelving all children's library materials
- Emptying book drops
- Shelf reading
- Shifting collections as needed
- Closing and cleanup procedures
- Attending meetings and training sessions
- Assisting users to the extent provided by library guidelines

Skills Required:

- Must be able to file library materials alphabetically and numerically
- Must have the physical ability to push and pull loaded book carts
- Must be able to bend, stretch, and kneel
- Must be able to communicate to staff and the public verbally and in writing
- Must be able to work without direct supervision

Other Requirements:

- Must be at least 16 years old
- Must be available for work evenings and weekends as required
- Must be willing to work with others and be cooperative
- Must be willing to do other duties as assigned

(Tunstall, 2010, p. 89)

School librarian job descriptions are often described in terms of standards. This would include such things as

- Possess the ability to teach information literacy
- Have efficient and ethical information-seeking behavior
- Can successfully promote reading and literacy
- Is able to cooperate with teachers
- Has knowledge of learners and learning and is an effective teacher
- Is a good program administrator who can manage the collection, human resources, and planning and assessment (Woolls and Loertscher, 2005, pp. 165–167)

A staffing plan should also include information on the chain of command—that is, who reports to whom, what reports are required about staffing, and guidelines for handling problems with staff. The staffing plan also includes grievance procedures and anti-harassment policies and specifies the training provided to new and continuing employees.

PROCESS OF HIRING

After the library board approves a new position, the department will work with the chief librarian and the library's personnel officer to find the most appropriate person to fill it. In almost all library systems, job openings are posted first within the system and often within the municipality. If there is no suitable candidate within the system, an advertisement is placed in library journals and professional mailing lists, and recruitment may be done at professional conferences or library schools.

Any advertisement for a position must meet government standards for fairness and follow the format approved by the municipality. It should be specific enough to encourage qualified applicants and discourage those without sufficient education or experience. A few words about the community and the library may arouse interest among applicants.

SAMPLE AD FOR CHILDREN'S LIBRARIAN

YOUTH LIBRARIAN. Become part of a winning team in an active library system serving a five-county region in scenic Idaho. Wild River Public Library is seeking an energetic individual who will bring imagination and creativity to all aspects of service including programming, outreach, and collection development. Requirements include an MLS from an accredited library school, a current driver's license, and the willingness to work some evenings and weekends. Starting salary range $32,500–$38,500 plus competitive benefits. Visit www.wildriverpl.org. Send resume to Jane Doe, Wild River Public Library, 200 Grizzly Road, Wild River ID. Emailed resumes can be sent to janedoe@wrpl.org

---

The ads published in recent issues of *American Libraries* or on electronic mailing lists may suggest ideas for wording and details to include.

Interviewing

In large school and public library systems, preliminary screening of job applicants is usually done by the Human Resources Department. In smaller libraries, the chief librarian and the head of the children's department may go over each application. Whatever the procedure, it is important for the person in charge of children's services to be closely involved in selecting new children's librarians and other department or school library staff. Experience with children is the best background for understanding the demands of the job and the suitability of individual candidates. The higher the responsibility, the more important it is to hire individuals with experience with children and library service.

Most libraries like to interview five or six candidates for each open position. If there are many out-of-town candidates, some of the interviewing may be done by telephone, but personal interviews are preferable. Often a library conference offers an opportunity to conduct interviews with several candidates.

In preparing to interview a candidate, a librarian should

- Carefully review the application
- Check references
- Prepare questions to allow the candidate to demonstrate knowledge and skills
- Establish procedures and decide which people will be included in the interview

In some library systems the HR officer conducts a preliminary interview and passes on the most promising candidates to the head of the children's department and finally to the chief librarian. Other libraries prefer a more informal group meeting with three or four librarians present. Whatever the method, the purpose is to find the best individual for a particular position.

The interview should always be held in a private, welcoming atmosphere, either an office or a meeting room. Water should be provided for the candidate and often tea, coffee, or a soft drink is offered. This allows the interviewers to establish a pleasant, friendly tone. A few minutes of small talk can help to ease the way into the more formal interview.

Both the interviewers and the candidate use the interview as an opportunity to learn more about each other and to assess how well they might work together. When interviewing several candidates for a job, it is useful to ask the same questions of each candidate so comparisons can be made. At the same time, each candidate should be allowed to talk freely and to express ideas, so each interview may move in a slightly different direction.

Before deciding on the questions to ask the candidate, interviewers must think about the qualifications needed. The job application supplies information about formal qualifications such as undergraduate and professional degrees and past experience in libraries. The interview should focus on the personal characteristics and attitudes of each applicant. If a new librarian is to work in a small branch library without direct supervision, decision-making skills and initiative are important. If the new librarian will be working with several diverse language and cultural groups, then language skills and cultural sensitivity should be assessed. If a school librarian needs to reorganize the collection, attention should be paid to knowledge of materials and cataloging.

The interviewer will want to open the conversation by briefly describing the job and the objectives of the interview. The candidate has already read a job description, but some talk about it gets the interview started, and there may be questions. Be sure you have a thorough understanding of what the job involves. You don't want to exaggerate the difficulty of the job, but give a fair estimate of the pace and rigor of the work and the amount of support available from other staff. If there have been behavior problems with children in the school, for example, you want to find a candidate who will view that as a challenge rather than an overwhelming problem.

The next step after telling the candidate about the position is to ask questions. Open-ended questions are often best because they give a candidate a chance to reveal how they think and how they would react to the job. Try to avoid questions that can be answered with "yes" or "no." Instead of asking "Have you worked with preschool children before?" you might phrase it "Tell me about your experience working with preschoolers." Also, avoid questions that put words in the candidate's mouth. Don't say, "You have helped to set up a website before, haven't you?" but rather "What experience have you had working with websites?"

Observe the way candidates answer questions and their body language. Both can tell you a great deal about a candidate's attitude and confidence.

Typical questions asked in an interview might include:

- Why do you want to be a children's librarian?
- What part of the job do you look forward to the most?
- What has been your experience with public libraries as a library user?
- What age group of children are you most comfortable with? Or the least comfortable?
- How would you handle a situation in which a parent complained that a book was inappropriate for children and should be removed from the library?

All questions in a job interview must ask for information relevant to the position. Asking personal questions is not acceptable. All questions must conform to the guidelines issued by the Equal Employment Opportunity Commission. Examples of questions that are prohibited include the following:

- How old are you?
- Are you healthy?
- Do you smoke?
- Are you married?
- Do you have children?
- Do you have any plans to become pregnant?
- What are your childcare arrangements?
- What is the occupation of your spouse?
- What kind of discharge did you receive from the military?
- Have you had any major illnesses in the past five years?
- Have you ever been treated for drug addiction or alcoholism?

In general, all non-job-related questions are prohibited, although some specific questions about physical abilities are acceptable.

Keep careful notes during each interview so comparisons between the candidates can be made. The same questions should be asked of each candidate, although follow-up questions may vary. Try to maintain a neutral attitude throughout the interview and do not indicate to the candidate what their chances are. After allowing a few days for consideration, all the people involved in interviewing the candidates should discuss each interview. If the group does not agree on which candidate was the strongest, you may need a second interview. Eventually a decision must be made and the successful candidate offered the job. As soon as the position is accepted, other candidates should be thanked for their applications and told the position has been filled.

Orientation of New Staff

No matter the job, new staff will do better, work more quickly, and be happier in their work if some thought is given to what job orientation is needed. Some schools and libraries have a set first-day routine and offer orientation for all new staff to cover workplace regulations and welcome new workers. Children's department and school library workers will also need an orientation specific to the library. Orientation can take a few hours for clerks or shelvers or several months for new professional librarians.

ORIENTATION GOALS

- Make all employees feel welcome
- Review library or school policies and employee rules
- Meet current staff and understand who reports to whom
- Begin to learn about what the job entails, learn skills, and identify activities for future training

---

Orientation to the physical environment of the library is important because libraries are complex organizations. Every employee needs to know the location of various departments and services, all entrances and exits, staff lounges and facilities, and the location of other branches in the system. A floor plan of the library often helps to orient new employees. Within the department, new employees need to know the location of various sections—the reference, picture book, and program areas—as well as that of computers and photocopiers, meeting rooms, public access washrooms, and public telephones. It is easy for a person who has worked in one building for several years to forget to mention some of these facilities. A checklist can help to avoid this and serves as a reminder of information to be covered during the tour.

Introducing a new employee to people working in the department, as well as relevant people outside the department, is as important as giving the tour of the building. Whoever is conducting the tour should be sure to introduce each person who works in the department and should make notes to ensure that the people who are off duty will be introduced as soon as possible. A welcoming and personal introduction to the department, as opposed to being thrust into a new situation without knowing coworkers, can make a crucial difference in shaping the newcomer's attitude.

In some departments, it is customary to have a coffee hour or staff meeting to introduce new staff. This occasion gives both new and old staff members an opportunity to talk casually and to fix identities firmly in mind. It also gives the department head a chance to explain the new person's role and set the tone for a smooth and pleasant transition.

Social customs such as contributing to a coffee fund, taking turns bringing refreshments, or having an annual staff potluck supper should be explained at this time. Details about who is responsible for making coffee in the morning and where employees are expected to park may not seem important, but they make a difference in establishing friendly working relationships.

The time involved in teaching a new employee the procedures to be mastered varies with the position. A new page may be expected to shelve and check materials in and out with an hour or two of training, while a new librarian will spend many weeks learning different aspects of the job. Whatever the level of training, the department head should make sure it is effective. Simple procedures should be clearly described and demonstrated. The new employee should watch someone perform the task and then practice. Few people can remember oral instructions for long, so a written description of the procedure should be available for future reference.

STAFF RETENTION

Library jobs are complex and demanding, and loss of a staff member causes difficulties throughout the department. All staff at every level need support from supervisors and appropriate training to be successful. A library manager should work hard to make sure all staff members find their jobs challenging and satisfying, so they will be less likely to look for other employment and more likely to provide excellent services. The value of a library to its patrons depends on the quality and dedication of its staff. Library managers should never take staff members for granted but should consider thoughtfully the best ways to help them develop skills and professionalism.

Ongoing Staff Training

Schools, libraries, and communities change, so staff often need training to keep up. This training must be continuous because libraries frequently introduce new practices and modify old ones. Conferences and workshops offer training, especially for professional staff, and an effective administrator encourages staff members to attend such meetings because they not only learn specific skills but also have a chance to discuss new ideas with colleagues. Meeting colleagues from other libraries or other professions often leads to an exchange of ideas, which can broaden the scope of a library's work. Beware of the danger that a staff member will choose to attend workshops in only one area—storytelling or puppetry, for example—and will resist suggestions that a course in website design might be more valuable. Most library departments need staff members who are proficient in a variety of skills, and one of the tasks of the department head is to encourage a broad-based continuing education program.

Large library systems often provide educational opportunities for children's librarians within the system. This program may be directed by a youth services coordinator, or each branch may take a turn planning a workshop. Depending on the budget, these workshops may be directed by outside experts or allow local library staff to exchange ideas. In either case, getting together to share ideas about programming or services generally benefits the staff and should be encouraged on a regular basis. The stimulation of new ideas can enliven a department's services and prevent staff burnout.

No matter how extensive the opportunities for continuing education outside the department, some staff training within the department is necessary. The introduction of new technology frequently requires formal staff training. When a school library is planning a major change, such as installing a new computer system, careful thought should be given to staff training. The usual practice is to have outside experts instruct a small group of library staff members. Those staff members train other staff members and teachers until eventually everyone can handle the new technology. All staff members must have the opportunity not only for instruction but also for sufficient practice to become comfortable with the system. The department head may require all employees to use new equipment because employees who do not practice at least twice a week tend to lose skills. After the skills have been mastered, most staff members will incorporate use of the new technology into their normal work practices.

Introducing even minor changes, starting a staff blog in the children's department, for example, requires carefully planned staff training. Each individual should be given ample time to practice until he or she feels comfortable. Staff members show various degrees of interest in new technology, but few people are actively hostile to it. All staff members who might be called upon to help patrons with computers must become comfortable in dealing with them. When one or two staff members are allowed to become the resident experts and monopolize the computer facilities, service usually suffers.

Not all staff training involves technology. Changing community demographics may call for continuing education sessions about working with different cultural groups, people with disabilities, or the aging. Legislative changes may mandate training in copyright regulations or internet policy. Social conditions may make it necessary to teach staff members better security measures. Some library or school administrators make all decisions about how to deliver staff training; others leave the decision to the discretion of the department head. The department head should always try to remain aware of the issues and be ready to give suggestions or provide training when necessary.

Although testing is rarely an acceptable way to check what the staff has learned, reminders can be effective. Short questions and answers in the staff wiki or social network, especially questions phrased in a humorous way, can remind staff of what they heard at a workshop. Although administrators often initiate ideas for staff training, asking staff members to suggest topics can lead to more active learning. Managers are sometimes unaware of staff members' areas of concern.

Figure 13.2
Elements of Educational Presentation

Introduction	Be sure the staff understands the scope of the topic: what will be included and what is excluded. Sometimes a video, PowerPoint, or other media presentation can introduce a topic and arouse interest.
Motivation	It is important that staff members believe the training is necessary and the topic important. An authoritative outside speaker is often more persuasive than the department head or another staff member.
Explanation	Experts from inside or outside the library can present detailed information. Sometimes a panel of experts can present different facets of the topic. When possible, information should be given in more than one format: print, visual, audio, for example. Interactive sessions with opportunities for questions and discussion engage people more than passive presentations. If the training includes suggested actions, such as the way to react to a hostile intruder, role-playing makes the learning more realistic and memorable than straight presentation.
Reinforcement	Print materials help people remember what they have heard and seen. The library website or a departmental blog is a good way to facilitate ongoing staff discussion and provide reference materials. Most effective training includes several types of reinforcement.

Rewarding Staff Achievement

Financial benefits to library staff are controlled by city or school administrators who make the salary decisions for all employees. Unlike many managers in profit-making organizations, the library manager usually has little control over library salaries. This is particularly true in a unionized library, but generally applies to all school and public libraries.

Managers in public sector organizations should be aware of the ways in which non-monetary rewards can be used to recognize employee achievement. Libraries benefit when employees are happy in their jobs.

In the public library, for example, among the non-monetary rewards that have been used, one of the most popular is flexible scheduling of work. Flex-time allows employees the freedom to plan work schedules that fit their life patterns. Because the library is a public service organization, this freedom is limited by the need to have the library staffed during busy hours of the day and days of the week. Even working within these constraints, however, a manager can often find a way to allow employees some voice in their scheduling. For school librarians, being assigned to a school close to home or with grades of particular interest can be a reward for good work.

Celebrations of achievement through public recognition of a project completed or particularly outstanding service makes employees feel appreciated. Writing a note to an employee who has done an outstanding job is welcome, as is recognition in a meeting or newsletter. The only danger of this kind of recognition is that some employees may decide the manager has a few favorite employees who are valued more highly than others. When a department head recognizes achievement, he or she must be sure all individuals have an equal chance to be honored. Let all staff know about the achievements of individual staff members. We thrive on success, so share recognition of staff when they do well (Hakala-Ausperk, 2011, p. 46).

A manager should recognize the benefits of rewarding staff achievement, but be aware of the danger of playing favorites. A balanced approach should allow each employee's strengths to be recognized and encourage greater job commitment.

HANDLING POTENTIAL CONFLICT SITUATIONS

Managers like to believe that relationships within the department are friendly and supportive; they are often shocked and unprepared when a conflict erupts. Unfortunately, no matter how well managed the department, disagreements between staff members or between a staff member and the department head occur. A department head should never react as though disagreements are a personal attack or a reflection upon individual management styles (even if they are). Instead, the conflict should be treated objectively as a normal part of life within any institutional setting.

Conflict about Work Habits

Most library departments are small enough for all of the employees to fall under the direct supervision of the department head. In a school the library staff may be under the direction of the principal, or a district coordinator, or both. The small size allows direct relationships and frequent opportunities for face-to-face meetings. The department head wants to be friendly and approachable, but this congeniality may occasionally conflict with the need to maintain an efficient workflow.

Because of the small size of work groups, library workers often have greater flexibility than workers in factories or large offices. For example, a new staff member who tells the department head that she has instructed her eight-year-old son to call her every afternoon as soon as he arrives home from school may be encouraged to receive this call. If one day the department head notices three patrons are waiting for the attention of this staff member, who is on her cell phone giving detailed instructions about which play clothes to wear, the supervisor is likely to feel that library service is suffering. What is the most effective form of intervention?

The supervisor may solve the immediate problem by offering to help the patrons, and the call will probably end quickly. More direct discussion is needed. The supervisor should speak to the staff member privately to ensure that the situation does not occur again.

The supervisor must set limits on the calls and see that the limits are adhered to. A warning may be sufficient to remind the employee of other obligations and reduce the number and length of calls. The supervisor must unobtrusively observe whether the librarian is spending an unacceptable amount of time on the telephone. It might be desirable for the child to call another library employee, with whom he will not be tempted to talk for long, to say he has arrived home safely. If the child needs to talk with his mother for a longer time, the employee might be encouraged to schedule her break, or even her lunch hour, when the child returns home. Then, the longer conversations can be conducted in the staff lounge.

Most employees recognize that the library has a right to maintain working efficiency. They accept limitations on their behavior as long as they believe that the entire staff is being treated in the same way. In fact, a manager who does not require appropriate work habits is not likely to be respected as well as one who enforces reasonable and fair regulations. The department head should have close, friendly relationships with staff but owes it to the library to maintain effective library service.

Whether the problem is librarians shopping online instead of helping students, shelvers exchanging text messages while working, or circulation clerks making inappropriate comments about children's book choices, the principles are the same. The supervisor should first ask questions to find out what is going on and whether the incident is a unique occurrence or a habitual pattern. Then the supervisor should interview the employee privately. The supervisor should always treat the employee with respect and try to understand the reasons for the problem behavior. Whatever steps are taken to resolve the issue should be based on changing the behavior, not on punishing the individual. The supervisor should explain why the behavior is a problem and describe appropriate behavior. Finally, it is up to the supervisor to suggest a solution. Usually it is better to suggest a different behavior than prohibit problem activities. A clerk who makes disparaging comments about the books children choose might be advised to give each child a book list and suggest that they might enjoy those books.

A summary of the discussion should be recorded in writing for the staff member's personnel file. After choosing a solution, the supervisor must observe whether the undesirable activities cease. If the behavior occurs again, the supervisor should have another meeting with the staff member and follow up by sending the individual a written description of the agreed solution. The supervisor must keep a complete written record of problem behavior, because it may eventually lead to dismissal. To terminate employment there must be a complete written record of the unsatisfactory performance and of all of the ways in which the supervisor worked with the individual to try to resolve the problem.

Dealing with Grievances

Schools and libraries have standard procedures to be followed when an employee has a complaint concerning a management decision. A department head should be familiar with the steps to take when a formal complaint, or grievance, is filed. School and library unions often take an active role in resolving grievances. Unions clarify work rules, working conditions, and salaries and as such can be helpful in ensuring fair treatment for all employees (McCook, 2011, p. 154).

The supervisor must take every complaint seriously and listen to what the employee says. Employees have the responsibility to bring grievances to the supervisor in a clear and timely fashion. Careful listening is a sign of respect for any employee. Occasionally a supervisor reacts to a complaint as if it were an idle comment. The supervisor's friendship with staff members should not interfere with the role of manager and the responsibility for mediating between the library administration and the staff.

After allowing the staff member to explain the grievance, the supervisor may need to ask other staff members about the facts of the case. Were the vacation schedules drawn up without working out overlapping requests? Did the circulation clerk fail to tell the pages they could go on their breaks? Has one librarian been assigned to work every Saturday for a month? Was a new circulation assistant scolded in front of students and teachers? Supervisors must determine the accuracy of the charges before making any decision. Often, complaints are caused by misunderstandings that disappear when the facts are made clear.

If one employee treats another badly, the department head should try to rectify the situation and make sure it does not happen again. If someone did not receive the required break time, nothing can undo that action, but an apology and perhaps some extra break time will help to make up for the mistake. The supervisor's most important task is to correct the person who made the mistake and firmly impress upon him or her that it should not happen again. This means the supervisor should have a private interview with the individual, explain why the action was inappropriate, and request a change in behavior. A written account of this interview should be placed in the offender's personnel file so it will be available if something similar happens later.

A supervisor should try to find out how similar grievances have been handled in the past. A new supervisor can do this by looking at personnel records or talking with a human resources officer or with the chief librarian. Making a sharp break with tradition is usually unwise. Staff members expect the library's response to be consistent with past practice.

The steps to be taken when an employee makes a complaint, in summary, are:

1. Listen carefully to the employee's explanation of what happened
2. Check the facts with library records and other staff members
3. Find out who was responsible for the offending action
4. Examine how previous grievances of the same type have been handled
5. Speak privately to the employee who made the mistake and state clearly that the incorrect behavior must not happen again
6. Offer an apology to the person who complained
7. File a written record of the incident
8. Check at appropriate times to ensure the offensive behavior does not happen again

---

Preventing grievances is far better than trying to handle them when they arise. A supervisor should be sensitive to the mood of the department, not only among the librarians but also among the clerical staff and pages. Is there bickering, snide comments, or a set of cliques? These often indicate divisions among staff members that may cause problems later. If the library is undergoing changes, a large growth in community population, or substantial building renovations, the added tension fosters an increase in complaints.

When these conditions exist, the department head should make an effort to develop a good spirit in the department. The department head should request additional staff members or budget increases if the workload is growing. If the staff believes the department head is trying to improve working conditions, they are likely to feel happier about their jobs. A manager who is seen to be working fairly and consistently to increase the library's effectiveness and who treats staff members with respect usually has fewer problems with grievances than one who appears remote and uninterested in or unaware of staff problems.

PERFORMANCE APPRAISAL

Evaluating a staff member's work is an important part of being a supervisor, and it is important for the staff being appraised. While formal appraisals may be uncomfortable for both managers and the staff receiving the appraisal, it is a key to good staff management. Supervisors need to give a fair and honest work review and "represent" the school or public library administration. This review is a way to help workers understand and correct problems with their work and get formal praise for their strengths. Workers get a chance to ask questions, lodge complaints, get help, and have a sense of how they are doing on the job. Evaluating another person's work requires objectivity as well as sensitivity to the strengths and weaknesses of each employee. Tact is especially important in evaluating a colleague with whom you work closely on a day-to-day basis.

Preparing to write a performance evaluation starts with keeping a personnel folder (in either paper or electronic format) up-to-date and complete throughout the year. When a patron tells you that so-and-so found just the right materials for her child's homework project, or when you observe a page being particularly helpful to a child searching for a book, add a note to the personnel file. Complaints or failures such as tardiness or mistakes should, of course, also be recorded. This file gives you the basis for an evaluation.

Usually the evaluation process starts with a request to each employee to write a statement about the year's goals, projects, and events. The employee should evaluate his or her own performance and record achievements on the job and in professional activities.

Most libraries have standard forms for performance evaluations.

PERFORMANCE REVIEW

NAME:
POSITION TITLE: DEPARTMENT:
REVIEW COMPLETED BY: DATE:

1. RESPONSIBILITIES

2. AREAS WHERE PERFORMANCE STANDARDS ARE BEING MET

3. AREAS WHERE IMPROVEMENT IS REQUIRED

4. HOW ARE IMPROVEMENTS GOING TO BE MADE?

5. EMPLOYEE'S COMMENTS

Employee's signature _____ Date

Supervisor's signature _____ Date

The responsibilities listed are based on the employee's job description. An employee should not be faulted for not taking on responsibilities beyond those listed in the job description. This is why a well-written job description is so important. On the other hand, if an employee goes beyond the standards required by the job, while at the same time meeting all of the stated requirements, this achievement should be commended.

The most important part of the performance appraisal is the one-to-one interview with each staff member. This may be quite informal, especially for a long-time employee whose appraisals are consistently good, but it should not be omitted. The interview gives an opportunity to step back from daily work and consider what is being done on a yearly basis. This may lead to a discussion of new projects, or changes in routine. The supervisor may learn about new ideas and professional plans of an employee, which do not come up in the ordinary course of work.

For a new employee, or for one whose performance has not met expectations, the interview is crucial. If there is any chance that an employee might be laid off or not achieve tenure, every step of performance appraisal must be fully documented. Documentation of the failure in the form of written complaints, records of tardiness or absence, statistics on programs conducted or books selected in comparison with other employees should be available. After some discussion of possible reasons for the inadequate performance, the supervisor and employee should agree on steps to be taken to improve the rating for the following year. This agreement must be in writing and signed by both parties.

Although confronting staff members about negative performance is a difficult task for most supervisors (and staff), it is an important function of management and must be done throughout the year, not just during the annual performance appraisal. In most schools and libraries, a first or second minor offense such as being late for work or failing to attend a required meeting calls for an oral reprimand. If the offense is repeated, the supervisor should send a memo to the person describing the behavior and stating that the offenses must stop. A written report should also be sent to administration officials. (A serious offense, for example, using abusive language toward a patron or staff member, requires immediate written reprimand with a copy to higher administrators.) If the behavior does not change, the individual should receive a strongly worded reminder laying out the further disciplinary action that will be taken if the offenses continue.

Like other important personnel records, memos concerning unsatisfactory performance should be printed out, dated, and signed by both the supervisor and the employee. Electronic documents may not be acceptable in formal procedures if the individual contests any of the actions taken. Copies should remain permanently in the individual's file. Performance appraisal may not be as pleasant as other aspects of a manager's job, but it is an important part of maintaining a well-run department. A supervisor who is known as a fair and objective evaluator is likely to win the respect of both employees and administrators.

USING VOLUNTEERS

Whether the school uses student help to keep the library running or the children's department at the public library recruits volunteers to tell stories or shelve books, it is important to organize your volunteers so that it is a win-win experience for the volunteers and the library. Whether you have one or two volunteers or your library is large enough to have a volunteer office that manages hundreds of volunteers, it is important to have a plan to recruit, train, and reward volunteers.

As with paid staff, school and public librarians should have a volunteer plan that describes what jobs volunteers can do (and not do!) and sets the rules and policies that will be used to manage volunteers. Unlike staff, who are hired because they have the qualifications for the work, volunteers are accepted because they want to help and are willing to try to do what is needed. The volunteer plan needs to view volunteers as a valuable resource that can be used to improve library service to children. Even in small libraries there should be a volunteer handbook that documents the program.

A Volunteer Program Includes:

- Goals and outcomes—what the library gains by using volunteers
- Goals and outcomes—what benefits volunteers will gain
- Job descriptions
- Applications and record-keeping forms
- Recruitment plan
- Training procedures for staff who supervise volunteers
- Training procedures for volunteers
- Program rules—policies and procedures
- Volunteer recognition program

In large school districts and libraries there will be standard forms and procedures for the staff to use when working with volunteers. At a minimum, anyone volunteering to work with children should have a formal background check, not be left alone with children, and understand the safety and legal requirements of working in the school or public library. The key, however, to volunteers being successful is that they do work they enjoy and have the training to do it effectively, and they feel welcomed and comfortable with library staff. Most libraries have a variety of volunteers from students or their parents to senior citizens to workers whose companies encourage or require work with community nonprofits. "The strength of your volunteer program will lie in your ability to . . . ensure all volunteers receive the necessary support from their supervisors and adequate on-the-job training" (Driggers and Dumas, 2011, p. 11).

The heart of any volunteer program is what jobs volunteers do; librarians should make sure the work is enjoyable and rewarding. You may be desperate for help with shelving or entering data into your circulation system, but asking a volunteer who wants to work directly with children to do this for hours might not be the best way to handle this volunteer job. Break up the clerical routine with helping with a program or reading with individual children. Find out what the individual volunteer wants to do, let them try several jobs or activities, and then agree on where the best "fit" for this volunteer is.

POSSIBLE VOLUNTEER JOBS

- Read to children; listen to children read; help with storytime; lead a book discussion
- Help or supervise children at library computers
- Help with homework; tutor
- Shelve materials; data entry or filing; help with program registration
- Proctor school exams
- Make name tags; prepare craft materials; clean up after programs; move furniture
- Help with non-English-speaking library users

Some libraries recruit volunteers by asking users to help out or placing an "ad" on the library bulletin board. Some libraries recruit from the local United Way or advertise in local papers. Some participate in community volunteer fairs or visit with volunteer coordinators at local high schools and colleges to ask for help. Most communities have lots of willing volunteers, so the task is to let these potential volunteers know about opportunities at the library.

SOURCES OF VOLUNTEERS

- Elementary/middle school students attending your school or from schools in your community
- PTO or other parent groups
- High school or college students who have a community service requirement
- Education majors or social work students who have a preservice requirement to work with children
- Older adults
- Church, civic (Lions, Rotary, etc.), service fraternities
- AmeriCorps; Volunteers for America
- Welfare to work, job training programs, court-ordered community service
- Unemployed individuals
- Library Friends groups and individual adults

Several ways are available to learn more about using volunteers with children. Most United Ways offer short courses on volunteer management; and some city, county, or extension offices help to train volunteer supervisors. Volunteers may help with recruiting volunteers. The Girl Scouts of America have a well-organized website (http://www.girlscouts.org/for_adults/volunteering/; accessed Sept. 1, 2012) that might give librarians some ideas of how to start or improve their volunteer program.

Human resources in the form of staff and volunteers are the heart of any school or public library service to children. Developing the skills and taking the time to manage these resources are essential to doing the best for the children you serve.

IF YOU WANT TO KNOW MORE . . .

Adkins, Denice, and Lisa K. Hussey. 2005. "Unintentional Recruiting for Diversity." *Public Libraries* 44 [July/August]: 229–233.

Crittendon, Robert. 2002. *The New Manager's Starter Kit: Essential Tools for Doing the Job Right*. New York: American Management Association.

Driggers, Preston, and Ellen Dumas. 2011. *Managing Library Volunteers*. 2nd ed. Chicago: American Library Association.

Giesecke, Joan, and Beth McNeil. 2010. *Fundamentals of Library Supervision*. 2nd ed. Chicago: American Library Association.

Hakala-Ausperk, Catherine. 2011. *Be a Great Boss: One Year to Success*. Chicago: American Library Association.

McCook, Kathleen de la Pena. 2011. *Introduction to Public Librarianship*. 2nd ed. New York: Neal-Schuman.

Panszczyk, Linda A. 2004. *HR How-To—Intergenerational Issues: Everything You Need To Know about Dealing with Employees of All Generations in the Workplace . . . HR How-To*. Chicago: CCH Knowledge Point.

Staerkel, Kathleen, Mary Fellows, and Sue McCleaf Nespeca, eds. 1995. *Youth Services Librarians as Managers: A How-to Guide from Budgeting to Personnel*. Chicago: American Library Association.

Tunstall, Patricia. 2010. *Hiring, Training and Supervising Library Shelvers*. Chicago: American Library Association.

Wendover, Robert W. 2002. *Smart Hiring: The Complete Guide to Finding and Hiring the Best Employees*. Naperville, IL: Sourcebooks, Inc.

Woolls, Blanche, and David V. Loertscher. 2005. *The Whole School Library Handbook*. Chicago: American Library Association.

14

Leadership and Staff Communications

Leadership and communication are two sides of a coin. A leader supplies the vision that sets the tone for a department or an institution, but other people will not be able to pursue this vision unless the leader communicates it freely and clearly. Libraries are complex systems with several layers of administration; strong leaders are needed at every level to be sure that communication within departments as well as between departments, with governing bodies, and with the public are maintained. This chapter deals with leadership and communication within the department and the organization. As libraries become less building-centered, effective communication is more important than ever in maintaining a shared focus for the system. In coming years, staff members may work from various locations such as community centers, social services facilities, or elsewhere; some may do their work completely online and work from home or other location.

The communication patterns for individual libraries vary greatly: a branch library that is part of a big city system has much more complex communication links with other staff and administration than does a children's department of a one-building library in a smaller community. School libraries have a different pattern of administration. Many school librarians are the only librarian in the building; their colleagues are teachers, principals, and other professionals. Whatever the differences, the underlying patterns of staff communication are similar for all service organizations. Some lines of communication go from the department level up to administrators and other decision makers while some go from one colleague to another within the department or building, or between staff and volunteers. Department heads also communicate with professional organizations and other outside groups.

WORKING WITH OTHER DEPARTMENTS

Adult and children's services are complementary in a public library, just as teachers and library staff are complementary in a school setting. Individual

Figure 14.1
Basic Communication Links in Public Library

patrons and students have interactions with both groups at various times. Most library users are introduced to the library through the children's department. If they enjoy the experience, children often become users of adult services. The patron's transition between departments should be smooth and easy; this happens when the departments work closely together. In a similar fashion, children encounter school first through the individual teacher in a classroom. When librarians work closely with teachers, they can cooperate in serving the child who moves seamlessly from classroom to library as they work on school projects.

When budgets are allocated, the importance of children's services or the school library should be apparent to administrators and other people in the system. Some children's librarians believe that if they work hard and provide good programs and materials the rest of the library or school staff will notice their achievements without prompting. Unfortunately, people are so busy with their own work that they can easily miss what is happening in other departments. In a large library the children's department must publicize their work to avoid having staff members in other departments view the children's department as providing essentially the same materials and services it did five or ten years ago.

Figure 14.2
Basic Communication Links in School Library

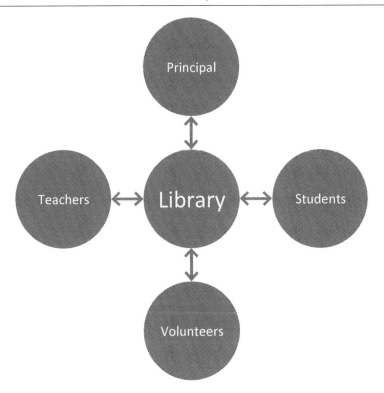

Because of the specialized work and the physical isolation of some school libraries and children's departments, people who work there may be unfamiliar to staff members in other departments. The school librarian should participate in curriculum meetings and school activities outside the library such as sports events. The head of children's services should encourage staff members to attend social events, staff and committee meetings, and other all-library activities.

Youth services personnel should get to know other staff members and tell them about what is going on in the children's department. They can develop informal contacts with staff in other departments and by participating in general library work. Children's staff should volunteer for committees and show an interest in the activities of all library departments.

Service on library or school committees is an important way for staff members to work together on issues that affect the entire organization. Children's librarians who demonstrate expertise in technology or reference service and who offer sound suggestions about solving library problems earn the respect of colleagues. Their organizational abilities and clever ideas can be demonstrated in committee work. When the library staff and school personnel come to know children's and school librarians as bright, knowledgeable professionals, they are more likely to respect the work of the children's department and school library.

CREATING AN EFFECTIVE DEPARTMENTAL TEAM

The first steps in creating an effective departmental team are based on simple everyday friendliness and good manners. Be sure to recognize and greet everyone in the department at the start of your day. Pay attention to each staff member; learn the names of the people who work in the library, both professional and support staff, and remember the basic facts of their lives—the names and ages of their children, the length of their commuting trip, the milestones in their lives such as graduations, engagements, and special achievements. Establish friendly everyday relationships by commenting briefly on local events such as the victory of a sports team, the opening of a new shopping mall, or a sudden change in the weather.

Even though paying attention to staff members and chatting with them is important, keep personal conversations during working hours brief and unemotional. Don't get drawn into long conversations about politics or world events. Save the stories about your vacations or household events for coffee breaks or lunch hours. Never, ever gossip about one staff member with another. This can create a suspicious and bitter attitude in the workplace. Any personal information about a staff member that you learn because of your job should be kept strictly confidential.

When interacting with staff members about work-related issues, maintain an open attitude and encourage frank and open discussion of decisions that have to be made:

1. Listen to other people's ideas. Even though many suggestions for changes or improvement may be impossible to implement, it is useful to have a wide range of opinions from which to choose.

2. Prioritize work. Try to keep the tasks of the department in perspective. Recognize that some tasks must be handled in a timely fashion, while other things can be postponed during busy periods. Try not to get flustered about minor items, but focus on the work that is most important for your public.

3. Solve problems quickly. Not making a decision is often worse than making one that is not perfect. Very few departmental decisions have a drastic permanent effect; most can be reversed if, after a reasonable trial, they don't work out. Dragging out a decision, on the other hand, can be demoralizing for the staff and affect the quality of service for patrons.

4. Be enthusiastic. No one can start work every morning feeling full of cheer and optimism, but if a leader is unable to be enthusiastic about the overall work of a department, the attitude can put a damper on the entire staff. Colleagues and patrons often feel the underlying tone of the leader and react to it. If you have personal or family problems that make you tense, try not to let them affect your attitude toward work and your colleagues too much. When these issues become serious, it is best to seek counseling or perhaps consider a leave of absence or a career change. Most often a lack of enthusiasm in a department leader stems not from serious issues but from a feeling that enthusiasm about the work being done is just not cool and sophisticated. On the contrary, great leaders, whether in business, services, or the arts, are usually openly enthusiastic about their work and encourage their colleagues to share their dedication and interest.

BALANCING COMMUNICATION CHANNELS

Communication is essential within an organization, and libraries have dozens of different tools to help us communicate, but as George Bernard Shaw once wrote: "The single biggest problem in communication is the illusion that it has taken place" (http://thinkexist.com/quotation/the_single_biggest_problem _in_communication_is/155222.html, accessed Aug. 30, 2012). Choosing the most effective and appropriate way to keep staff and patrons informed about the department and services is an important skill to develop.

Face-to-Face Communication

Advantages
- immediate feedback on message
- speaker can modify the message if listener indicates a problem
- allows two-way communication
- speaker can invite immediate comments and questions

Disadvantages
- listener may not listen carefully or take message seriously
- listener may argue
- unexpected response may throw the speaker off balance
- speaker may be tempted to reply hastily and inappropriately to a comment

In talking with an administrator, a department head should think about the style of presentation. Sometimes it is difficult to achieve a balance between acting like an assured, knowledgeable professional without being too aggressive or confrontational. People working within a department generally see the entire institution, whether it is a school or a library, from the vantage point of their own concerns. When talking to a principal or a chief librarian, it is a good idea to listen carefully to what is being said and to try to view your own concerns within the context of the larger institution. When both individuals are listening carefully and responding to what is being said, meaningful progress can be made. Too often individuals talk past each other instead of listening and addressing concerns.

If an important discussion is held face-to-face, it is often useful to follow up the meeting by writing a memo or email message outlining the main points that were made. This gives everyone involved in the meeting a chance to correct misperceptions or misinterpretations of what was said or agreed on. It also serves as a useful point of reference if questions arrive days or months later.

Telephone Calls

Most library staff members have a mobile phone available at all times, so more and more communication is handled through them. Telephone communication shares many of the advantages of face-to-face communication because feedback is fast, questions can be raised, and explanations given immediately; however, one big difference is that it is impossible to see the listener's body language. The speaker has to develop sensitivity to small clues such as silences and clearing of the throat. Chief librarians and other administrators often have secretaries to screen their office calls, but many librarians do not; for the latter a call may interrupt an important task or duty. When you call, ask if you are calling at a convenient time. It is better to call back when the individual can give your message full attention than to talk to a person who is distracted by other duties. When someone calls you at an inconvenient time, ask if you can return the call later. Communication suffers when either person is trying to cope with more than one thing simultaneously. If you promise to return a call, you should do so as soon as possible. Playing telephone tag is annoying and can sabotage communication. Some people find it worthwhile to set aside a certain time for telephone calls, perhaps the first hour in the morning, before the department is busy, so calls can be taken or returned without distraction.

Because telephone calls are often sandwiched between other activities, they may be easily forgotten. When you receive a call it is usually wise to make notes about the caller, the date, the subject, and any action to be taken. These notes will remind you of promises and agreements. When an important agreement is reached on the telephone, follow it up with an email or memo formalizing and recording the decision.

Texting

For many cell phone users, texting has almost replaced traditional calling. The advantage is that a text message is less obtrusive and does not interrupt other activities as much as a phone call does. Texts can be received in a quiet office or meeting without annoying anyone else in the vicinity. Texts do not require immediate response and can be answered when convenient. They also leave a record of the message, which can be referred to at a later time. Texting is very convenient for passing information about a book title, author, or call number, for example, to a patron or staff member. Young people who have cell phones are usually very comfortable with texting, although older patrons or staff may not be.

Electronic Mail

Email messages are a major communication format in most libraries. They take the place of all but the most formal memos and can be sent quickly to individuals or groups within the system or elsewhere.

Advantages
- take little effort and are easy to send
- usually arrive more quickly at the recipient's mailbox than other formats
- can be printed to provide a record of the message
- can be erased if message is ephemeral
- do not interrupt other people and can be read at the receiver's convenience

Disadvantages
- some people do not check their in-boxes frequently
- may be lost in number of spam messages received
- unless a receipt notification is requested, the sender does not know whether the message has been received
- technical problems can delay receipt of message

USING EMAIL EFFECTIVELY

1. Do not send unnecessary or trivial messages.
2. Make the subject heading clear and useful. If a message is particularly important, add URGENT to the subject line, but be careful of overdoing this. If a message does not require a response, add FYI (for your information) to the subject line.
3. Delete outdated subject headings. A string of messages with the same old subject heading is confusing.
4. Never write a one-word message. Saying "yes" or "agreed" without quoting the previous document forces the recipient to waste time checking back.
5. Be concise. Most people do not like to read long blocks of text online.
6. When including a link, write out the entire address so the recipient can link directly to the site. It is convenient to put a link on a separate line.
7. Using ALL CAPS to call attention to a particular section of a message is often considered rude, so use it sparingly.
8. Avoid the use of graphic emoticons except in messages to people you know well. They can appear unprofessional, and some email programs do not accept them.
9. Use a spell checker to avoid careless mistakes and typos.
10. Add a signature to your emails. Generally, a professional signature should include your name and title, the name of the library, and a link to the library website.
11. When replying to an email message, choose the "reply" option if only the writer of the message needs the information you are sending, and "reply all" if the information would be useful to everyone who received the original message.
12. Copy your message to the people who would receive copies of a written memo on the subject: an administrator, individual staff members, or a professional colleague.
13. Keep a record of any important message sent or received electronically by archiving it.
14. If your library or school has a policy or guidelines for e-communications, be sure to follow those carefully.

PUT IT IN PRINT

Memos are one of the most frequently used forms of communication in any organization. The name "memo" comes from the Latin word "memorandum," meaning something that should be remembered. Today many memos are written and stored in digital form, but that does not change their function, which is to preserve a permanent record of events, decisions, and actions. Dean Acheson, a postwar American statesman, famously quipped that "A memorandum is not written to inform the reader but to protect the writer" (Acheson, 1977). Most administrators find memos an efficient way of keeping in touch with what is going on in various departments. A department head will usually keep the chief librarian informed by memos of activities within the department, issues that may grow into problems, suggestions for changes in library procedures, and requests for increased budget or other services. Most memos are now sent as email attachments, but they are often printed out to provide a permanent record.

Occasions for Sending Memos

- Record decision made at a meeting or in a telephone call
- Document an issue that may become a problem within the department

- Suggest a change in policy or procedures
- Remind people of a meeting and send an agenda
- Protest an action taken by a supervisor or other personnel
- Announce the schedule for holidays or other events
- Transmit information about changes in the library system
- Ask questions or get permission for an action
- Make suggestions for positive change to services or to solicit suggestions from staff

Memos are used in following up on whether decisions are implemented, problems solved, and plans followed. They are also used in writing annual reports. For this reason, a department head should try to ensure that important departmental issues are documented in memos. Memos are generally filed by subject matter, so each memo should be devoted to a single issue. Otherwise, the less important issue may be lost or ignored.

When memos serve as documentation for decisions, they become formal communications. Whenever a memo dealing with an important issue is sent, a copy should be kept in the department files for verification. This is particularly important if the memo deals with a request for action. If, for example, an agreement has been reached that an additional computer will be installed in the children's room, it is important to record the date of the agreement. If the action is not taken within a reasonable period of time, the department head can follow up with a reminder.

A memo that deals with a personnel problem is filed in the individual's personnel file. These memos serve as important reminders to supervisors preparing performance assessments and are invaluable if disciplinary measures are needed. Memos of commendation are also important for writing performance assessments and for writing recommendations for employees who are leaving the library.

Although it is important to keep files of memos, the files should be weeded frequently. Memos, whether paper or electronic, that refer to specific events or ephemeral matters should be discarded at regular intervals. Memos can also be used as legal or procedural documents. Many libraries have records management rules that should be followed carefully when memos are to be discarded.

Letters

Letters are written between departments in a library system to document changes in status such as promotions, increases in salary, formal reprimands or commendations, and resignations. Because letters give the title and position of the writer and recipient, they are preferable to memos whenever the document may need to be made available outside of the library system. Even though much communication occurs through informal channels today, it is important to remember that formal, signed letters are needed for many formal statements. Communications with individuals, corporations, or unions that may at some time become part of a legal case should be carefully formulated and preserved. The school or library's administrative officers and lawyers can give guidance to school librarians at the building level and department heads on how to manage these documents.

REACHING THE ENTIRE DEPARTMENT

Communication is not always between individuals. Any organization generates news that should be shared with everyone working in the department. A good leader tries to be open about letting staff members know what is going on in the library: what changes are being considered, which staff members may be changing responsibilities, what events are being planned. The difficulty is that the amount of information coming from all the meetings and deliberations of various committees and individuals can be overwhelming in a large system. A good leader organizes information so the more important items are emphasized and details are available to those who want them. The channels used for communication should suit the preferences of staff members. Available formats include:

- Face-to-face meetings—a method that helps put faces to the messages, but is time-consuming, and it is often difficult to arrange a time that fits everyone's schedule.
- Printed notice on staff bulletin boards—a method that is being abandoned in many libraries today because of the waste of paper and lack of interest in reading print notices.
- Notices sent on staff email lists—not as often used as previously because the volume of email causes many staff members to delete many notices without reading them.
- Text messages sent to all staff—useful for those staff members who are accustomed to texting.
- Staff wikis—maintained in many libraries because notices can be posted by administrators and department heads and staff. Comments and questions can be raised and answered.
- Restricted social media—a number of private social media sites are available; examples are Yammer and Jive. Only people with a valid institutional email address can sign on to them, so privacy is maintained.

In today's world of social media, people are becoming more used to interactive communication and often resent having no chance to respond to messages. That's one reason why wikis and social media are becoming such important parts of communication within organizations. Because most staff members are accustomed to responding to announcements and comments on sites such as Facebook, they pay more attention to organizational communication that also allows interaction. Many young staff members are accustomed to using wikis and restricted social networks in college and library school classes and will participate eagerly in library or departmental use of these tools. Older staff members may need some encouragement to sign on and become active users, but for the most part library staff members are flexible and willing to try new technology, especially if the library leaders participate actively.

The format most commonly used in libraries and other institutions for sharing online information is the wiki. Almost everyone who uses a library is familiar with Wikipedia, the popular online encyclopedia, so they have experience reading a wiki. Most staff members will find it easy to switch to actively participating in a wiki.

Webster's dictionary defines a wiki as a website that allows visitors to make changes, contributions, or corrections. Free wiki platforms are available from several online sites. You can sample some library and school wikis that are available online and choose a format that seems most appropriate for your library or department. If wikis have not been used in your library, you may want to ask for a small group of volunteers to help set up a wiki before unveiling it to the entire staff.

The basic principles of setting up and using a departmental wiki:

- Provide an introduction and directions for using the wiki for every staff member. This should include librarians, teachers, clerical and maintenance staff, and student assistants.
- Encourage every staff member to contribute to the wiki when they have information to share with the department.
- Allow small groups to set up a wiki page for group projects, such as planning summer reading projects or special events.
- Set a good example by using the wiki for posting schedules, changes in procedures, holiday closings, and other information.
- Assign one individual the task of doing daily maintenance to set up new users, reviewing changes to be sure they are appropriate, eliminating obsolete pages, and backing up the wiki.

Like any other management tool, the wiki for a library or school will not remain the same forever. At least once a year, it should be reviewed to be sure it is functioning as intended for the department. New developments in technology will no doubt offer new tools that will replace your library wiki and offer even better formats for sharing staff ideas and solving problems.

SHARING IDEAS WITH OTHER YOUTH LIBRARIANS

Most librarians spend their working days with colleagues in their library and community and with the patrons they serve. Work patterns can become standardized, and the library may continue to offer fairly traditional services year after year even though both the patrons and their community have changed. Reaching out to the wider world of youth librarians who share a professional viewpoint and set of problems can keep librarians from falling into a rut. Librarians have always networked, and technology has made it easier and more efficient than ever before to maintain contact with colleagues far beyond the individual library.

Networking within a System or Region

The logical place to start with face-to-face professional networks is to engage with librarians working in other branches of your library system or other schools in your district. Large library systems or school districts often have an association of children's librarians, which meets regularly to select materials, listen to speakers, discuss issues, or attend events. The coordinator of children's services or the district school library director or, in the absence of this person, one school librarian may be asked to chair the group, and generally plans and chairs these meetings. In smaller systems, children's librarians may maintain contact through periodic meetings at the main library or a branch. The head of the main library's children's department often takes the lead, but sometimes each librarian takes a turn in planning meetings. In some jurisdictions, a number of libraries form a regional system that meets for materials selection and professional development. Independent schools or small libraries sometimes form a local association to share ideas.

Part of the value of meeting colleagues is to enjoy social contacts, but beyond this purpose is the larger professional aim of improving children's services. Each individual has a responsibility to bring to the meetings helpful information and ideas. If one branch has discipline problems, discussing them with other librarians may help resolve them. If particular programs or specific materials have proved notably successful, it is important to share this information. A willing, cooperative spirit generally leads to better service for the entire community or region.

At any meeting, one person should have the responsibility of taking notes and distributing them by email to each participant. Be sure to follow up suggestions and requests. If someone offers to share the outline of a particularly successful program, and it does not arrive, send a reminder. Take time to send a thank-you when the material does come. Similarly, be sure to carry through on promises to send information or materials.

Visiting other local school libraries or children's departments enables librarians to see how well different room arrangements, decorations, or materials actually work. Some systems and regions hold rotating meetings so librarians eventually see most of the departments, but other jurisdictions hold all meetings at one central location. Making an effort to visit other departments and other school libraries is worthwhile even on your own time. You can gather many ideas in twenty minutes or so.

Meetings with local librarians need not be limited to professional staff. These meetings can become opportunities to recruit other staff members into the profession. Many people become librarians because they have worked in a library, and librarians have taken an interest in their career plans. Encouraging staff to enter library programs is a good way to increase diversity in the workplace. When employees in the library show an aptitude for the work and appear to be capable of undertaking graduate education, it is worth discussing the possibilities. Library assistants who are interested in becoming professionals should be invited to attend conferences and workshops to learn more about the range of options in the field. Recruiting effective new librarians is one of the major obligations of library professionals.

Broadening Your Network

Colleagues within one system or region are a starting point, but many librarians also belong to larger professional groups, such as a state or provincial organization. These groups allow librarians working in different systems to share information and experiences, and they can offer workshops or programs that are too expensive for an individual system. For many librarians, especially those in the larger states and provinces, these groups continue to be the major focus of their professional life. Beyond the state level, the wider world of youth librarians includes national and international associations where librarians can meet their counterparts in widely varying locations, receive national journals, and attend national and international conferences.

Choosing a Professional Association

Membership in professional associations is expensive, so new librarians usually should choose carefully.

TIPS FOR CHOOSING THE RIGHT ASSOCIATION

- If you are in library school, join several associations at the student rate
- Read association journals to discover which is closest to your interests
- Check association websites to see which is most useful to you
- Find out what support you can expect from your library
- Ask colleagues about associations they belong to and conferences they attend
- Attend a conference or workshop before deciding to join

Most library systems regard membership and participation in professional associations as a sign of commitment to librarianship. They may reward this work with commendations on annual reviews and sometimes with merit pay increases. Encouragement from the library is an important factor, but individuals must choose for themselves which associations will be most helpful in their professional development. State, regional, and provincial associations offer less expensive conferences and workshops than national groups, but the national associations offer exposure to a more diverse group of librarians who work under a wide variety of conditions. National associations can present specialized programs and publications dealing with particular groups such as deaf children, new immigrants, or native children. The large conferences sponsored by national associations attract many exhibitors and are one of the major benefits of attending a conference. For many librarians, the exhibits are the most important part of conferences because they provide an opportunity to see new materials and equipment, to contact salespeople, and to get on distribution lists from important publishers. The American Library Association is the largest national professional library association in the United States, and the Canadian Library Association is its counterpart in Canada. Both of these associations include sections for children's librarians in public libraries and for school librarians. The Association for Library Services for Children (ALSC) is the oldest division of the ALA, and it offers publications, conference programs, and media evaluations and prizes of interest to people who work in libraries for children. The American Association of School Librarians (AASL) provides the same type of services for school librarians.

International associations such as the International Federation of Library Associations and Institutions (IFLA) or the International Association of School Librarians (IASL) hold conferences throughout the world and publish journals of interest to youth librarians, but few library systems encourage or support participation in their work. The costs of attending international conferences are high. A decision to participate in an international organization is usually made by an individual librarian who has a personal interest in widening the horizons of his or her professional life.

In some communities, multiagency groups of people serving youth form associations. These offer valuable networking opportunities for librarians, and their meetings and programs are worth attending. Libraries are not always highly visible and may be overlooked unless the librarians make an effort to find out about and join these local associations.

While librarians may join nonlibrary professional associations, the major focus of association work is usually on library groups. Professional library associations not only provide professional development opportunities for members, they also lobby to enhance the status of the profession. The groups also work to alert the public to the importance of libraries in the community, the state, and the country. Participation in association work may bring enhanced career performance and professional visibility (which can lead to increased job opportunities) as well as offer professional contacts that often develop into long and rewarding friendships.

Attending Conferences

Attending a professional conference is expensive in time and money, yet many librarians find them worth the cost.

Benefits of attending a conference:

- Participating in professional workshops
- Learning from well-known speakers
- Meeting professionals from other libraries
- Examining new materials and equipment at exhibits
- Practicing skills in chairing committees and speaking in public
- Making new friends who share professional interests

Unlike conferences in some other professions, most library programs do not offer many presentations of research findings. Programs tend to focus on topics of practical concern and to feature speakers who have had experience in the area. A typical program format is for one speaker to give an overview of the topic, serving homeless children or selecting graphic novels, for example, followed by a panel of four or five librarians who respond. The value of the program depends on the speakers. Some speakers talk almost exclusively about the policies of their library, while others draw from a wider background. Because the audience is diverse, speakers must balance their talks to be of interest to new librarians as well as experienced administrators. This is not an easy task. Fortunately, organizers have a large pool of speakers, and most panels have at least two or three speakers who give new information or fresh viewpoints. No one program will make the entire conference worthwhile. The librarian should look for a number of sessions on topics of interest and attend at least half a dozen of them.

Talks by authors of children's books are popular features at most professional conferences. Authors are generally fluent and entertaining speakers, and many of them have wide experience in public speaking. Their talks deepen a librarian's appreciation of the author's books, but do not necessarily improve library services. They are cultural rather than professional events, and despite their inherent interest, they should not dominate a librarian's conference schedule. The authors can often be seen at their publisher's booth during book-signing periods.

Contacts made at conferences can help you solve professional problems, gather new information, and enlarge your view of the profession. The most long-lasting contacts are usually made through committee work.

Exhibits are also a valuable part of most conferences and one of the major reasons why librarians attend conferences year after year. For librarians in small systems or solo school librarians, conferences may be their best opportunity to see new materials and equipment. Children's publishers have booths at many large conferences, and librarians can browse through the new books to decide what to order. Conferences also offer opportunities to examine the newest technology and see demonstrations of new software. Librarians can compare brands and ask questions of the salespeople at each booth. A large conference such as the American Library Association's Annual Conference has thousands of exhibitors offering an overwhelming variety of products. Any conference attendee should allow several sessions of two or three hours each to look at the exhibits. Talking to the editors and sales representatives at exhibit booths is informative and can establish relationships that may be useful over the years.

Schools and libraries support conferences because they increase knowledge about the profession and heighten commitment to it. A good conference lifts an individual out of a particular job and offers a glimpse of the wider world of librarianship.

Competition for funds to attend a conference is often strong. Membership in the association, or on a committee, may be required. Applying early for funding is a good idea. If the application is approved, check on the time and money that will be allowed for attendance and the expense records that will be expected. Most institutions reimburse expenses only with a receipt. Another frequent requirement is a written report to be circulated to other staff members, or an oral report at a staff meeting. If staff members win awards or present programs at conferences, accounts of the event may be posted on the library website.

When more than one person from a library goes to a conference, they should attend different sessions to achieve greater overall coverage. If the library or school district pays expenses, the administration expects each individual to attend meetings useful to the institution, which may mean missing some meetings that might be more interesting to the individual. Writing good reports and demonstrating a professional attitude toward conference attendance is likely to lead to greater support in the future.

IF YOU WANT TO KNOW MORE ...

Acheson, Dean 1977. *Wall Street Journal*, September 8. Available at http://www.quotations page.com/quote/3986.html (accessed Aug. 30, 2012).

Matthews, Joseph R. 2005. *Strategic Planning and Management for Library Managers*. Westport, CT: Libraries Unlimited.

Shipley, David, and Will Schwalbe. 2008. *Send: Why People Email So Badly and How to Do It Better.* Rev. ed. New York: Knopf.

Woods, Dan, and Peter Thoeny. 2007. *Wikis for Dummies.* Indianapolis, IN: Wiley.

Zsulya, Andrea Stewart, and Carlette Washington-Hoagland, for the Library Leadership and Management Association (LLAMA), ed. 2012. *Staff Development: A Practical Guide.* 4th ed. Chicago: American Library Association.

Section VI

Looking toward the Future:
Challenge and Change

Libraries have evolved over the centuries from collections of treasured texts for society's elite into busy hubs of activity where valued resources are made available to everyone who chooses to access them. The pace of change has picked up in recent years, and many librarians believe that the changes of the next decade will be even more dramatic than those of the past fifty years. The question for the library profession is not whether school and public libraries will change, but how we will manage the inevitable changes that are occurring.

CHALLENGE AND CHANGE

Libraries are firmly established as an important part of our school or community life, but today some commentators believe that they are, or soon will be, obsolete. Most children's and school librarians believe libraries have a bright future, but few can predict exactly what that will be. Steve Jobs once said, "The best way to predict the future is to invent it" (Isaacson, 2011, p. 95). Today's librarians will invent the future for our libraries and decide the shape it will take. Our final chapter discusses some of the factors affecting what that future will be and how we can shape it.

15

Changing Media—Changing Services

Nothing is permanent except change.

—Heraclitus

Libraries are institutions dedicated to preserving books and other resources that are of benefit to the user. School and children's librarians try to give children access to the ideas and entertainment stored in media. At times there has been agreement on the importance of many children's books; these were the classics that have survived the test of time. Tastes seemed to change slowly and grandparents, parents, and children shared many of the same materials. To some extent this is still true, but in recent decades there have been so many changes in media that the presentation of even familiar literature has been altered. Children watch fairy tales on tablet computers and view realistic stories on smartphones. Libraries feel harried by the need to keep up with the shifting demands of their patrons. There is no reason to think that this climate of change will not continue for decades to come, so librarians must prepare for more of it.

TRANSLITERACY

One concept that has affected thinking about libraries as well as other disciplines is the notion of transliteracy, defined as "the ability to read, write and interact across a range of platforms, tools and media from signing and orality through handwriting, print, TV, radio and film, to digital social networks" (Transliteracy.com, http://nlabnetworks.typepad.com/transliteracy/; accessed Aug. 30, 2012). Librarians and educators are aware that children today must learn to understand messages sent in a variety of formats. For this reason libraries are collecting resources in visual and auditory as well as print formats. In most libraries, as of 2012, books are still the dominant format available. Libraries in coming years will probably have fewer physical books in their collections but will offer more access to books for the average user. What does the emphasis on literacy across all media mean for libraries? Both school and public librarians help young people learn how to discover information in books and other media. In a public library the teaching is usually informal, although in some communities school classes may visit a public library to find information about some topics, such as local history. Homeschooled children also use the public library as a major source of information resources, and librarians may help them in searching for materials. School librarians work with teachers to teach information literacy across many platforms. Library sessions may be an important part of a school project or assignment.

The concept of transliteracy covers activities that have been going on for many years—gathering information from books, pictures, other people, or any other source. It is currently being used by some educators as a synonym for information literacy, but other commentators think of it as a broader field, including using various media for entertainment as well as learning. Changes in technology are related to transliteracy because they have presented us with many different formats from which to gather impressions, ideas, or facts. Transliteracy is the broader term that includes the use of technologies and the ways in which people interact with resources. The ways in which the concept of transliteracy is beginning to affect library practices range from merging media platforms, to increasing interactivity, and serving patrons across different ages and groups.

Merging Media Platforms

The distinction between print books and visual media becomes less clear. Digital books that are primarily text will include embedded videos, pictures, website links, and audio CDs. The artificial separation that now exists between print books and audiovisual materials such as DVDs is already breaking down. DVDs and other stable digital products are likely to disappear from libraries as most visual media will be streamed from online repositories. Librarians will want to have this material noted in catalogs so that users can identify all sources of information on the topic of interest. The separation of various formats into different sections of the library may also be questioned. Graphic novels and nonfiction picture books may be most useful if interfiled with more traditional print products instead of being classified and shelved separately. Catalogs can integrate listings of both these formats along with digital products on the same topic.

Encouraging Interactivity in the Library

As the volume and variety of information sources continue to grow, it becomes increasingly evident that working in groups is an effective way of learning about a topic. Librarians will encourage clusters of children to work together to find and assess available materials with their help. A group can examine more material than an individual can and therefore find more aspects of a topic. Some of the skills of transliteracy are shown in an ability to react to information and assess sources. By working together students can learn more about an issue and practice presenting information to a group. Librarians will want to support these skills by making interactivity easier and encouraging children to work together productively without going off topic.

Inclusive Services for All Media for All Patrons

One of the consequences of the emphasis on transliteracy is the diminishing of age-limited services and materials. Although preliterate children will be provided with picture books and media on topics of greatest interest to preschoolers, patrons of all ages will be encouraged to use these materials when they are appropriate. Many middle school children and English-language learners find picture books useful for information and enjoyable for reading and browsing.

At the other end of the children's age group, children in middle school are more likely to use resources designed for adults. Much online material is not designated for audiences of a particular age, so children and their parents share much digital recreation and information sources. Public librarians will find it useful to allow young people greater access to adult collections in print and digital formats, and school librarians are likely to increase access to materials designed for all ages. Some parents and other adults are likely to find this trend disturbing. Challenges to books and other materials have certainly not diminished, even though definitions of unsuitable materials have changed dramatically every decade for the past fifty years for both school and public libraries.

Another issue that is likely to have increased in importance as more materials appear in digital format is that of access for physically challenged individuals. Librarians should be aware that embedded videos in print sources should be captioned for the hearing-impaired, and assistive devices for the visually impaired should be available. The 2010 standards of the Americans with Disability Act (ADA), which became effective in March 2012, will make buildings more accessible and perhaps increase the number of people using library collections in some areas (2010 Standards for Accessible Design, available at http://www .ada.gov/2010ADAstandards_index.htm; accessed Aug. 30, 2012). The greater the variety of materials offered, the more important accessibility issues become.

Along with greater accessibility to materials in the building, libraries will increase services to people accessing resources from outside of the building. Online reference services are now offered by many libraries, and with the increasing use of mobile media, these services will be in high demand. This is likely to lead to a reassessment of how space is allocated in the library as a number of librarians may spend most of their working time interacting with patrons online.

CHANGING WORLD OF PUBLISHING

The traditional print publishing world has been in turmoil ever since ebooks were introduced to the general public by Amazon's Kindle e-reader in 2007. Before that some ebooks had been produced and used by scholars on computers, but specialized book-reading devices expanded the market dramatically. Other companies introduced rival book platforms, including Apple's iPad and Barnes & Noble's Nook, and sales of ebooks took off. These sales have increased every year for the past four years, as have sales of e-readers and tablet computers. Amazon has announced that sales of ebooks are greater than the sales of print books.

When e-readers were first introduced, they offered books in a black-and-white text version. Later devices such as the iPad and Kindle Fire offer full-color screens and embedded links to websites and videos. Ebooks were first offered primarily for adult book readers, but the introduction of color and illustrations has led to a large market for digital picture books for young children. By 2012 thousands of picture books were available as apps for the iPad and other platforms. Some are reproductions of older picture books enhanced with sound and videos. As ownership of e-readers increases, it is likely more picture books will be produced in this format, and libraries will have to decide how they will make them available to their patrons.

Books for middle grade children are also popular in digital versions. Rick Riordan's series of Olympian books as well as Tolkien's *The Hobbit* were among the early favorites in ebooks available for Barnes & Noble's Nook reader. Although the majority of children in 2012 do not own an e-reader, more and more of them have smartphones and other devices on which to read books. When schools start buying e-readers for use in classrooms, the sales of ebooks for children are likely to grow quickly.

Several publishers are trying the concept of *bundled books*, sold in both ebook and print format. Producing an ebook as a by-product of publishing a print book is comparatively inexpensive because books are written in digital format. The book manuscript is edited and prepared for publication electronically even for a paper edition. Producing an ebook version of the material does not require much additional labor. The advantage to readers is that they can read the book on their favorite e-reader and then have the print copy as a permanent format to keep. They can also switch back and forth between digital and print formats depending on their location, so they have the best of both worlds. It remains to be seen how much extra a purchaser will pay to have a book available in dual formats; there are also questions about royalties to authors and illustrators if two versions of the same book are sold together. The advantage to libraries seems clear, because it would enable the purchase of ebooks for readers who prefer those and then ensure that the library has a print copy that can be preserved for future use or reference.

Among the first books to be available as ebooks were the traditional out-of-copyright classics that are included in many children's libraries. Many of these classics, including the works of Louisa May Alcott and Lucy Maud Montgomery, are available either free of cost or at prices of less than two dollars for e-readers. These books are not as popular as more recent titles, but many children still read and enjoy them, often at the urging of parents or grandparents. Teachers, too, might want to include some of these heritage books in classes. A library that provides e-readers can include all of these books to an individual child for almost no cost. If an entire class wanted to read one, there might be additional costs for the e-readers. This publishing initiative means that many libraries will be able to include a range of classic children's books in their collection without necessarily buying expensive print versions.

ACQUIRING AND PROVIDING DIGITAL MATERIALS

Methods of acquiring digital materials follow a number of different patterns. Publishers and vendors are still experimenting with business models.

Some publishers sell or lease materials as subscriptions; others group a series of ebooks together for sale. This is especially true of nonfiction series that are used for curriculum backup in school libraries. (See chapter 8 for more about acquisitions.) The important thing for librarians to remember is that publishers and vendors are still experimenting with various ways of making digital materials available to libraries. This topic is an important professional issue that deserves serious discussion in professional associations. One of the benefits of attending library conferences is the opportunity to talk with vendors and publishers about plans and changes that may affect libraries.

A complementary issue about the provision of digital materials is the need to educate children and parents about copyright law. Like many other aspects of digital culture, copyright law is in flux and likely to remain so for years to come. Congress is in the process of drafting legislation regulating the rights of individuals to download and use content. What the final legislation will look like and how it will stand up in court challenges are topics of importance to librarians and their patrons.

Some basic steps that help to get the message across:

- Provide links to basic information about copyright. One starting point is a curriculum guide developed by the Electronic Frontier Foundation and available for free download online at http://www.teachingcopyright.org/ (accessed Aug. 30, 2012). Other sources for information about copyright are listed at the end of this chapter.
- Most libraries have printed sheets of warnings about copyright infringement posted near photocopy machines. Similar warnings about downloading material should be posted near library computers.
- Library websites should have a copyright notice and warning visible to users at the bottom of each screen.
- Needless to say, library websites should be careful about not posting materials that infringe copyright. Caution is needed in using images from book covers or illustrations.
- Librarians in school libraries should inform teachers about the limitations on using copyright material and also about the dimensions of fair use policy. It is useful to provide this material in print and online documents and newsletters and to occasionally address the subject in meetings with teachers.
- Both school and public librarians should be aware of policies within local school districts about the use of possibly copyrighted materials in assignments and guide students accordingly.
- Finally, it is important for librarians to be aware of the most recent legal decision affecting copyright. This can be done through a digital alert system such as Google alerts.

MAINTAINING AN ATMOSPHERE THAT WELCOMES CHANGE

Librarians have been changing their ways of serving patrons ever since they first unchained books from the medieval bookstands. The trend ever since has been to make books and other resources more accessible to more people. Closed stacks gave way to open plans with books freely available on open shelves. Now children's libraries offer baskets full of books for toddlers to browse through and electronic versions to be viewed on smartphones or tablets in the car or shopping cart. But every change that is made meets with some resistance from staff, children, or parents. How can a librarian encourage changes in the library and win the cooperation of those affected by them?

Encourage New Ideas and Suggestions

Habits develop easily in the workplace. "We've always done it this way," is a familiar response when any suggestion is made to change, but successful librarians do not get into a rut of keeping old habits. Dieter Rams, the celebrated industrial designer, suggested that we should "Question everything generally thought to be obvious" (Rams, 2011), and his questions led to the design of some of the best products of the 20th century. Children's librarians are lucky because they have an endless source of new ideas in the patrons they serve. Children don't come to libraries with preconceptions about what a library should be like (although they soon learn to expect the familiar), and if adults listen to their suggestions, many good ideas may be discovered. Many of the children's ideas may be on the lines of "Let's have ice cream at storytimes" or "We could have a pet giraffe" or other unworkable ideas, but some of the suggestions are useful. At the very least, the department will open up communication and establish an atmosphere in which patrons can feel like partners rather than just customers.

If the library has high school or college students working as shelvers, encourage them to express their ideas about library procedures and resources. They are closer in age to the patrons and often more comfortable with technology than staff are, so they can provide a new, fresh outlook on library services.

The most important element in welcoming change is to make the entire staff partners in developing services. A rigid hierarchy of decision making is not the most effective way to keep an organization relevant and useful to its clients. Everyone who works in the library should be encouraged to suggest ideas for change, and should have a procedure for doing so. Useful ideas for change may come from a clerk with twenty years of experience in circulation, or from the newest hire fresh from library school. Sorting through them and reaching decisions takes time, but it strengthens the organization and usually ensures better cooperation when changes are made.

Allow Experimentation

Allowing experimentation with small, inexpensive changes can encourage ideas and suggestions for larger change. If all of your storytime programs are offered in the morning on a drop-in basis, try a series of early-evening theme-related programs for which parents register their child in advance. This will give you an idea about whether parents in your community are willing to plan ahead to ensure their child will have a place. If it is successful, you might try to organize a parent group to give input into themes for future programs and various ways of informing the public of their availability. If it fails, you can go back to your earlier schedule of storytimes. *An experiment that fails is not a failure for the library;* it gives useful information about how to plan for the future. Analyze why particular projects were not successful and decide how they can be modified to meet the needs of your community. An individual who suggests an experimental program, only to have it fail, should be encouraged to try again.

Of course you can't go on trying every impractical idea that is suggested, but encouraging honest experimentation is the only way to ensure a steady flow of new ideas. Many of them will eventually prove valuable.

Allow Criticism of Imposed Change

Many changes are introduced into library services and resources. Most of them meet with some resistance from staff and sometimes patrons. The more dramatic the change, the more resistance is likely to be felt, so plans have to be made to handle the complaints. Changes in the children's department or school library that will affect many patrons, for example, no longer offering Sunday hours or not being open before school starts in the morning, should be planned well in advance. Reasons for the change should be explained honestly. "Budgetary problems" is often cited as a reason for any cutback or change, but it is not a sufficient explanation in itself. Adjusting to a drop in funding allows decisions to be made about which services or resources should be cut. Explaining why a particular cut was made helps those affected adjust to the situation. These explanations are easier if the library has data to back them up on the basis of value to users. That is one reason why it is so important to have statistics on the use of resources, attendance at programs, and requests for additional items.

Channels for receiving input from the public about changes in the library are important. A comment box in the library as well as on the library webpage and Facebook page allows people to give their opinions. It is usually preferable to have people address the librarian directly rather than resort to writing letters to the local newspaper or making comments on community radio shows or, in the case of the school librarian, directly to the superintendent or school board. The channels for comments should be publicized, but public comment on major changes need to be restricted in time, just as public comment on community government projects have a specific time frame.

People like to get responses to their comments, but the volume of responses to a public library system change sometimes dictates a general rather than specific answer. It is always appropriate to thank people for taking the time to give an opinion and to express respect for their point of view. Detailed complaints or suggestions should be answered individually whenever possible.

Feedback from staff members often calls for a staff meeting where individuals can give their opinions about changes. Sometimes informal meetings work best. Some library departments find that brown bag lunch meetings at which staff can discuss changes in technology or resources help individuals to learn from one another and accept changing procedures.

Don't Stop Talking

When a change has been implemented, individuals will accept it according to their different styles. As one business writer has stated, "on average, in any organization, about 15 percent of the people will go with the management whatever they do. About 15 percent don't really like the management at all and will resist them whatever they do. You're really playing to the 70 percent in the middle" (Roberts, 2007, p. 55). A school librarian will usually find that some teachers are eager to hear about and try out new items in the library while others cling to what they have used in the past. The same is true about patrons and staff in a public library. Some people are eager to try out new technology, or demonstrate new resources to children; others prefer to avoid a change they may have only grudgingly accepted. Within limits, it is usually best to let individuals set their own pace, while at the same time making it clear that changes are here to stay. Sometimes a reluctant staff member can work with a more change-friendly one until gradually becoming comfortable with the change.

Information professionals sometimes refer to the current climate of constantly changing software, systems, publishing methods, and media use as being in "perpetual beta." Libraries as part of the information world have entered a state of perpetual data. In other words, we can expect changes in the buildings we work in, the resources we offer, the way we deliver services, and the people we serve. Libraries are not monuments to the past but pathways to the future, and they will continue to survive just as long as they maintain their commitment to help people move toward that future.

IF YOU WANT TO KNOW MORE . . .

Curzon, Susan C. 2005. *Managing Change: A How-To-Do-It Manual for Librarians*. New York: Neal-Schuman.

Isaacson, Walter. 2011. *Steve Jobs*. New York: Simon & Schuster.

Rams, Dieter. August 27, 2011–February 20, 2012. "Question Everything Generally Thought To Be Obvious." Exhibition @ San Francisco Museum of Modern Art: Less and More—The Design Ethos of Dieter Rams.

Roberts, John. 2007. "Dealing with Opposition to Culture Change." In *Managing Change*. Boston: Harvard Business School Press.

Russell, Carrie. 2012. *Complete Copyright for K–12 Librarians and Educators*. Chicago: American Library Association.

Teaching Copyright. Electronic Frontier Foundation. Available at http://www.teaching copyright.org/ (accessed Aug. 30, 2012).

References and Additional Resources

2011 State of America's Libraries Report. 2011. Chicago: American Library Association.

About Strategic Planning. Available at http://managementhelp.org/plan_dec/str_plan/str_plan.htm (accessed Aug. 30, 2012). Free Management Library.

Acerro, Heather. 2011. "Keeping a Work Journal." ALSC Blog, May 6. http://www.alsc.ala.org/blog/?p=2353 (accessed Aug. 29, 2012).

Adams, Helen R. 2008. *Ensuring Intellectual Freedom and Access to Information in the School Library Media Program.* Westport, CT: Libraries Unlimited.

Adams, Helen R. 2011. "The Privacy Problem." *School Library Journal*, April, 34–37.

Adkins, Denice, and Lisa K. Hussey. 2005. "Unintentional Recruiting for Diversity." *Public Libraries* 44 [July/August]: 229–233.

American Association of School Librarians. 2009. *Empowering Learners: Guidelines for School Library Programs.* Chicago: American Association of School Librarians.

American Association of School Librarians. 2009. *Standards for the 21st Century Learner.* Chicago: American Association of School Librarians.

American Association of School Librarians. "Position Statement on the Confidentiality of Library Records." Available at http://www.ala.org/aasl/aaslissues/positionstatements/conflibrecds (accessed Aug. 30, 2012).

American Library Association. 2010. *Intellectual Freedom Manual.* 8th ed. Chicago: American Library Association.

Basic Guide to Outcomes-Based Evaluation. Available at http://managementhelp.org/evaluatn/outcomes.htm (accessed Aug. 29, 2012).

Baumbach, Donna J., and Linda L. Miller. 2006. *Less Is More: A Practical Guide to Weeding School Library Collections.* Chicago: American Library Association.

Bernstein, Joan E., and Kathy Schalk-Greene. 2006. "Extreme Library Makeover: One Year Later [April]." *American Libraries* 37: 66–69.

Bertot, John Carlo, Paul T. Jaeger, and Charles R. McClure, eds. 2011. *Public Libraries and the Internet.* Santa Barbara, CA: Libraries Unlimited.

Bisson, Casey. 2007. "Open-Source Software for Libraries." *Library Technology Reports,* Vol. 43:3. Chicago: American Library Association.

Bostwick, Arthur. 1914. *Library and School: The Relationship between the Library and the Public Schools.* New York: HW Wilson.

Breeding, Marshall. 2008. "Open Source Integrated Library Systems." *Library Technology Reports,* Vol. 44:8. Chicago: American Library Association.

Bromann, Jennifer. 2005. *More Booktalking That Works.* New York: Neal-Schuman.

Brophy, Peter, and Kate Coulling. 1996. *Quality Management for Information and Library Managers.* Brookfield, VT: Aslib Gower.

Brown, Anita. 2004. "Reference Services for Children: Information Needs and Wants in the Public Library." *Australian Library Journal* 53 (3): 261–274.

Brown, Carol R. 2002. *Interior Design for Libraries: Drawing on Function and Appeal.* Chicago: American Library Association.

Bryan, Cheryl. 2007. *Managing Facilities for Results: Optimizing Space for Services.* Chicago: Public Library Association/American Library Association.

Burnett, Ken. 2006. *The Zen of Fundraising: 89 Timeless Ideas to Strengthen and Develop Your Donor Relationships.* San Francisco: Wiley.

Cerny, Rosanne, Penny Markey, and Amanda Williams. 2006. "Knowledge of Client Group." In *Outstanding Library Service to Children: Putting the Core Competencies to Work.* Chicago: American Library Association.

Chronicle of Philanthropy. *Fund Raising.* Available at www.philanthropy.com/fund raising (accessed Aug. 29, 2012).

Circle, Alison. 2012. "A New Player in Marketing." *Library Journal* 137 (2): 30–31.

Coleman, Tina, and Peggy Llanes. 2009. *The Hipster Librarian's Guide to Teen Crafts.* Chicago: American Library Association.

Cooper, Linda Z. 2002. "A Case Study of Information-Seeking Behavior in 7-Year-Old Children in a Semistructured Situation." *ASIS* 53 (11): 904–922.

Cooper, Linda Z. 2005. "Developmentally Appropriate Digital Environments for Young Children." *Library Trends* 54 (2): 286–302.

Crittendon, Robert. 2002. *The New Manager's Starter Kit: Essential Tools for Doing the Job Right.* New York: American Management Association.

Curzon, Susan C. 2005. *Managing Change: A How-To-Do-It Manual for Librarians.* New York: Neal-Schuman.

Data Center 2012 from Kids Count. http://datacenter.kidscount.org (accessed Sept. 6, 2012).

Diamant-Cohen, Betsy. 2010. *Children's Services: Partnerships for Success.* Chicago: American Library Association.

Doucett, Elisabeth. 2008. *Creating Your Library Brand: Communicating Your Relevance and Value to Your Patrons.* Chicago: American Library Association.

Dresang, Eliza. 2005. "The Information-Seeking Behavior of Youth in the Digital Environment." *Library Trends* 54 (2): 178–196.

Dresang, Eliza T., Melissa Gross, and Leslie Edmonds Holt. 2006. *Dynamic Youth Services through Outcome-Based Planning and Evaluation.* Chicago: American Library Association.

Driggers, Preston, and Ellen Dumas. 2011. *Managing Library Volunteers.* 2nd ed. Chicago: American Library Association.

Druin, Allison, Elizabeth Foss, Hilary Hutchinson, Evan Golub, and Leshell Hatley. 2010. *Children's Roles Using Keyword Search Interfaces at Home.* Mountain View, CA: Google Inc.

Druin, Allison, Elizabeth Foss, Hilary Hutchinson, Evan Golub, Leshell Hatley, Mona Leigh Guha, and Jerry Fails. 2009. "How Children Search the Internet with Keyword Interfaces". In Proceedings of Interaction Design and Children (IDC 2009), Cuomo, Italy, 89–96.

Duncan, Arne. 2012. "After 10 Years, It's Time for a New NCLB." *Washington Post*, January 8. Available at http://www.ed.gov/blog/2012/01/after-10-years-its-time-new-nclb/ (accessed Aug. 29, 2012).

East, Kathy. 1995. *Inviting Children's Authors and Illustrators: A How-to-Do-It Manual for School and Public Librarians*. New York: Neal-Schuman.

Eisenberg, Michael B., Carrie A. Lowe, and Kathleen L. Spitzer. 2004. *Information Literacy: Essential Skills for the Information Age*. 2nd ed. Westport, CT: Libraries Unlimited.

Erikson, Rolf. 2009. *Designing a School Library Media Center*. Chicago: American Library Association.

Feinberg, Sandra, and James R. Keller. 2010. *Designing Space for Children and Teens in Libraries and Public Places*. Chicago: American Library Association.

Feinberg, Sandra, Barbara Jordan, Kathleen Deerr, Marcellina Byrne, and Lisa Kropp. 2007. *The Family-Centered Library Handbook*. New York: Neal-Schuman.

Feinberg, Sandra, Joan Kuchner, and Sari Feldman. 1998. *Learning Environments for Young Children*. Chicago: American Library Association.

Fielding, Lynn. 2006. "Kindergarten Learning Gap" [April]. *American School Board Journal* 193 (4): 31–35.

Fincke, Mary Beth, Mary Frances Zilonis, and Carolyn Markuson. 2002. *Strategic Planning for School Library Media Centers*. School Librarianship Series. Lanham, MD: Scarecrow Press.

The Foundation Center. *Knowledge to Build On*. Available at http://foundationcenter.org (accessed Aug. 31, 2012).

Fox, Mem. 2001. *Reading Magic: Why Reading Aloud to Our Children Will Change Their Lives Forever*. New York: Harcourt.

Ghoting, Saroj Nadkami, and Pamela Martin-Diaz. 2011. *Early Literacy Storytimes @ your library®: Partnering with Caregivers for Success*. Chicago: American Library Association.

Giesecke, Joan, and Beth McNeil. 2010. *Fundamentals of Library Supervision*. 2nd ed. Chicago: American Library Association.

Gould, Mark R., ed. 2009. *The Library PR Handbook: High Impact Communications*. Chicago: American Library Association.

Gregory, Vicki L. 2011. *Collection Development and Management for 21st Century Libraries*. New York: Neal-Schuman.

Gutnick, Aviva Lucas, Michael Robb, Lori Takeuchi, and Jennifer Kotler. 2010. *Always Connected: The New Digital Media Habits of Young Children*. New York: The Joan Ganz Cooney Center at Sesame Workshop.

Hakala-Ausperk, Catherine. 2011. *Be a Great Boss: One Year to Success*. Chicago: American Library Association.

Hanson, Cody W. 2011. "Issues for Information Access on the Mobile Web." In *Library Technology Reports*. Chicago: American Library Association.

Harris, Frances Jacobson. 2011. *I Found It on the Internet: Coming of Age Online*. 2nd ed. Chicago: American Library Association.

Hill, Chrystie. 2009. *Inside, Outside, and Online*. Chicago: American Library Association.

Holt, Leslie Edmonds, Glen E. Holt, and Lloyd Stratton. 2006. *Library Success: A Celebration of Library Innovation, Adaptation and Problem Solving.* Newton, MA: EBSCO Publishing.

Hughes-Hassell, Sandra, and Jacqueline Mancall. 2005. *Collection Management for Youth: Responding to the Needs of Learners.* Chicago: American Library Association.

Intner, Carol F. 2011. *Homework Help from the Library: In Person and Online.* Chicago: American Library Association.

Intner, Sheila S., Joanna F. Fountain, and Jean Weihs. 2011. *Cataloging Correctly for Kids: An Introduction to the Tools.* 5th ed. Chicago: American Library Association.

Irving, Jan. 2004. *Stories NeverEnding: A Program Guide for Schools and Libraries.* Englewood, CO: Libraries Unlimited.

Isaacson, Walter. 2011. *Steve Jobs.* New York: Simon & Schuster.

Johnson, Peggy. 2004. *Fundamentals of Collection Development & Management.* Chicago: American Library Association.

Kane, Laura Townsend. 2011. *Working in the Virtual Stacks: The New Library & Information Science.* Chicago: American Library Association.

Kenney, Brian. 2011. "Things Are Changing Fast. SLJ's 2011 Tech Survey." *School Library Journal,* May, 28–33.

Krug, Steve. 2006. *Don't Make Me Think: A Common Sense Approach to Web Usability.* 2nd ed. Berkeley, CA: New Riders Publishing.

Landis, Cliff. 2010. *A Social Networking Primer for Librarians.* New York: Neal-Schuman.

Levinson, Jay Conrad, Frank Adkins, and Chris Forbes. 2010. *Guerrilla Marketing for Nonprofits.* Irvine, CA: Entrepreneur Press.

Manley, Will. 1996. "The Manley Arts." *Booklist,* March 1, 1108.

Martin, Barbara Stein, and Marco Zannier. 2009. *Fundamentals of School Library Media Management.* New York: Neal-Schuman.

Matthews, Joseph R. 2005. *Strategic Planning and Management for Library Managers.* Westport, CT: Libraries Unlimited.

McCook, Kathleen de la Pena. 2011. *Introduction to Public Librarianship.* 2nd ed. New York: Neal-Schuman.

McGinn, Howard F. 2006. "Getting Started: Case Histories. Carlson Library, Clarion University." In ALA (American Library Association). Public Information Office, Campaign for American Libraries. Available at http://www.ala.org/advocacy/advleg/publicawareness/campaign@yourlibrary/prtools/academicresearch/successful academic (accessed Sept. 1, 2012).

McNeal, James U. 1999. *The Kids Market: Myths and Realities.* Ithaca, NY: Paramount Market Publishing.

Morgan, Candace D. 2010. "Challenges and Issues Today." In *Intellectual Freedom Manual.* 8th ed. Chicago: American Library Association.

Morris, Betty J. 2010. *Administering the School Library Media Center.* Westport, CT: Libraries Unlimited.

Murphy, Tish. 2007. *Library Furnishings: A Planning Guide.* Jefferson, NC: McFarland.

Mutz, John M., and Katherine Murray. 2010. *Fundraising for Dummies.* Hoboken, NJ: Wiley.

Naidoo, Jamie Campbell, ed. 2011. *Celebrating Cuentos: Promoting Latino Children's Literature and Literacy in Classrooms and Libraries.* Santa Barbara, CA: Libraries Unlimited.

National Center for Education Statistics. 2011. http://nces.ed.gov/pubsearch/pubsinfo.asp?pubid=2012008 (accessed Aug. 29, 2012).

Norfolk, Sherry, Jane Stenson, and Diane Williams. 2006. *The Storytelling Classroom: Applications across the Curriculum.* Englewood, CO: Libraries Unlimited.

North American Council for Online Education. 2007. http://www.inacol.org/research/docs/KeepingPace07-color.pdf (accessed Aug. 29, 2012).

Osborne, Robin, ed. 2004. *From Outreach to Equity: Innovative Models of Library Policy and Practice.* Chicago: American Library Association.

Panszczyk, Linda A. 2004. *HR How-To—Intergenerational Issues: Everything You Need To Know about Dealing with Employees of All Generations in the Workplace . . .* HR How-To. Chicago: CCH Knowledge Point.

Pfeil, Angela B. 2005. *Going Places with Youth Outreach: Smart Marketing Strategies.* Chicago: American Library Association.

Polanka, Sue. 2010. *No Shelf Required: E-Books in Libraries.* Chicago: American Library Association.

Queen, Barbara, and Laurie Lewis. 2012. "Distance Education Courses for Public Elementary and Secondary School Students: 2009–10." In *National Center for Education Statistics,* ed. J. Coopersmith. Washington, DC: U.S. Department of Education.

Rainie, Lee. 2012. Tablet and E-book reader Ownership Nearly Double over the Holiday Gift-Giving Period. Washington, D.C.: Pew Internet Project. http://pewinternet.org/Reports/2012/E-readers-and-tablets.aspx (accessed Aug. 29, 2012).

Rams, Dieter. August 27, 2011–February 20, 2012. "Question Everything Generally Thought To Be Obvious." Exhibition @ San Francisco Museum of Modern Art: Less and More—The Design Ethos of Dieter Rams.

Rideout, Victoria. 2011. *Zero to Eight: Children's Media Use in America. Common Sense Media.* Available at http://www.commonsensemedia.org/sites/default/files/research/zerotoeightfinal2011.pdf (accessed Aug. 29, 2012).

Rideout, Victoria, Ulla G. Foehr, and Donald F. Roberts. 2010. *Generation M(2) : Media in the Lives of 8- to 18-Year-Olds.* Menlo Park, CA: Henry J. Kaiser Family Foundation Study. http://www.kff.org/entmedia/upload/8010.pdf (accessed Sept. 5, 2012).

Roberts, John. 2007. "Dealing with Opposition to Culture Change." In *Managing Change.* Boston: Harvard Business School Press Lessons Learned Series, pp. 53–60.

Rubin, Rhea Joyce. 2006. *Demonstrating Results: Using Outcome Measurement in Your Library.* Chicago: American Library Association.

Ruefle, Anne E. 2009. *Creating a Culture of Literacy: Programming Ideas for Elementary School Librarians.* Santa Barbara, CA: Libraries Unlimited.

Russell, Carrie. 2012. *Complete Copyright for K–12 Librarians and Educators.* Chicago: American Library Association.

Sass, Rivkah K. 2002. "Marketing the Worth of Your Library." *Library Journal* 127 (11): 37–38.

Scales, Pat R. 2009. *Protecting Intellectual Freedom in Your School Library: Scenarios from the Front Lines.* Chicago: American Library Association.

School Library Journal. *The Digital Shift. LJ/SLJ Ebook Summit: More School Libraries Offer Ebooks; Increased Demand, Rise in Circulation.* Available at http://www.thedigitalshift.com/2011/10/ebooks/ljslj-ebook-summit-more-school-libraries-offer-ebooks-increased-demand-rise-in-circulation/ (accessed Aug. 27, 2012).

Shipley, David, and Will Schwalbe. 2008. *Send: Why People Email So Badly and How to Do It Better.* Rev. ed. New York: Knopf.

Siddiqi, Anooradha Iyer. 2010. *Library Book, The: Design Collaborations in the Public Schools.* New York: Princeton Architectural Press.

Silverstein, J. 2005. "Just Curious: Children's Use of Digital Reference for Unimposed Queries, and Its Importance in Informal Education." *Library Trends* 54 (2): 228–244.

Smallwood, Carol, ed. 2011. *The Frugal Librarian: Thriving in Tough Economic Times*. Chicago: American Library Association.

Staerkel, Kathleen, Mary Fellows, and Sue McCleaf Nespeca, eds. 1995. *Youth Services Librarians as Managers: A How-to Guide from Budgeting to Personnel*. Chicago: American Library Association.

Steele, Victoria, and Stephen D. Elder. 2000. *Becoming a Fundraiser: The Principles and Practice of Library Development*. Chicago: American Library Association.

Stephens, Claire Gatrell, and Patricia Franklin. 2007. *Library 101: A Handbook for the School Library Media Specialist*. Westport, CT: Libraries Unlimited.

Suffolk Public Library System. http://www.suffolk.lib.va.us/ldnd_template/youth -services/library-tip-sheets/weeding.html (accessed Aug. 27, 2012).

Sullivan, Michael. 2010. *Serving Boys through Reader's Advisory*. Chicago: American Library Association.

Swan, James. 2002. *Fundraising for Libraries: 25 Proven Ways to Get More Money for Your Library*. New York: Neal-Schuman.

Teaching Copyright. Electronic Frontier Foundation. Available at http://www.teaching copyright.org/ (accessed Aug. 30, 2012).

"'Things Are Changing Fast' SLJ's 2011 Technology Survey." 2011. *School Library Journal*, May, 28–33.

Thomas, Nancy Pickering, Sherry R. Crow, and Lori Franklin. 2011. *Information Literacy and Information Skills Instruction*. Santa Barbara, CA: Libraries Unlimited.

Toor, Ruth, and Hilda Weisburg, 2011. *Being Indispensable: A School Librarian's Guide to Becoming an Invaluable Leader*. Chicago: American Library Association.

Transliteracy.com. http://nlabnetworks.typepad.com/transliteracy/ (accessed Sept. 6, 2012).

Tunstall, Patricia, 2010. *Hiring, Training and Supervising Library Shelvers*. Chicago: American Library Association.

U.S. Bureau of Labor Statistics. *Occupational Outlook Handbook, 2010–11 Edition*. Available at http://www.bls.gov/oco/oco2003.htm (accessed Aug. 29, 2012).

Wallace, Linda K. 2004. *Libraries, Mission & Marketing: Writing Mission Statements That Work*. Chicago: American Library Association.

Walter, Virginia A. 1992. *Output Measures for Public Library Service to Children: A Manual of Standardized Procedures*. Chicago: American Library Association.

Walter, Virginia A. 2010. *Twenty-First Century Kids, Twenty-First Century Librarians*. Chicago: American Library Association.

Weber, Sandra, and Shanly Dixon. 2007. *Growing Up Online: Young People and Digital Technologies*. New York: Palgrave Macmillan.

Wendover, Robert W. 2002. *Smart Hiring: The Complete Guide to Finding and Hiring the Best Employees*. Naperville, IL: Sourcebooks, Inc.

West, James A., and Margaret L. West. 2009. *Using Wikis for Online Collaboration: The Power of the Read-Write Web*. 1st ed. San Francisco: Jossey-Bass.

Willis, Margaret Sabo. 2005. *Kid's Rooms*. Menlo Park, CA: Oxmoor House.

Woods, Dan, and Peter Thoeny. 2007. *Wikis for Dummies*. Indianapolis, IN: Wiley.

Woolls, Blanche. 2008. *The School Library Media Manager*. Westport, CT: Libraries Unlimited.

Woolls, Blanche, and David V. Loertscher. 2005. *The Whole School Library Handbook*. Chicago: American Library Association.

Zilonis, Mary Frances, Carolyn Bussian Markuson, and Mary Beth Fincke. 2002. *Strategic Planning for School Library Media Centers*. Lanham, MD: Scarecrow Press.

Zsulya, Andrea Stewart, and Carlette Washington-Hoagland, for the Library Leadership and Management Association (LLAMA), ed. 2012. *Staff Development: A Practical Guide*. 4th ed. Chicago: American Library Association.

Index

"Acceptable Use of the Internet" policy, 108
Acheson, Dean, 187
Acquisitions, 93–94
  of databases, 96
  of materials, 94–96
    and bidding on contracts, 94–95
    and online accounts, 95–96
Adults, 24, 35, 45, 77, 83, 105, 107, 127, 148, 149, 150
  appropriate library furniture for, 71, 72
  and children's libraries, 10–11
  and privacy issues, 117
  providing an adult-friendly space in libraries, 71
  as threats, 11
  use of e-readers by, 24
  use of library catalogs by, 99
  use of library computers by, 108–109
Advertising, 131, 148, 149
  paid advertising, 158
African Americans, 11, 19
Alcott, Louisa May, 202
Allen, Jennifer, 97
Amazon, 95, 201
American Association of School Librarians (AASL), 90, 117, 192
American Library Association (ALA), 11, 43, 106, 109, 111, 120, 192
  Office of Intellectual Freedom, 116

and the protection of privacy for library patrons, 117
  top ten most challenged books of, 107 (box)
American Library Association Bill of Rights, 105, 106, 110
  interpretation of, 111–114
American Library Association Intellectual Freedom Manual, 110
Americans with Disabilities Act (1990), 12, 75
  revised standards of (2010), 201
Anglo-American Cataloging Rules (AACR2), 97
Annual reports, 47
  audiences for, 49
  for the general public, 47
  preparation of, 48–49
  release of, 51
  themes of, 49–50
  use of graphics in, 50
  use of pictures in, 50–51
Apple Corporation, 21–22, 201
Asian Americans, 11
Assessment. *See* Evaluation
Association for Library Services to Children (ALSC), 90, 192
Associations. *See* Professional associations
Audiences, 6, 142, 148, 149, 154, 201
  for annual reports, 47, 49

Audiences (*continued*)
 attracting audiences for enrichment
  programs, 131
Audiovisual materials, 101
 See also Videos
Author/illustrator visits, 132–133
planning checklist for, 132–133 (box)
Automated systems, 93–94, 96
 for cataloging and classification, 96–97,
  99
  electronic catalogs, 96–97
  group catalog instruction, 99
  specific cataloging systems, 97
 changes in, 99–100

Barnes & Noble, 95, 201, 202
Bibliographies, 102
Blogs, 39, 85, 90, 119, 130, 150
Book fairs, 61–62
Bookmarks, 51, 100
Books, 4, 87
 audiobooks, 83, 84, 137
 bundled books, 202
 categories of children's books, 13
 digital books, 24, 121
 display of in libraries, 101–102
 multilingual books, 11
 nonfiction picture books, 200
 print books, 79
 top ten most challenged books of the
  American Library Association
  (ALA), 107 (box)
 See also E-books
Bostwick, Arthur, 135
Braille, 101
Branding strategies, 148–149
Bring Your Own Device (BYOD), 22
Brochures, 140, 153
Brooklyn Children's Museum, mission
 statement of, 33
Budgets/budgeting, 53–54, 182
 budget checklist, 133 (box)
 budget narrative, 58
 budgeting for staff time, 58
 capital budgets, 54
 managing budgets, 59
  accountability for, 59–60
 for new programs and services, 58–59
 operating budgets, 54
 preparation of, 54–55, 58

Canadian Library Association, 192
Capital budgets, 54

Cataloging in Publication (CIP) data, 97
Catalogs, 74, 93, 99, 102, 200
 electronic/online catalogs, 13, 96–97
 See also Anglo-American Cataloging
  Rules (AACR2); Dewey Decimal
  System; Machine readable catalog-
  ing (MARC) system
CDs, 4, 8, 13, 87, 102, 200
Chain of command, 165
Charlotte Children's Theater, 76 (box)
Charlotte Mecklenburg Public Library,
 76 (box)
Chicago Public Library, 47
Child-service agencies, 142–143
Children, 19, 75, 102, 204
 basic facts concerning children in the
  United States, 19 (box)
 demographic changes concerning, 19–20
 disabled children, 76
 effect of employment outlook on children's lives, 25–26
 exposure of to media/media services,
  4–5, 22
 hospitalized children, 12
 library cards for, 50
 middle-school children and the use
  of library resources designed for
  adults, 201
 questions concerning suitable reading
  material for children, 106–108
 right of to privacy in public and school
  libraries, 116–117
 seating arrangements for children in
  libraries, 72–73
 special needs children, 6, 12, 20, 84, 101,
  103, 139
 transient children, 12
 using pets as children's reading
  buddies, 126
Children's Internet Protection Act (CIPA
 [2000]), 108, 109
Chronicle of Philanthropy website, 65
Circle, Alison, 147
Circulation, 73, 77, 94, 99, 100, 128, 204
 behavior of circulation clerks, 173, 174
 circulation figures, 43, 85
 circulation records, 117, 118, 120
 monitoring of, 89
  circulation rules, 100
  circulation system, 100, 177
 specific issues concerning, 100
 weeding of collections based on low
  circulation, 87

City Academy, 70
Collaborative study, 25
Collections. *See* Library collections
Committees, 37, 38, 73, 183, 189, 193, 194
   curriculum committees, 115
   intellectual freedom committees, 116
Communication, 16, 23, 35, 115, 136, 138,
     144, 204
   channels of, 128, 161
   electronic communication, 100, 153
   and outcome evaluation (OE), 42
   traditional patterns of, 161
   See also Email; Leadership, and staff
     communication; Networking
Communities, and libraries, 1, 3, 4, 5, 9,
     16, 19–20, 26, 30, 37, 38, 111, 125, 135,
     136–137, 139, 141, 142, 143, 169, 178
   and the care of preschool children, 25
   and change in a community, 1, 16
   community radio shows, 205
   composition of a community, 89
   cooperation of libraries with commu-
     nity groups, 11
   and cuts to library funding, 60
   forming of community associations, 193
   homeschooling parent groups in
     communities, 11
   immigrant communities, 23
   importance of foreign-language
     publishers and small presses to a
     community, 95
   importance of providing information
     about the library to the commu-
     nity, 15, 47, 147
     and the use of annual reports, 49
   low-income communities, 65
   reaching all children in a community, 34
   shared community values, 108
   upper-income communities, 22–23, 24
   See also Environmental scan
Computers, 22, 23, 71, 103
   computer work areas, 75
   public internet computers, 109
   See also Internet, the; Websites
Conferences, 73, 85, 90, 165, 191–192, 203
   attending conferences, 193–194
   international conferences, 192–193
   vendor exhibits at, 74
Conflict situations. *See* Work situation
   conflicts
Coordinators, 138, 172, 178
   children's services coordinators,
     190–191

library coordinators, 138
   youth services coordinators, 170
Copyright law, 203
Craft and activity programs, 130, 130 (box)

Data collection, 42–44
Databases, 13, 14, 81, 83, 94, 99, 104, 150,
     151, 154
   access to, 137
   acquisition of, 96
   electronic databases, 135, 159
   monitoring of, 89
Daycare centers, 14, 34
   daycare outreach programs, 144–145
Decision making, 166, 181, 184, 187, 193
   hierarchy of, 204
   in the hiring of library staff, 168
   See also Library services, managing of
Décor, 70–71. *See also* Library space,
     aesthetics of
Dewey, Melvil, 135
Dewey Decimal System, 97, 101
Dia de los Niños/Dia de los Libros (Chil-
     dren's Day/Book Day), 11
Digital materials, 23–24
   acquisition and provision of, 202–203
   policies concerning copyright law, 203
Digital recording devices, 23
Dina Dictionary, 149
Display, 101
   of artwork, 73
   of books, 70, 71, 72, 101
   display cases, 72, 73, 74
   display space, 73, 75
   of electronic resources, 103–104
Duncan, Arne, 21
DVDs, 4, 8, 13, 83, 87, 95, 102, 137, 200

Early education, 21
E-books, 13, 95
   e-textbooks, 21
   sales of, 201–202
Educational levels, 106, 111, 113
Educational programs and resources, 12,
     23, 113, 115
Educational records, 117
Educational trends
   e-textbooks, 21–22
   high-stakes testing, 21
   homeschooling, 20
   online schools and classes, 20–21
Eldorado Intermediate School, mission
     statement of, 32–33

Electronic Frontier Foundation, 203
Electronic links, 86, 99, 118, 200, 202, 203
Electronic media, promotion of, 103–104
Electronic/online catalogs, 13, 96–97
Email, 129, 138–139, 154, 186
    effective use of, 187 (box)
Emerson, Ralph Waldo, 53
Employment
    fastest-growing job sectors, 26
    jobs in service industries, 26
    and the outlook on children's lives,
        25–26
Enrichment programs, 129–130
    craft and activity programs, 130, 130
        (box)
    programs to increase library visibility,
        130–131
        attracting large audiences for, 131
        event and program preparation, 131
        miscellaneous programs, 133–134
        planning for author visits, 132–133
    reading clubs, 129–130
Environmental scan, 34–35
    and acquiring feedback, 35
    and collecting statistics, 35
    and information gathering, 34–35
Equal Employment Opportunity Com-
    mission, 167
E-Rate program, 65
E-readers, 75, 201, 202
Evaluation, 29
    and accountability, 15–16
    of achievement, 41
    annual assessments, 44
    of electronic services, 43
    of marketing and public relations, 159
    outcome evaluation (OE), 41–42
        and data collection, 42–44
    qualitative evaluation, 45
    reporting of evaluation results (*see also*
        Annual reports), 47
    of specific programs or activities, 44–45
    statistical evaluation, 45
    using the results of evaluation, 45–46
        and the causes of failing to meet
            objectives, 46–47

Facebook, 153
Families, 23, 24, 35, 53, 70, 71, 72, 121, 129,
    143, 147, 154
    attendance of at in-library programs,
        125
    economic challenges of, 19–20
    higher-income families, 22, 24
    lower-income families, 22
    non-English speaking families, 20, 125
    same-sex parent families, 20
    single-parent families, 20, 108
    view of and use of libraries by, 14–15, 16
    young/preschool families, 145, 148
    See also Homeschooling
Filipino-American communities, 44, 45
Folktales, 11
Foundation Center, 65
Friedman, Milton, 41
Friends group, 62
Fundraising, 60–61
    from corporations, 63
    from foundations, 62–63
    from friends and parents, 61–62
    goals of, 61
    from grants, 64
        steps in preparing grant proposals, 64
        locating grant sources, 64–65
        proposal writing, 65–66
    and marketing, 66
    menu of fundraising activities, 62 (box)

Gates Foundation, 65
Gift policy, 89
Girl Scouts, 42
Goals, 6, 7, 14, 29, 32, 35, 39, 49, 50, 54, 88,
        112, 123, 136, 141, 143, 144, 159
    achievement of, 35, 36, 41, 44, 47
    departmental goals, 32, 33–34, 37, 39, 41,
        54, 55, 58, 139, 150
    educational goals, 14, 21
    evaluation of, 34
    fundraising goals, 61
    instructional goals, 6
    organizational goals, 34
    specific goals of children's libraries, 33
Google, 24
    children's use of, 24, 127
    Google analytics, 43
Grants, 6, 7, 53, 61, 158
    applying for, 65–66
    foundation grants, 62–63
    for the support of children, 61
    See also Chronicle of Philanthropy
        website; E-Rate program; Founda-
        tion Center; Gates Foundation;
        Institute for Museum and Library
        Services (IMLS); Library Services

and Technology Act (LSTA [1996]);
    Target Stores literacy funds
Graphic novels, 38 (box), 46, 51, 97, 101,
    129, 137, 193
Grievance process, 165, 173–175
    conflict concerning work habits, 172–173
    steps to take regarding employee com-
        plaints, 174 (box)
work situation conflicts, 172

Handouts, 140, 141, 152, 153
Harris, Frances J., 103
Head Start, 8, 144
Hennepin County Library Foundation,
    63 (box)
Heraclitus, 199
Hiring procedures. *See* Staff/staffing, and
    the hiring process
The Hobbit (Tolkien), 202
Homeschooling, 11, 20, 34, 142, 200
    percentage of homeschooled children
        in the United States, 20
Homework, 129

Indicators, 36
Information services, 14, 126–127
    alternate delivery programs, 128–129
    and help with children's homework, 129
    managing of in libraries, 127–128
Information technology, 13
Instant messaging (IM), 128
Institute for Museum and Library
    Services (IMLS), 65
Intellectual freedom, 79, 105
    and digital resources, 108–110
    issues concerning, 105–108
    steps for the preservation of, 110
        Step One: Knowledge of documents
            supported by the ALA, 110, 111
        Step Two: Have a selection policy in
            place, 114
        Step Three: Prepare to deal with
            challenges, 114–115, 116
Interactive media, 119
Interior planning. *See* Library space
International Association of School
    Librarians (IASL), 192
International Federation of Library Asso-
    ciations and Institutions (IFLA), 192
Internet, the, 4
    "Acceptable Use of the Internet" policy
        of libraries, 108

filtering of internet access, 109
    and information communication, 154
    internet access for library patrons, 108,
        109
    policies concerning, 108–110, 119, 170
    public internet computers, 109 (box)
    See also Email; Social media/networks;
        Websites
Internet User Agreements, 109
iPad, 23, 84, 201, 202

Kaiser Foundation, 22
Kane, Laura, 93
Kindle, 23, 84
Kindle Fire, 202

Leadership, and staff communication, 181
    balancing of communication channels,
        185
        effective use of email, 187 (box)
        electronic mail, 186
        face-to-face communication, 185, 189
        telephone calls, 185–186
        texting, 186
    communication with an entire depart-
        ment, 189–190
        basic principles for using a depart-
            mental wiki, 190
        methods of departmental communi-
            cation, 189
    creating departmental teams, 184
    serving on school committees, 183
    sharing of ideas with youth librarians,
        190
        attending conferences, 192–194
        broadening a network, 191–192
        choosing professional associations,
            192–193, 193 (box)
        use of networking for, 190–191
    using print materials, 187
        letters, 188
        proper occasions for sending memos,
            187–188
    working with other departments,
        181–183
Librarians, children's, 1, 15, 23, 29, 59–60,
    63, 69, 70, 84, 93, 100, 190–191, 199,
    204
    and information literacy, 200
    and the need to prepare students for
        reading at the next level, 10
    responsibilities of, 97, 99

Librarians, children's (*continued*)
  specialties of in early education, 21
  and the use of digital materials, 24–25
Librarians, public, 103–104
Librarians, school, 70, 72, 93, 100, 102–103,
    126, 183, 199
  job descriptions for, 165
Libraries, children's, 3, 29, 102, 103, 145
  access to, 93–94, 100
  challenges faced by, 1
  changing priorities of, 1, 3–4, 199
  department plan of for children, 36
    (box)
  encouraging and welcoming change in,
    203–204
    allowing for criticism of change, 205
    allowing for experimentation,
      204–205
    encouraging new ideas, 204
    and the importance of communica-
      tion, 205–206
  future of, 197
  goals of, 33
  mission statements of, 32–33
    goals of, 33 (box), 34
  purposes of, 4–5
  shelving materials for, 101–102
  types of, 6–7 (*see also* Public libraries;
    School libraries; Special libraries)
  typical users of, 8 (box)
  webpages for and web access to, 13–14
  work environment of, 161, 163
Libraries, children's, marketing of,
    147–148, 147 (box)
  branding strategies, 148–149
  developing a marketing plan, 149–150
  evaluation of, 159
  specifics for marketing to children,
    149–150
  steps for effective marketing, 149
  See also Public relations
Librarianship, 93–94
Library Bill of Rights. *See* American
    Library Association Bill of Rights
Library circulation, 100
Library collections, 69, 79, 81, 137
  changing nature of, 81, 83–84
  gift policies of, 89
  housing of, 74
  links of to children, 121
  marketing of, 102–103
  purpose of, 83

and the selection of digital materials,
    84–86
  specific considerations concerning, 85
selection policies, 88–89
selection specifics for print materials, 84
and the sharing of resources, 86
staying current with changing needs,
    89–90
weeding collections, 86–87
  and the MUSTY (Misleading, Ugly,
    Superseded, Trivial, Your collec-
    tion's use) list, 87
  specifics of, 87
Library of Congress, 97
Library Journal, 74
Library policies, 12, 115, 128, 155
  collection development policy, 108
  e-communication policy, 187
  fair use policy, 203
  gift policy, 89
  internet policy, 108–110
  selection policy, 84, 88–89, 115
talking points concerning, 120
Library services, managing of, 121
  challenges of, 121
  changes involved in, 4–5, 121–122
  and information that needs to be pro-
    vided on the web, 154
Library services, planning and provision
    of, 3–4, 7–8, 29
  adult services, 10–11
  department plan for children, 36 (box)
  and differences in children unrelated
    to age, 11
    children with special needs, 12
    ethnic diversity, 11
    homeschooled children, 11–12
    unattended children, 12
  preschool children's services, 8–9
  school-age children's services, 9
  transitional user services, 9–10
  types of services provided, 12–13
    collection building, 13
    delivering information services, 14
    and the evaluation of services, 15–16
    marketing services, 15
    outreach programs, 14–15
    providing accessibility to collections,
      13–14
    providing educational and recre-
      ational programs, 14
  See also Strategic planning

Library Services and Technology Act
(LSTA [1996]), 65
Library space, 69
    aesthetics of, 70–71
    changing/moving of spaces, 71–72
    day-to-day issues involved in, 70
    furnishings, 74–75
    housing of collections, 74
    infrastructure, 75
    miscellaneous considerations, 75–76
    new libraries, 76–77
        evaluation of space in, 77–78
    planning of interior space, 72–73
    planning for technology, 75
    providing an adult-friendly space, 71
    virtual tour of children's library spaces,
        76 (box)
LibraryThing.com, 99
Literacy through School Libraries
    program, 65

Machine readable cataloging (MARC)
    system, 97, 99
Magazines. See Periodicals
Mailing lists, 131, 158, 165
    electronic mailing lists, 51, 165
Marketing. See Advertising; Libraries,
    children's, marketing of; Public
    relations; Publicity
Materials acquisition, 94–96
    and bidding on contracts, 94–95
    and online accounts, 95–96
McGraw-Hill Publishers, 21
McNeal, James, 149–150
Mead Public Library, 47
Media and technology, changing uses of,
    22–23, 85–86
    and changes in information seeking, 24
        digital resources, 24–25
        group searching, 25
    and changes in reading formats, 23
        in public libraries, 24
        in schools, 23–24
    interactive media, 119
    and mobile media/technology, 22, 25
    See also Networking; Social media/
        networks
Meetings, 126, 138, 145, 155, 169, 190–191,
    193, 194
    committee meetings, 183
    curriculum meetings, 183
    daycare meetings, 145

face-to-face meetings, 161, 172, 189
    informal meetings, 205
    rotating meetings, 191
    staff meetings, 14, 38, 39
    with teachers, 203
Memphis Public Library, 142
Mission, of libraries, 6–7
Mission statements, 31, 33 (box)
    for children's libraries, 33
    for public libraries, 31–32
    for school libraries, 32–33
    See also specifically listed individual library
        mission statements
Montgomery, Lucy Maud, 202
Mount Laurel Library, 72
Museums, 7, 15, 33, 66, 73, 77, 86, 93, 132,
    158
MUSTY (Misleading, Ugly, Superseded,
    Trivial, Your collection's use) list, 87

National Center for Educational
    Statistics, 21
National Museum of Play, 76 (box)
Networking, 150, 153, 154, 193
    broadening of, 191–192
    within a system or region, 190–191
    See also Social media/networks
New York Public Library, mission state-
    ment of, 31
Newberg, Pamela, 97
News releases, 49, 131, 155–156, 157
No Child Left Behind legislation (2002), 21
Nook, 84, 201, 202
North American Council for Online
    Learning, 20

Objectives, 40, 41, 45, 54, 58, 59, 66, 112,
    113, 131, 150, 167
    assessment of, 39, 43–44
    example of, 38
    failure to meet objectives, 45–47
    and goals, 32, 34
    hallmarks of, 36
    realistic objectives, 37–38
    short-term objectives, 36
    specificity of, 36
    stages of, 35–36
    and strategy formation, 35–36
    working with objectives, 38–39
Online Public Access Catalog (OPAC), 99,
    102
Operating budgets, 54

Outcome evaluation (OE), 45
  benefits of, 42
  enhancement of, 42
*Output Measures for Public Library Service
    to Children: A Manual of Standard-
    ized Procedures* (Walter), 43
Outreach programs, 71, 135, 152–153, 165
  communication issues concerning,
    137–139
  outreach to after-school programs,
    142–143
  outreach to daycare, 144–145
  public library outreach, 143–144
  and resource sharing, 137
  school and public library cooperation,
    135–137
  and space sharing, 141–142
  successful outreach programs, 136,
    143–144

Partnerships, 15, 62
Patrons, 22, 24, 25, 32, 41, 42, 47, 61, 101,
    120, 129, 130, 131, 172, 190, 201–202,
    204, 205, 206
  access of to library materials, 79, 81, 117,
    128
  changing needs of, 89–90
  impact of library services on, 45
  internet access for, 108, 109
  and library space, 72
  needs of, 33, 89
  privacy of, 79
  reasons of for using libraries, 43
  value of a library to, 169
  and weeding of collections for patron
    use, 86, 87
Periodicals, 83, 94, 102
"perpetual beta," 206
Pew Research Center, 24
Planning, 8, 11, 12, 14, 16, 125, 165, 170
  for budgets, 54, 59
  for collections, 74, 81, 84, 101
  for cooperative services, 136
  for facilities, 29
  for the future, 51, 133
  for grant proposals, 64
  for new libraries, 76–78
  for online learning development, 20
  program planning, 71, 131, 145, 158
  for workshops, 170
See also Author/illustrator visits, plan-
    ning checklist for; Library services,

planning and provision of; Library
    space; Reading enhancement
    programs, steps in planning a
    storytime; Strategic planning
PowerPoint, 93, 152
Presentations, 23, 93, 152, 159, 193
  oral presentations, 51, 194
  pictorial presentations, 155
  PowerPoint presentations, 93, 152
Privacy, of library users, 116
  children's (minors) right to privacy,
    116–117
  sample privacy policies, 118
  steps for preserving the privacy of
    library users, 117
    Step One: Developing a privacy
      policy, 118
    Step Two: Reviewing privacy
      policies, 118
    Step Three: Protecting children from
      social media misuse, 118–119
Problem management, 172
  of conflicts concerning work habits,
    172–173
  dealing with grievances, 173–175
  steps to take regarding employee com-
    plaints, 174 (box)
Professional associations, 192–193, 203
  tips for choosing an association, 192
    (box)
Proposals. *See* Grants
Public Internet computers, 109 (box)
Public libraries, 6, 15, 16, 20, 53, 66, 88, 123,
    128, 171, 177
  afterschool outreach programs of,
    142–143
  benefits of public libraries operating
    with schools, 135–137
  and group catalog instruction, 99
  relationship to schools, 88–89
  school visits to public libraries, 139–142
    and handouts for children, 141
    and librarians' book talks, 140–141
    preparing for class visits, 140
  services to children in homeless
    shelters, 142
  special testing offered by for children,
    143
  use of electronic catalogs by, 97
  use of digital materials by, 24
  wireless service of, 75
See also Outreach programs

Public relations, 147 (box), 150–151
  activities of, 151
  and branding, 147 (box), 148–149
  electronic media promotion services,
      153–154
  evaluation of, 159
  logo development, 148–149
  media interviews, 156–157
    preparation for, 157
  news releases, 155–156
  paid advertising, 158
  public service announcements (PSAs),
      156, 158
    example of, 156 (box)
  and quality library services, 151–152
  use of handouts (flyers, posters, book-
      marks, and brochures), 153
  when speaking to or meeting with the
      public, 152–153
Publicity, 59, 126, 138, 144, 151–152, 157
  for special events, 14, 63, 131, 133
Publishing, changes in, 201–202

Radio shows/stations, 15, 51, 150, 155, 156,
      157, 158, 199
  community radio shows, 205
Rams, Dieter, 204
Reading clubs, 129–130
Reading devices, 22, 24
Reading enhancement programs, 123–124
  lapsit programs, 123, 124
  providing programs for offsite
      children, 125–126
  questions to be answered concerning,
      125
  reading development programs, 126
  storytime programs, 123–124
    drop-in storytimes, 125
    steps in planning a storytime,
      124–125
    target groups for, 125
Recreation
  recreational activities, 9, 140
  recreational materials, 3, 4, 7, 9, 21, 90, 120
  recreational needs of children, 113
recreational programs, 14, 139, 140
recreational reading, 21, 139, 140
Recruitment of staff. See Staff/staffing,
      and the hiring process
Reference questions, recording of, 43
Renovation, 69, 72, 101
  See also Library space

Reports, 65, 165, 194
  budget reports, 54, 59
  development of, 47
  oral reports, 51
  See also Annual reports
Resources Description and Access
      (RDA), 99
Restaurants, and library publicity, 63
Retention, of staff, 169
  through ongoing staff training, 169–170
  through rewarding of staff achieve-
      ments, 171–172
Riordan, Rick, 202
Robin Hood Foundation, 76 (box)
Rochester Public Library, 76 (box)

School Library Journal, 83
School libraries, 6–7, 15, 16, 43, 53, 66, 69,
      123, 128, 177
  adult-friendly features of, 71
Schools, 53
  differences between schools and day-
      cares, 144–145
  public funding for, 161
  relationship to public libraries, 88–89
  security of, 141
  use of media devices by, 23–24
  See also School libraries
Science, Technology, Engineering, Math
      (STEM) subjects, 26
Search engines, 25
Sears List of Subject Headings, 97
Seattle Public Library, mission statement
      of, 31, 32
Security, 79, 133, 141, 170
Selection, 25, 58, 81, 108
of digital materials, 84–86
  of material for teens, 10
  selection policies, 84, 88–89, 114, 115, 120
  selection specifics for print materials, 84
Services. See Library collections; Library
      services, planning and provision of
Shaw, George Bernard, 185
Shelving, 101–102
Skype, 23
Smartphones, 103
Social media/networks, 25, 99, 119
  safety issues for children's use of, 119
Space management. See Library space
Space sharing, 141–142
Special events, 49, 61, 130–131, 155, 190
  attracting audiences for, 131

Special events (*continued*)
  author visits, 132–133
  budgeting for, 133 (box)
  finding cosponsors for, 131
  preparation for, 131
  publicity for, 14, 63, 131, 133
  and working with community leaders, 131
  See also Enrichment programs; Reading enhancement programs; Recreation
Special libraries, 7
  church libraries, 7
  medical libraries, 7
  museum collections, 7
Special needs children, 6, 12, 20, 84, 101, 103, 139
St. Louis Public Library, 148–149
Staff/staffing, 163, 181
  and chain of command, 165
  and the hiring process, 165
    sample employment ad for a children's librarian, 165 (box)
    interviewing of potential employees, 166–168
      preparation for, 166
      questions prohibited in interviews, 167
      typical questions asked in interviews, 167
  orientation of new staff, 168–169
    orientation goals, 168 (box)
    and social customs, 169
  performance appraisal, 175–176
    sample of performance review, 175 (box)
  retention of staff, 169
    ongoing staff training, 169–170
    rewarding staff achievement, 171–172
  staffing plans, 163–165
  work situation conflicts, 172
    conflict concerning work habits, 172–173
    dealing with grievances, 173–175
    steps to take regarding employee complaints, 174 (box)
  See also Leadership, and staff communication; Volunteers
Statistical evaluation, 45
Storytimes, 11
drop-in storytimes, 125
  steps in planning a storytime, 124–125
  target groups for, 125

Strategic planning, 31, 51
  importance of mission statements, 31, 33 (box)
    for children's libraries, 33
    for public libraries, 31–32
    for school libraries, 32–33
  transitioning from mission statements to departmental goals, 33–34
  collaborative planning, 37–38
  environmental scan, 34–35
  strategy formulation through objectives, 35–36
  useful objectives, 36
  working with objectives, 38–39, 38 (box)
  visualizing the strategic planning process, 39–40
Student tests/testing, 21
Suffolk County Public Library, Community Resources Database of, 10
Supervision, 12
  adult supervision, 9
  direct supervision, 8, 164, 166, 172
Supervisors, 116, 169, 176, 177, 188
  and dealing with work conflicts, 172–175
  performance appraisal duties of, 175–176
  volunteer supervisors, 178

Target Stores literacy funds, 65
Teachers, 14, 37, 138–139
  links to, 127–128
  meetings with, 203
  use of media by, 24, 25
Technology, 59, 71, 170
  growth of, 25
  information technology, 13
  See also Media and technology, changing uses of
Television, 123, 131, 133, 150, 155, 157, 158
  access to, 4, 23
  amount of viewing by children, 22–23
  and the broadcast of public service announcements (PSAs), 15, 51, 156
  public television, 14
Texting, 128
Theo Thesaurus, 149
Training, 42, 49, 142, 177
  in cataloging rules, 97
  curriculum training, 15
  inservice training, 115

of library staff, 15, 143, 163, 165, 169–170
of students, 137
of teachers, 145
Transliteracy, 199–200
encouraging interactivity in libraries, 200–201
and inclusive media services, 201
and the merging of media platforms, 200
Twitter, 153

United Nations' Universal Declaration of Human Rights, 105–106
United States Census (2010), 19
United States Department of Education, 20, 65
United States Supreme Court, 108
United Way, 42, 65

Vendors, of library supplies, 74, 94, 100, 130, 202–203
establishing discounts with, 95–96
See also Materials acquisition
Videos, 22, 23, 43, 51, 126, 130, 132, 154
e-video, 99
online video collections, 25
video book reviews, 8
video stores, 95
video zooms, 86
See also YouTube
Volunteers, 61, 176–178
sources of, 178 (box)
steps for a volunteer program, 177 (box)

use of ads to recruit volunteers, 178
volunteer jobs, 178 (box)

Websites, 13, 39, 73, 81, 83, 86, 93, 102, 131, 142, 150, 154, 192, 202
access to, 107, 107
advertising on, 158
for children, 4
and fundraising, 61
library websites, 203
placing of library reports on websites, 47
school websites, 118, 132
seasonal websites, 104
use of for public service announcements (PSAs), 156
See also Social media/networks
Weeding, 86–87
Wikis, 189–190
Willis, Margaret, 69
Work situation conflicts, 172
conflict concerning work habits, 172–173
dealing with grievances, 173–175
steps to take regarding employee complaints, 174 (box)
Workshops, 45, 65, 73, 148, 169, 170, 191, 192, 193

Young Adult Library Services Association (YALSA), 90
YouTube, 8, 15, 25, 153

Zoos, 143, 158

About the Authors

ADELE M. FASICK, PhD, specializes in public library service to children and young adults. She taught at the library school at the University of Toronto, Ontario, Canada, and at the School of Library and Information Science (SLIS), San Jose State University, California. Her most recent publication is Libraries Unlimited's *From Boardbook to Facebook: Library Services for Children in an Interactive Age*. Fasick received a bachelor's degree from Cornell University, a master's degree in library science from Columbia University, and a doctorate from Case Western Reserve University.

LESLIE EDMONDS HOLT, PhD, consults with libraries, schools, and child-serving agencies. She worked at the St. Louis Public Library as Director of Youth Services from 1990 through 2004. Holt is a past president of the Association of Library Service for Children (ALSC) and has been active for many years in ALA, PLA, ALSC, and other state and regional library associations. She is coauthor of *Public Library Service to the Poor: Doing All We Can*. Holt received her bachelor's degree from Cornell College, master's degree in library science from the University of Chicago, and doctorate from Loyola University of Chicago.

Made in the USA
Columbia, SC
20 August 2021